Localities (ASCS
1. Anton 2. Flag
8. Towner 9. F
13. Harrison 14.

N E B
K A

omas
Colby

n

Scott   Lan

Finney

Garden
City

Gr

Haskell

s   Seward

Liberal

K L A H O M A

nd

Moundridge ●

● Hutchinson

ford

Wichita ●

nonresident farming has been cor
Moreover, the author includes a close-up
view of the coming of the suitcase farmer,
especially as reported in contemporary local
newspapers and checked against the assessors' records in Kansas. A significant number of records of the Agricultural Stabilization and Conservation Service (ASCS) have
been analyzed in reconstructing the place
of the nonresident farmer in Kansas and
Colorado. These records, now in the main
destroyed, show that while suitcase farming has been remarkably persistent in the
heart of the Kansas-Colorado Dust Bowl,
the percentage of those operating wheat
farms from a distance has decreased.

A native of Oklahoma, LESLIE HEWES at-
tended the University of Oklahoma (B.A.,
1928) and the University of California,
Berkeley (Ph.D., 1940). He is a member of
the Council of the Association of American Geographers and has received their
Meritorious Contribution Award. His numerous articles on the Great Plains have
appeared in *Economic Geography, Geography Review,* and *Annals of the Association of American Geography,* and other
scholarly publications. In 1958–59 Mr.
Hewes was a Fulbright lecturer at the University of Vienna. He is professor of geography at the University of Nebraska.

25   0   25   50   75   100

Miles

The Suitcase Farming Frontier

The Suitcase Farming Frontier

A Study in the Historical Geography of the Central Great Plains

Leslie Hewes

UNIVERSITY OF NEBRASKA PRESS · LINCOLN

Contents

LIST OF FIGURES AND PLATES   ix

LIST OF TABLES   xi

PREFACE   xiii

1. INTRODUCTION   1
   The Setting   1
   Introducing the Suitcase Farmer   4
   The Coming of the Suitcase Farmer   8

2. GREELEY COUNTY, KANSAS, AS PART OF THE SUIT-
   CASE FARMING FRONTIER   11
   Introduction   11
   Beginnings of Suitcase Farming   12
   Importance of Out-of-County Wheat Farmers, 1930-33   21
   Persistence of Local and Out-of-County Wheat Farmers   29
   Conclusion   30

3. THE EARLY SUITCASE FARMING FRONTIER: SOME
   FURTHER CLOSE-UPS   31
   Hamilton County   31
   Stanton County   37
   Miscellaneous   41
   Summary   47

4. EARLY SUITCASE FARMING IN WESTERN KANSAS:
   SUMMARY AND INTERPRETATION   49
   Geographical Distribution, 1933   49
   Farmers from Adjacent Counties   53

Source Areas: Where Did They Come From? 54
The Making of the New Wheat Country 56
Factors in the Development of Suitcase Farming 62
Summary 70

5. THE EARLY COLORADO SCENE 73

6. PAUSE AND RETREAT 83
Introduction 83
Greeley County 84
Elsewhere in Western Kansas 90
Land Use of Suitcase and Local Farmers 94
Summary 96

7. A RENEWAL OF SUITCASE FARMING 97
Introduction 97
New Activity in Greeley County 97
Hamilton County, Kansas 101
Eastern Colorado 104
General Considerations 116

8. THE SUITCASE FARMING FRONTIER IN THE EARLY
1950s 121
Introduction 121
Geographical Distribution of Suitcase Farmers 124
Sources of Suitcase Farmers in Eastern Colorado 126
An Interpretation of the Spatial Aspects of the Second Suit-
case Farming Frontier 127
Decline of Suitcase Farming in Western Kansas 134
Some Comparisons of Suitcase and Local Farming 134
Conclusion 138

9. AFTERMATH: SUITCASE FARMING IN THE 1960s 139
Introduction 139
Incidence of Suitcase Farming about 1960 140
Source Areas about 1960 146
Spatial Relationships of Suitcase Farming about 1968 147
Some Aspects of Suitcase Farming in the 1960s 150
Conclusion 158

10. BLOWLAND AND THE ABSENTEE   161
    Introduction   161
    Measures of Wind Erosion on Absentee- and Locally Owned
        Land   164
    Conclusions   173

11. SUMMARY, INTERPRETATION, AND PROSPECT   175
    Summary   175
    Interpretation   178
    The Future of Suitcase Farming   185

APPENDIX A: FIGURES   189

APPENDIX B: TABLES   231

BIBLIOGRAPHY   257

ACKNOWLEDGMENTS   273

INDEX   275

Figures and Plates

Figures
1. Setting of Suitcase Farming Frontier   189
2. Hard Winter Wheat Region   190
3. Suitcase Farmers in Western Kansas, 1923   191
4. Home Bases of Suitcase Farmers, Greeley County, 1920-32   192
5. Wheat Farms in Colony Township, 1933   193
6a. Home Bases of Suitcase Farmers, Hamilton County, 1924-32   194
6b. Home Bases of Suitcase Farmers, Hamilton County, 1960   194
7. Out-of-County Wheat Farmers in Western Kansas, 1933   195
8. Home Bases of Suitcase Farmers in Western Kansas, 1930   196
9. Post Offices of Suitcase Farmers in Western Kansas, 1936   197
10. Improved Land, Western and Central Kansas, 1920   198
11. Cropland in Wheat, 1924   199
12. Tractors in Western Kansas, 1922   200
13. Level Land, Western Kansas and Eastern Colorado   201
14. Land Owned by Nonresidents, 1936   202
15a. Home Bases of Suitcase Farmers, Greeley County, 1940   203
15b. Home Bases of Suitcase Farmers, Greeley County, 1959   203
16. Increase in Cropland, 1939-54   204
17. Suitcase Farmers in Western Kansas and Eastern Colorado, 1954   205
18. Suitcase Farmers in Eastern Colorado, 1954   206
19. Suitcase Farmers in Eastern Colorado, 1954 (dot map)   207
20. Chief Wheat Areas of Eastern Colorado, about 1954   208
21. Sources of Suitcase Farmers in Eastern Colorado, 1954   209
22a. Home Bases of Early Suitcase Farmers, Haswell Area   210
22b. Home Bases of Suitcase Farmers in Haswell-Arlington, 1954   210
23. Addresses of Suitcase Farmers, Colorado, 1954   211

ix

24. Baughman Land in Eastern Colorado, 1948   212
25. Sod Ordinances and Land Utilization Projects, Colorado   213
26. Suitcase Farmers, about 1960   214
27. Suitcase Farmers by Communities in Eastern Colorado,
    1961-62   215
28. Change in Percentage of Suitcase Farms, 1954-60   216
29. Landownership by Nonresidents, 1969   217
30. Suitcase Farms in Conservation Reserve, 1961-62   218
31. Home Bases of Suitcase Farmers, about 1960   219
32a. Home Bases of Suitcase Farmers, Haswell-Arlington, 1961   220
32b. Home Bases of Suitcase Farmers, Haswell-Arlington, 1968   220
33. Suitcase Farmers in Western Kansas and Eastern Colorado,
    1967-68   221
34. Suitcase Farmers in Eastern Colorado, 1968   222
35. Change in Percentage Suitcase Farms, 1954 to about 1968   223
36. Suitcase Farming Frontiers in the Central Great Plains   224
37. Trends in the Percentage of Suitcase Farmers in Kansas   225
38. Trends in the Percentage of Farmers in Colorado   226
39. Variability in Wheat Yields, 1926-48   227
40. Changes in the Value of Land, 1930-40 and 1940-50   228

Plates   *following*
1. Portable cookshack of G. A. and Loren Snell, 1915 or 1916   8
2. Trued brothers breaking sod for Simon Fishman, northeast of
   Tribune, Kansas, May, 1925   16

Tables

1. Greeley County, Kansas, Wheat, 1912-27   231
2. Large Wheat Farms, Suitcase and Local, Greeley County, Kansas, 1920-25   231
3. Wheat Yields, Suitcase and Local, Greeley County, Kansas, 1920-25   232
4. Residence of Greeley County, Kansas, Wheat Farmers, 1933   232
5. Farms of Out-of-County Wheat Farmers, Greeley County, Kansas, 1933   233
6. Farms of Resident Rural Wheat Farmers, Greeley County, Kansas, 1933   234
7. Farms of Greeley County Town Farmers, 1933   235
8. Percentage of Farm Land Sown to Wheat, Greeley County, Kansas, 1930-33   236
9. Average Wheat Yields, Greeley County, Kansas, 1930-32   236
10. High and Low Yields of Wheat, Greeley County, Kansas, 1930-32   237
11. Owner and Tenant Operations, Colony Township, Greeley County, Kansas, 1933   238
12. Ownership of Rented Wheat Farms, Colony Township, Greeley County, Kansas, 1933   238
13. Hamilton County, Kansas, Wheat Farms, 1933   239
14. Average Wheat Yields in Hamilton County, Kansas, 1930-32   240
15. Stanton County, Kansas, Wheat Farms, 1933   241
16. Land Use, Sample Area, Haskell County, Kansas, 1936 and 1925   242
17. Wheat Growing, by Old and New Farmers, Kansas, 1920 and 1927   243

18. In-County Kansas Farmers Growing Wheat, 1933   244
19. Residence of Reported Nonresident Farmers, Kansas, 1936   245
20. Percentages of Wheat Abandoned in Kansas, 1910-34   246
21. AAA Payments in 1935   246
22. Summer Fallow and Strip Cropping, Greeley County, Kansas, 1936-40   246
23. Land Use, Whitewoman Township, Wichita County, Kansas, 1939-40   247
24. Land Use, Greeley County, Kansas, 1939-40   247
25. Land Ownership in Colorado Counties, 1936   248
26. Land Use, Eastern Colorado, Early 1950s   248
27. Comparison of Fallow and Wheat Acreages, Colorado, 1951-53   249
28. Wheat Abandonment in Colorado, 1951-53   249
29. Land Use, Western Kansas, 1951-53   250
30. Comparative Statistics, Persisting and Nonpersisting Farmers, 1954-61/62   251
31. Land Use and Productivity, Colorado Counties, 1961-62   251
32. Land Use, Farmers Not Participating in Conservation Reserve, 1961 or 1962   252
33. Land Use, Farmers Partly in Conservation Reserve   252
34. Acreages Planted and Left for Harvest, Colorado Counties, 1964-67   253

Preface

The semiarid grasslands in the Dust Bowl portion of Kansas and Colorado were transformed from stock raising and general farming to mainly wheat farming in a thirty-year period, from 1920 to 1950. The wheat farmer replaced the stockman in west-central and southwest Kansas and a corner of Colorado in the 1920s and early 1930s. After the great drought of the 1930s there was a second advance, this time in Colorado. In all, the hard winter wheat country expanded about two hundred miles. Nonresident farmers, so-called suitcase farmers, led both advances. As pioneers of a sort, taking part in the westward movement, they were agents of change, innovators who introduced the technology, methods, and experience of established wheat farming. So significant was the role of these farmers from a distance that the new wheat country can be designated a suitcase farming frontier.

The suitcase farmers operated in the northern half of the Dust Bowl area. The conditions for suitcase farming were, first, the existence of nearly empty grasslands adjacent to the fairly well occupied specialized wheat country of central Kansas. Then, in the 1920s, when increasing mechanization cut labor requirements drastically, the stage was set for a rapid advance in wheat farming by nonresidents. From the relative security of farms mostly located in central Kansas, suitcase farmers trucked their equipment—often the same that they had used at home—west to the grass-lands, to break sod, sow, and harvest.

Absentee farmers have been distributed in a consistent geographical pattern around a core area at the western margin of important wheat farming at least since 1933. In the earlier of the two advances of the

xiii

suitcase farming frontier, the highest percentage of nonresident farmers was found in westernmost Kansas, while the core of the second frontier lay immediately to the west in Colorado. This study will be restricted to the Kansas and Colorado portions of the Great Plains, which include the major concentrations of suitcase farming and provide a sufficiently large area to be meaningful.

Focal concerns of this inquiry are, first, the determination of the role of the suitcase farmer in a portion of the frontier of wheat farming; second, the description and analysis of the spatial patterns of suitcase farming; and, third, a comparison of farming by suitcase and other farmers. Related considerations are the relative degree of persistence of the two groups of farmers and a comparison of their stewardship of the land, especially in respect to the problem of blowing dust. Finally, there is the question of whether nonresident farming is a cause or result of high failure—or are both high failure and suitcase farming evoked by an unusually hazardous region?

It is difficult to escape the conclusion that the Dust Bowl area, obviously one of high agricultural risk, has qualities especially conducive to suitcase farming. Thus, the hypothesis advanced here includes the following parts: The land lay open and available to the suitcase farmer because resident farmers had been discouraged by high crop failure. The resulting low land values attracted buyers from the outside interested in speculative gains. Some absentee owners became suitcase farmers and other absentees became tenants of nonresident owners. Rainy years, high prices, and technological advances encouraged prairie plow-ups by absentee wheat farmers. The combination of variable precipitation, extremely variable yields, absentee ownership, and suitcase farming continues to characterize much of the Dust Bowl area of Kansas and Colorado. Variable yields and absentee ownership, as well as level land and an uncertain semiarid climate, are essential elements of suitcase farming.

The body of this study will consist primarily of a presentation and analysis of the evidence on which the generalizations stated above are based. Breadth of coverage in order to determine areal patterns of suitcase farming was considered necessary. Probing in depth was required for the identification of the processes of change by noting significant actions of individuals and groups. *Where* suitcase farming happened, *who* was involved, *how*, and, if possible, *why* it happened are all fundamental concerns.

It should be noted that a full-fledged attempt at description and analysis of the economic and social effects of absentee farming will not be attempted. These are matters for the agricultural economist and sociologist. Nor will more than incidental attention be given to the description and analysis of the landscapes of the areas studied.

It is hoped that this study of suitcase farming will shed light on the character—the personality—of an area. The record of man-land relations would be far from complete without attention to the farmer operating from a distance. Transforming hundreds of thousands of acres from grassland to wheat fields is one significant way in which this part of the surface of the earth has been altered. Hence, it is an important aspect of the changing geography of the area, an essential part of its historical geography.

Sources basic to this survey of suitcase farming included the following: ASCS records, among them the wheat listing sheets for 1954 and 1957 and official records of wheat farms of later years; annual assessors' reports for counties in western Kansas; newspaper files in various historical society libraries; and annual reports of county agents to state agricultural extension services. Pre-1960 ASCS records were examined at the Federal Records Centers in Denver and Kansas City, with the exception of a few found at county offices in Kansas. I examined those for later years at state and in some instances county offices. Most of the ASCS records are no longer available, having been disposed of by the various holding agencies.

The Suitcase Farming Frontier

CHAPTER ONE

Introduction

The Setting

The suitcase farming frontier, as a geographical area, consists of most of the Kansas and Colorado portion of the Dust Bowl (see fig. 1). It is a semiarid plains region covered mainly by short grasses. The annual precipitation averages over twenty inches in the east but less than twelve in the southwest, along the Arkansas River. The variability of the precipitation—above and below the average—constitutes a major problem. In terms of land use, the study area, extending from about the one hundredth meridian in western Kansas to the Rocky Mountains, is made up of the west-central part of the hard winter wheat region and its grazing margin (fig. 2).

Seen in larger perspective, the Great Plains of the United States are among the new lands that have been called upon to provision the burgeoning city populations of the world. The plow-up of the semiarid grasslands in the United States and elsewhere came late, largely in the twentieth century. Generally, they were remote, unfamiliar, and hazardous lands. With the use of new technology in agricultural machinery, transportation, fencing, and well drilling, such lands have become parts of the industrial-commercial world. Walter Prescott Webb has identified those innovations as important in the transformation of the Plains.[1]

The occupation of the western grassland was hazardous. As the farming

1. Walter Prescott Webb, *The Great Plains* (New York: Ginn and Co., 1931).

frontier edged into the semiarid plains in the 1870s, John Wesley Powell, in an often quoted warning, emphasized that the proper use of most of the semiarid land was grazing and that crop farming without irrigation would fail.[2] Nevertheless, farming has been attempted almost everywhere throughout the region. Included in their attempts was the so-called dry farming movement of the turn of the twentieth century, as reported by M. W. M. Hargreaves for the northern Plains.[3] However, the movement had little effect in the area later to become known as the Dust Bowl, where wheat was of little importance until the arrival of the suitcase farmer.

Early in the period of introspective stocktaking of the use and condition of American resources in the 1930s, Carl O. Sauer recognized the Great Plains as a "large speculative fringe of agriculture." In the four-way developmental classification of regions according to economic condition that he proposed, the Great Plains serve as exhibit number one of "*the marginal areas in which instability* rather than continuing change in a particular direction is characteristic." At times, the Plains qualified nicely also as a frontier area, one of the "*areas of vigorous development,*" another of the types Sauer recognized.[4] On two of the occasions (before and after the drought of the 1930s) when the central Great Plains was an expanding frontier, nonresident farmers were in the thick of change. Perhaps the retreats from the Plains have been more dramatic—and better recorded. This was the pioneers' "first great crushing defeat," borrowing the term Harlan Barrows used to describe the flight from the Plains of the 1890s.[5] C. W. Thornthwaite, the Great Plains Committee, Frederick Clements, and others have reported the retreat of the 1930s,[6] when every

2. John Wesley Powell, *Report on the Lands of the Arid Region of the United States, with a More Detailed Account of the Lands of Utah,* United States Geographical and Geological Survey of the Rocky Mountain Region, 2d ed. (Washington, D.C.: GPO, 1879).

3. Mary Wilma M. Hargreaves, *Dry Farming in the Northern Great Plains. 1900-1925* (Cambridge: Harvard University Press, 1957).

4. Carl O. Sauer, "Land Resource and Land Use in Relation to Public Policy," Appendix 9, *Report of the Science Advisory Board,* July 31, 1933, to September 1, 1934 (Washington, D.C.: September 20, 1934), pp. 251, 249, 250.

5. Harlan H. Barrows, *Lectures on the Historical Geography of the United States as Given in 1933,* ed. William A. Koelsch, University of Chicago, Department of Geography Research Paper, no. 77 (Chicago, 1962), p. 231. The defeat was judged to be permanent, according to W. D. Johnson, in *The High Plains and Their Utilization,* 21st Annual Report, U.S. Geological Survey, 1899-1900, part 4, Hydrology (Washington, D.C.: GPO, 1901), pp. 609-741.

6. C. W. Thornthwaite, "The Great Plains," in *Migration and Economic Opportunity: The Report of the Study of Population Redistribution,* ed. Carter Goodrich (Philadelphia: University of Pennsylvania Press, 1936), pp. 202-50; *The Future of the Great Plains,* Report of the Great Plains Committee (Washington, D.C.: GPO, 1936);

state from Oklahoma to North Dakota lost population.

As the great drought of the 1930s was getting under way, Isaiah Bowman expressed a perceptive judgment when he wrote, "How far one can go in reaping the bounty of the land and yet escape the penalties of recurrent drought is the perennial question of the dry-farming and farming-ranching country of the West."[7] Nonresident, or suitcase, farming was one way of seizing the rewards of good years while minimizing the risks of the poor ones. Absentees, mainly part-time, were prepared to move in rapidly and, being less committed than the residents, could withdraw or cut back more readily.

The conclusion is hard to escape that the Dust Bowl area, obviously one of great risks, has qualities that were especially conducive to suitcase farming. The hypothesis advanced includes the following parts: the land lay open, available to the suitcase farmers, because resident farmers had been discouraged by high crop failures. Low land values resulted. The low land values attracted land buyers from the outside interested in speculative gains. Some of the absentee owners became suitcase farmers and other absentees became tenants of nonresident owners. Rainy years, high prices, and technological advances encouraged plow-ups led by absentee wheat farmers.

The combination of variable precipitation, extremely variable yields, absentee ownership, and suitcase farming continues to characterize much of the Dust Bowl area of Kansas and Colorado. Variable yields and absentee ownership, as well as level land and an uncertain semiarid climate, are essential parts of the setting of suitcase farming.

As part of the economic climate, American agricultural policies have had some effects on suitcase farming. Some are obvious; others are not. Nonresident farming began despite the agricultural depression of the 1920s and neared a peak at the time that the Hoover administration was partially successful in supporting farm prices. Beginning in 1933, government payments for acreage control and conservation practices kept both suitcase and local farmers in business for nearly a decade. Under Dust Bowl conditions, absentees were less successful than residents in "farming the government." With the rainy years and high wheat prices of the mid- and late

Frederick E. Clements and Ralph W. Chaney, *Environment and Life in the Great Plains,* Carnegie Institution of Washington, Supplementary Publication, no. 24 (Washington, D.C., 1936); F. E. Clements, *Climatic Cycles and Human Population in the Great Plains,* Carnegie Institution of Washington Supplementary Publication, no. 43 (Washington, D.C., 1938).

7. Isaiah Bowman, *The Pioneer Fringe,* American Geographical Society Special Publication, no. 13 (Worcester, Mass.: Commonwealth Press, 1931), p. 112.

1940s, nonresidents led another assault on the grassland, pushing farming westward, even beyond the twelve-inch-average rainfall line. The anti-sod-breaking ordinances of several soil conservation districts and penalties enforced by local Agricultural Adjustment Act (AAA) committees against plow-ups did little to slow the surge, and it is doubtful that the suspension of acreage controls in 1943 aided the advance materially. When in the late 1950s the government was again trying to bail out farmers and retire poor lands from cultivation, loopholes in the regulations governing the conservation reserve of the Soil Banks permitted absentees to become landowners and nominal wheat farmers for the purpose of collecting government payments. Some of the resident farmers who took the occasion to "lease" part or all of their cropland to the government in the same program moved away, becoming actual or nominal absentee farmers. Perhaps the lower benefits, based on lower estimated yields, received by nonresident wheat farmers under recent wheat programs have contributed to a decline in the number and percent of absentee farmers. Probably lower yields themselves have hurt suitcase farmers more than the comparative disadvantages of agricultural policies.

Introducing the Suitcase Farmer

Suitcase, nonresident, and *absentee,* as adjectives to describe farmers and farming, will ordinarily be used synonymously in this study. The definition of suitcase farmer by Earl H. Bell—a farmer who lives more than one county away—will be used. According to Bell, "The typical suitcase farmer is conceded to be a man who farms so far away from home that he has to carry his suitcase to his farm work, but he has some brothers who live close enough to carry a dinner pail—they are frequently called town farmers. They live in a nearby town and farm land out in the country." Bell exemplified the lack of a precise definition by labeling farmers from neighboring counties as suitcase also.[8] In their definition of suitcase farming, Walter M. Kollmorgen and George F. Jenks used a distance of at least thirty miles to the post office address of the farmer from the edge of the county where he farmed.[9] Some suitcase farmers lived in distant towns,

8. Earl H. Bell, *Culture of a Contemporary Rural Community: Sublette, Kansas,* Rural Life Series, no. 2, USDA Bur. Agr. Econ. (Washington, D.C.: September, 1942), pp. 12, 11, 34. In effect, farmers living in bordering counties are classified as local.

9. Walter M. Kollmorgen and George F. Jenks, "A Geographic Study of Population and Settlement Changes in Sherman County, Kansas, Part I: Rural," *Transactions of the Kansas Academy of Science* 54, no. 4 (December 1951): 453.

resulting in some confusion between town, or "sidewalk," and suitcase farmers. The term *satchel farmer* was used in southwestern Nebraska,[10] and perhaps elsewhere. An investigation carried on in thirteen counties in the Great Plains from Texas to Montana about 1940, apparently centering on town farming, used satchel and suitcase farmer as synonyms.[11]

The first use of the term suitcase farmer known to me is found in the 1930 (first) annual report of the county agent of Greeley County, Kansas. Already considered a *type,* he was described thus in part: "This type of farmer lives here only during the summer months. He plants his crop and comes back for another planting." The 1932 report spoke of "our migratory or 'suitcase' farmers. The outside farmer coming to do wheat farming. He is here one month or year and is gone the next. A good crop year will draw new ones, and a poor year will drive out some of the old ones."[12] It is plain that the name suitcase farmer was intended as an epithet. The 1935 annual reports for Stanton and Scott counties, and later reports for several other counties, contained references to suitcase farmers. The 1936 instructions from the Kansas State Board of Agriculture sent to assessors included the order that "special care should be taken to see that all farms operated by absentee owners are listed. This applies particularly to the farms of the so-called 'suitcase' farmers of western Kansas."[13] The term suitcase farmer was noted in the assessors' reports for Wallace County in 1935, Finney County in 1936, and Greeley County in 1938. However, the words absentee and nonresident were used more often.

Insofar as the assessors recognized absentee operators of farms, living out-of-county was usually the test. However, some farmers listed with in-county addresses were listed as absentee, and some with addresses as distant as Wichita were placed on regular rather than absentee rolls. Identification with the community, as much as actual residence, seems to have been the governing consideration. In this study, however, place of residence—an address more than one county away—is used to identify suitcase farmers.

Newspaper editors, interested both in the development of their trade

10. John L. Champe of Lincoln, Nebraska, and his father carried on absentee farming in Keith County in western Nebraska in the 1920s. "Damned satchel farmers" was the epithet used by resident farmers until the nonresidents proved themselves. Interview with John L. Champe, January 3, 1970.

11. Richard Asby, "Town Farming in the Great Plains," *Rural Sociology* 6 (1941): 342.

12. All the annual reports of the county agents in Kansas cited were examined on microfilm at Kansas State University, Manhattan.

13. A copy now bound with the assessor's report for Thomas County in 1936, "Statistical Rolls, Agriculture," is in the library of the Kansas State Historical Society, Topeka.

territories, whether by local or absentee farmers, and in potential subscribers, usually spoke of nonresident rather than suitcase farmers. For example, the *Johnson City Pioneer*, the Stanton County paper, in 1928 and 1929 sometimes ran a "Non-resident Column." Even during Dust Bowl days, when nonresident owners and operators were blamed for much of the dust, the use of the term suitcase farmer was infrequent in newspapers of the area.

The term was used, however, in a letter to the editor of the *Topeka Capital* which was reprinted in the *Syracuse Journal* of September 11, 1931:

> This is what is occurring in the extreme western counties of Kansas. Much of this territory is farmed by what is known as "suit-case" farmers, that is, by people who live elsewhere and farm out here in the summer. Many of them are farmers in Central Kansas and transport their heavy machinery back and forth.[14]

At the time the first AAA wheat allotments were made, in 1933, the Kearny County newspaper complained that assessors' reports of acreage were too low because "so much wheat was grown by suitcase farmers living elsewhere that assessors were unable to turn in a complete agricultural report."[15]

The frequent use of the term suitcase farmer in contemporary publications suggests widespread knowledge of the word and the commonness of suitcase farming in the Dust Bowl during the 1930s.[16]

As mentioned, the most frequent designation of farmers from a distance was *nonresident*, although in some cases such farmers might be confused with local town-dwelling farmers. In a discussion of Stevens County, Kansas, in 1936, it was thought necessary to distinguish between nonresident farmers. Among them, there was "the operator who lives outside the county and who only occasionally visits his land. He trucks his

14. *Syracuse Journal,* September 11, 1931. All Kansas newspapers cited were examined in the library of the Kansas Historical Society, Topeka.

15. *Lakin Independent,* July 7, 1933.

16. The following list is representative. Avis D. Carlson, "Dust Blowing," *Harper's Magazine,* July 1935, p. 156; James C. Malin, "The Turnover of Farm Population in Kansas," *Kansas Historical Quarterly* 4 (1935): 350; Bryon Hunter et al., *Type of Farming Areas in Colorado,* Colorado Agricultural Experiment Station Bulletin, no. 418 (Fort Collins, September 1935), p. 122; Arthur H. Joel, *Soil Conservation Reconnaissance Survey of the Southern Great Plains Wind-Erosion Area,* USDA Technical Bulletin no. 556 (Washington, D.C., January 1937), p. 21; A. D. Edwards, *Influence of Drought and Depression on a Rural Community: A Case Study in Haskell County, Kansas,* Social Research Report, no. 7, Farm Security Admin. and Bur. of Agr. Econ. (Washington, D.C.: GPO, January, 1939), p. 50.

farming equipment into the county and out again after his crop is planted and possibly he never visits his land again until he returns for harvest, if he is lucky enough to receive one." In addition, full-time local town farmers and businessmen speculating in part-time farming were recognized as nonresident.[17]

Later descriptions of suitcase farming have changed little. For example, a statement repeated for most of the counties in western Kansas in which suitcase farming was common in the early 1950s reads: "Much of the land is still farmed by absentee owners and operators. These people live, in many cases, a distance of 200 miles or more from the land and visit the area only at seeding and harvest time. Many of them live in trailers, trucks, or cabin camps during their short visits to carry on farming operations."[18] This is still a much used description, although some nonresidents both at the outset of suitcase farming and since spent most of the summer one-half of the year in nonresident farming.

The failure to distinguish between nonresident ownership and nonresident operation of land was a cause of confusion. The distinction should have been clear-cut in the numerous cases in which local farmers rented absentee-owned land; perhaps the distinction was not important for the farms owned by absentees and rented to other absentees. Often the absentee landowner did his own farming, as described in the several quotations above; the absentee owner was, in fact, the farmer. However, arrangements by which the owner exercised control of farming without performing most of the farming operations constituted a kind of twilight zone. Among such arrangements were engaging a local agent or manager, the use of custom or contract farming for some or all farming operations regularly or occasionally, and the keeping of a hired man. According to the practices of the Agricultural Stabilization and Conservation Service (ASCS), and probably for the predecessor AAA, the landowner is considered the operator in such cases. It is understandable that in periods of stress the outsiders, both absentee owners and absentee farmers, were thought of as exploiters and responsible for the sorry state of affairs in both the Dust Bowl era and the drought of the early and mid-1950s. It was easy to group them together.

17. "Land Use Survey of the Southern Great Plains Region, 1936, Progress Report," Resettlement Admin., Land Use Planning Division, February 20, 1937, p. 83. In 1964 on file with the Extension Division, mimeographed, Kansas State University, Manhattan.
18. R. W. Eikelberry and C. L. Fly, eds., *Physical Land Conditions Affecting Use, Conservation and Management of Land Resources, Greeley County, Kansas,* USDA Soil Conservation Service and Kansas Agr. Exper. Sta. (Manhattan, December 1956), pp. 1, 2.

The Coming of the Suitcase Farmer

It is hard to pinpoint the beginning of suitcase farming in Kansas and adjoining areas. James C. Malin refers to suitcase farming by proxy—custom farming for absentees—in central Kansas back in 1881.[19] In 1915, G. A. and Loren Snell began farming in adjacent Logan County, Kansas, from their home in Colby. Beginning in late 1915 or 1916, their operation would qualify as suitcase farming because they had moved to a farm near Bird City, Kansas, farther from the land in Logan County. That they lived in a cook-shack (plate 1) while they were away from home perhaps foreshadowed the later trailer era of suitcase farming.[20] There were other scattered instances of actual raising of wheat by absentees before 1920. For example, the county assessors in western Kansas reported that two of the eleven farm operators living more than one county away emphasized wheat in 1918, but most of the eleven were carrying on stockraising or general farming, and probably depended on custom farming or had hired men.

In Deuel County, in the southeastern part of the Nebraska Panhandle, then near the frontier of important wheat farming, nonresidents were raising wheat as early as 1914 and 1915. Several brief notes and stories in the county newspaper are plainly descriptive of suitcase farming. In one instance, G. H. Wilkinson of Benedict, Nebraska, with one son in one mention, two sons in another, after harvesting 560 acres of wheat on his farm and reseeding a large tract, "left . . . with a car of stock and farming equipment." Their plan to construct some improvements, probably buildings, on the farm was held up as an example for other nonresident landowners. The following summer the Wilkinsons had returned from eastern Nebraska with stock and machinery.[21] The reference to a car of stock and equipment shows that the journey to and from the suitcase farming area was made by rail.

Some years later, a summary account of suitcase farming in Deuel County included the following statements:

> The demands for increased production and the greater perfection of
> motor machinery resulted in the inauguration of "big" farming in
> 1915. This type of operation has been steadily promoted and a large

19. James C. Malin, *Winter Wheat in the Golden Belt of Kansas: A Study in Adaption to Subhumid Geographical Environment* (Lawrence: University of Kansas Press, 1944), p. 129.

20. Letter from O. A. Snell, Carson City, Nevada, April 16, 1970. All correspondence cited in this study consists of personal letters to the author.

21. *Chappell Register,* October 8, 1914, and July 29, and August 5, 1915.

Plate 1. Portable cookshack of G. A. and Loren Snell used in their suitcase farming in Logan County, Kansas, in 1915 or 1916. Photograph courtesy of the Kansas State Historical Society.

part of the county is farmed by people from eastern Nebraska whose capital is attracted by the broad, level table-lands and their suitability for cultivation with tractors and other power machinery. Many of these people remain on the land only during the time of harvesting and reseeding. [22]

No doubt, mechanization aided suitcase farming, but the Chappell newspaper clearly records some earlier instances of nonmotorized suitcase farming.

Although there were earlier examples, absentee farming first became important in western Kansas in the 1920s. The earliest big operator identified was Simon Fishman, with 16,000 acres of winter wheat in Greeley County, as reported by the assessor in 1921. [23] In 1923, the county assessors in western Kansas listed more than two dozen farmers from a distance, at least one-half of whom emphasized wheat (fig. 3). In all probability, the number carrying on absentee wheat farming was actually much greater because the assessors made their reports in the spring of the year before the arrival of suitcase farmers. By 1923 suitcase farming was well under way and nonresident wheat farmers have been seasonal visitors ever since. For most of the Kansas suitcase farming frontier, the peak number was reached about 1933, the year when the first wheat allotments were determined under the AAA. The first suitcase farming frontier developed in the twelve-year period from 1921 to 1933.

22. Louis A. Wolfanger, A. W. Goke, and H. E. Weakley, "Soil Survey of Deuel County, Nebraska," Advance Sheets, Field Operations of the Bureau of Soils, 1921 (Washington, D.C.: GPO, 1924), p. 714.
23. Statistical Rolls, Agriculture, Greeley County, 1921.

CHAPTER TWO

Greeley County, Kansas, as Part of the Suitcase Farming Frontier

Introduction

A close look at an area in which suitcase farming was important at the time of great expansion in the raising of wheat might well throw some light on the principals involved, the processes that were in operation, and the results. Greeley County, Kansas, the fourth county north from the southwestern corner of the state, is well suited for this sort of study. In 1933, Greeley had the highest percentage of out-of-county farmers in Kansas. Suitcase farming became important in the decade 1920-30, when the amount of wheat sown increased by more than 100,000 acres. The choice of Greeley County is fortunate in that both the county newspaper editor and the county agricultural agents were aware of the seasonally migratory farmers and the long-established Tribune Experimental Farm of the Kansas State College of Agriculture and Mechanical Arts provided a convenient point for observation. Its long-time superintendent, T. Bruce Stinson, is a most knowledgeable authority on events of nearly half a century.

As noted earlier, the identification of absentee farmers from newspaper accounts is difficult because of the wide range of possibilities in farming by or for nonresident owners. In addition, there is the subjectivity of reporting—or failing to report—on the part of assessors. Their annual reports were made in the spring, before the suitcase farmers arrived. Perhaps it is surprising that as many were reported as were, some for a number of years running. Adding to the difficulty of identifying absentees is the apparent shifting of residence to and from the county, failure to report any farming in two of the three townships in 1921, and the lack of lists of inhabitants (heads and size of families) for the towns of Tribune and Horace in 1921, 1922, and 1923 and for a part of rural Colony Township in 1923. In those cases in which planting was reported with no harvest shown the following year, the explanation might be crop failure; but if a harvest was reported without a record of planting, it is clear that the record was incomplete. A comparison of newspaper accounts with assessors' reports leads to the same conclusion—the record of farming is incomplete, especially for nonresidents. Nevertheless, a general picture can be fashioned.

The Beginnings of Suitcase Farming

Table 1 (in the Appendix) shows plainly that wheat was not an important crop before 1921. On the assessor's report for that year a note was made, at the end in a different hand, of Simon Fishman, an absentee, as planting 16,000 acres of winter wheat in Harrison Township. The 16,000 acres constituted most of the wheat planted in the county.[1] The very high percentage of failure experienced during the preceding decade provides an adequate explanation of why virtually no one tried to raise wheat except as an occasional sideline. Lack of transportation was not the reason because the main-line Missouri Pacific Railroad, running across the county, had been available for years. Perhaps it required an optimist from the outside to make the gamble.

The early assessors' reports listed Fishman as a wheat farmer only in 1921 and in 1926 and 1927, with 3,200 and 10,210 acres, respectively, in Tribune Township for the Kansas Agriculture Development Company. However, the county newspaper noted his part in wheat farming in other years as well. The earliest such reference was to Fishman's 1920 wheat crop, west of Horace, making twenty-five bushels per acre.[2] Land preparation and the planting of this crop in 1919 would seem to have been Fishman's first endeavor in farming in the county.

1. The assessor's report for Greeley County for 1921 was examined at the library of the Kansas State Historical Society, Topeka. The assessors' reports on agriculture are called Statistical Lists, Agriculture. T. Bruce Stinson and H. H. Laude (*A Report of the Tribune Branch Agricultural Experiment Station*, Agr. Exp. Sta. Bull. 250, Kansas State Agricultural College, Manhattan, March 1930) show 19,616 acres for the county.
2. *Greeley County Republican*, August 19, 1920.

The big wheat-planting venture for 1921 was appropriately chronicled in the local press:

> The Fishman tractor outfits have changed the order of things mightily on their large tract south of town. The plowing is well done and the soil seems to be in the best of condition and ere long we are to have waving crops instead of Buffalo grass to picture that beautiful landscape.

> He commenced the development only last spring and has broken 32,000 acres of prairie most of which has produced a good crop of millet. A force will begin in a short while seeding all of this 32,000 acres to wheat.

> Simon Fishman and Louie Fine [Fishman's father-in-law] were over from Burlington, Colorado, last week doing the preliminary stunt toward starting the big development of this county about March 1st.

> The Fishman Land Company has started activities for the year in the presence of Lou Fine who is on the job looking after about 125 miles of fencing which he expects to have completed in about a month. . . . The gigantic problem the Fishman Land Company has this summer [is one of] harvesting over 20,000 acres and reseeding probably twice as much . . . .

> We have it from Lou Fine that the Fishman Land Company started 7 harvesting outfits in Greeley County Wednesday morning and expect to have 21 going by Saturday.

> Of the nearly 20,000 acres of Fishman wheat crop it is estimated that the poorest of it will produce 10 bushels per acre and that the general average will be around 12 1/2 bushels per acre.

> With the completion of the Fishman elevator Tribune will have the best elevator along the line of the Missouri Pacific. This with a 25,000 acre wheat crop, considering that one year ago we raised practically no wheat is a good enough record for one year.[3]

Although the Fishman Land Company may have shifted emphasis to land sales, wheat farming was an important objective for 1922, as shown by the following accounts from the Greeley County newspaper.

> The Fishman Land Company reported Saturday that they have already seeded more than 13,000 acres for next year's wheat crop. They will seed all told around 20,000 acres.

3. Ibid., May 8, 1920; August 19, 1920 (citing the *Kansas City Post*); February 17, March 31, June 30, and July 7, 1921.

> Simon Fishman is here this week starting things toward putting another crop on some land where the wheat is not making a good showing. However, he reports that most of his wheat is doing well.[4]

The Tribune Experiment Station report, although showing more abandonment in 1922 than in 1921, confirms that the 1922 harvest was good (table 1). The crop was described in the newspaper as fair to exceptionally good, with a large number of tractors, combines, header-stackers, and headers employed.[5] Before the harvest, Fishman was said to expect some thirty-five bushels of wheat to the acre. The results were not given, but late in the harvest season the Smid boys were reported to be threshing Fishman wheat in the southeastern part of the county,[6] although farming by neither the Smids nor Fishman was noted by the assessor.

It was reported that Fishman had about a dozen outfits employed fallowing for wheat for 1923, possibly partly on land that was not expected to make a wheat crop in 1922, but the county paper failed to show that Fishman either sowed wheat in the autumn of 1922 or harvested in 1923. Instead, in ambiguous fashion, the local paper noted in the spring that "Simon Fishman, the fellow who raises wheat on a big scale, came in the first of the week to look over the prospects." Later it was announced that "Simon Fishman, the big wheat operator is down from Denver and ready to take care of the wheat as it comes to his elevator." His nephew, Phil Fishman, was to act as his business manager.[7]

That autumn Fishman was characterized as "a land developer who has the grit to do things on a big scale and in great measure the big things had their origin with Fishman."[8] There seems to be nothing in either the local press or the assessors' reports after 1922 to show Fishman's direct participation in wheat farming until 1925, when he was listed as a resident of the county. However, a report in the *Kansas City Kansan,* reprinted at length in Hamilton County, bordering Greeley County, in 1924, said that he had 30,000 acres in wheat, from which he expected a harvest of 350,000 bushels.[9] The *Greeley County Republican* of October 1, 1925, signaled the activity of a new company with the announcement that "the Agricultural Development Company, under the management of Simon Fishman, is putting out 6000 acres of wheat this year." The assessor's report for 1926

---

4. Ibid., September 15, 1921, and June 1, 1922.
5. Ibid., July 6, 1922.
6. Ibid., June 15 and August 3, 1922.
7. Ibid., June 15, 1922; April 19 and July 5, 1923.
8. Ibid., September 6, 1923.
9. *Syracuse Journal,* January 4, 1924.

credited 3,200 acres of winter wheat in Tribune Township to the company.

Fishman might well have had his own career in mind when he said a few years later in a speech to the Rotary Club in the neighboring county seat town of Syracuse, "Corporation farming has been the instrument which brought about the breaking and farming of thousands of acres of land which would still be pasture if left to individual farmers." He added that the events of lifetimes had been compressed into a few years and that individual farmers had adopted methods and machinery introduced by the corporations.[10]

Statewide recognition of Fishman's achievement came in 1924, when he was called the "biggest wheat farmer in the world," and a Topeka newspaper story reported as follows:

> Last Wednesday Greeley county celebrated in honor of Simon Fishman, who has made 50,000 acres of wheat grow where none grew before. . . . [Two Greeley County men] went to Burlington, Colorado, where Fishman has converted sundry thousands of acres of buffalo grass into wheat and field crops and invited him to Tribune and Greeley county. . . . During the three years he has been operating there he has broken 31,000 acres of sod and farmers to whom he has sold land have broken an additional 20,000 acres. . . . [Before the Burlington, Colorado, and Greeley County operations] thousands of acres of land were developed in Cheyenne County, Nebraska, as a result of Fishman's demonstration in wheat farming for himself. He had never thought of dealing in land until a man from eastern Nebraska suggested that he sell some growing wheat for colonization purposes. A few weeks later that man appeared with fourteen of his neighbors. They all bought land.[11]

The *Topeka Capital* story added, "Fishman no longer operates his own machinery. He hires all the work done." This statement was confirmed by long-time residents of the Tribune area.

According to another account, Fishman had owned 3,000 acres in Cheyenne County, Nebraska, and had acquired and planted 40,000 acres near Burlington, Colorado, where the selling of newly broken land with growing wheat on it was practiced.[12] He was quoted as saying, "I have

10. *Syracuse Journal,* February 13, 1931.

11. Headline of story in the *Kansas City Kansan,* as reprinted in the *Syracuse Journal,* January 4, 1924. *Topeka Capital,* October 14, 1923. Fishman's wheat farming near Sidney, Nebraska, was said to have begun in 1907.

12. *Topeka Capital,* October 14, 1923; also interviews with Myrna Corns (Lincoln, Nebraska, May 19, 1964), a former resident of Burlington, who recalled the

tried to produce for the world the equivalent of two loaves where only one was before." This desire is understandable because his father reportedly had starved to death in Russia.[13]

If Fishman did not have a crop in 1923, it is likely that the "Trued aggregation," suitcase farmers from Ceresco, Nebraska, were the biggest wheat farmers in the county. The Tribune paper noted in sequence:

> About eight jolly boys southeast of Tribune, whom we know as the Trued aggregation have 4,000 acres of wheat all of which looks quite promising.

> The Trued brothers, Anton Nelson and the Wallin brothers from Saunders County, Nebraska, hove [sic] more than 5000 acres of *their own* [italics supplied] wheat and it is estimated they will have at least 75,000 bushels of wheat.[14]

In the August 16, 1923, issue of the *Greeley County Republican,* a picture showed five combines and two headers used in the harvesting of Trued-Nelson grain. The description in the newspaper three weeks later of the sowing of wheat by this group suggests a large-scale operation and emphasizes further the use of large equipment: "Seeding for next year's wheat crop is now getting under way. . . . The Trued outfit is running five 12-ft. drills across the field and you will easily understand that ere long their acreage will extend way up in the thousands."

In 1923 the assessor noted only that L. E. Trude (*sic*), whose address was given incorrectly as the town of Tribune, had 2,520 acres of wheat on a farm of 3,000 acres. The Wallins and Nelson were missed, with Nelson credited a year later with a 1923 harvest of 2,800 bushels and L. E. Trued with having harvested 17,800 bushels.

It is probable that the group from Saunders County, Nebraska, were attracted by Fishman. Anton Nelson and three Trueds were reported as leaving for home, at least several of them after working at wheat farming, in the autumn of 1921, the year of Fishman's first big wheat crop in Greeley County.[15] One of the group, Nelson, was described later as "a local farm machinery wizzard, who came to Greeley County to buy Fish-

---

fencing of Fishman land at the time of World War I. Wayne Boland, Cheyenne County, Colorado, ASCS office manager, in a November 21, 1968, interview, identified his father as one who broke land northeast of Burlington for Fishman at the end of the war.

13. Henry L. Carey, "The Rise of Simon Fishman," *B'Nai B'Rith Magazine* 48, no. 8 (May 1934): 274, 301; *Topeka Capital,* October 14, 1923.

14. *Greeley County Republican,* June 14 and July 5, 1923.

15. Ibid., September 22, October 6, and October 27, 1921.

Plate 2. Trued brothers breaking sod for Simon Fishman northeast of Tribune, Kansas, in May, 1925. Photograph courtesy of the Kansas State Historical Society.

man land."[16] A photograph of the Trueds breaking sod for Fishman north-east of Tribune four years later suggests continued association (plate 2).

The assessor reported some early suitcase farming in Colony Township, in the western part of the county, apparently mainly or entirely outside the area of Fishman's major early efforts. In 1922, E. J. Anderson of Kansas City, Missouri, was credited with 325 acres of winter wheat. Farms in Colony Township were not reported in 1921, but in 1920, "Anderson and Houk," with a post office address in the county and listed as inhabitants, had been shown with 350 acres. Possibly the suitcase farmer of two years later was a relative. L. W. Dickhut of Casper, Wyoming, one of the three nonresident farmers shown as farming in the township in 1923, had lived there earlier and later was again listed as resident. He was credited with 156 acres of wheat on a farm of 160 acres. The other two, who seemed to have no such local associations, were Walter Wetzel of Manila, Iowa, 1,060 acres of wheat on a farm of 1,280 acres and also 1,200 acres of wheat on a farm of 1,440 acres, and C. A. Wolf of Lincoln, Nebraska, with 155 acres of wheat on a farm of 160 acres. The double entry for Wetzel was probably a mistake. The county newspaper reported the planting of about 1,200 acres for him.[17]

Figure 4, based on identification of suitcase farmers from the local newspaper and assessors' reports, shows places from which nonresident farmers operated wheat farms in Greeley County in the early years of wheat farming. Repeaters are shown only once. Some traveled long distances. The prominence of Nebraskans as suitcase farmers was matched by the number from Nebraska who became residents. The combined census and assessor's report of 1925 shows that Nebraska was the leading source of farmers living in Harrison Township, the area in which Fishman's first large-scale breaking of prairie in the county took place.[18] The attraction of Greeley County for both suitcase farmers and settlers from Nebraska may well have been a carry over from their early associations with Fishman when he was operating in western Nebraska, as reported above. In addition, considerable credit is given to a long-time resident real estate man, Clement Wilson, originally from Nebraska, for effective real estate promotion in Nebraska.[19] When Fishman transferred his office force from

16. *Topeka Capital,* October 14, 1923.

17. *Greeley County Republican,* September 28, 1922.

18. What was called a census was combined with the usual agricultural data of the assessor's report of 1925. Library of Kansas State Historical Society.

19. Interviews with Margaret Pile and T. Bruce Stinson, Tribune, Kansas, November 16, 1968.

Burlington in the spring of 1921, he established them in Wilson's office.[20]

It seems safe to assume that the wheat farming by nonresidents was rarely adequately portrayed in the assessors' reports because the assessors made their rounds in the spring before the arrival of the suitcase farmers. Certainly the assessor of Greeley County missed many. At assessment time in 1924 he admitted underreporting of wheat, probably minimizing substantially the amount not reported: "Last year we were short several hundred acres due to the fact that some of the men who had large acreage were non-residents or were away at the time of assessment."[21] His report for 1924 was incomplete too. He listed only two suitcase addresses, both from northwestern Kansas, and one farmer from a neighboring county who proved to be a resident. In addition, he included L. E. Trued and the Wallin brothers as resident farmers, although only one of the Wallins was named in the lists of inhabitants. He missed the Wetzels, who were reported as planting 1,100 or 1,200 acres of wheat the previous autumn; Wetzel returned in June with two sons to "take care of their big wheat crop." Nor did he include the Ramm boys from Nebraska, who were described as "engaged extensively in farming in this county," since they had left for home in late November of 1923.[22]

Because lists of inhabitants for all three townships and the two towns of the county were included with the assessor's report for 1924, it was possible to determine which farmers were residents. Only thirty-two of the forty-seven individuals listed by themselves or in partnerships as having one hundred acres or more of winter wheat could be found as inhabitants of the county. The fifteen not shown as residents added to others identified in the newspaper, brings the proportion of the out-of-county larger wheat farmers to more than one-third. In Harrison Township, the site of Fishman's early big wheat venture, the ratio of nonresidents planting one hundred or more acres of wheat ran higher—nine of nineteen. Seven individual farmers and one partnership were listed by the assessor as having 560 acres or more; five of these farmers were residents and four were not. Two of the five then resident had started as suitcase farmers a few years earlier.

Altogether, the assessor reported forty-nine tractors and ten combines in the county in 1924. The resident farmers with 100 acres or more of wheat were shown as having sixteen tractors and three combines; those not found as inhabitants had nine tractors and six combines. If the two trac-

20. *Greeley County Republican,* March 31, 1921.
21. Ibid., April 3, 1924.
22. Ibid., November 1 and 29, 1923; June 26, 1924, and November 27, 1923.

tors of the Wallin brothers (one resident and one not) are divided, the nonresidents having 560 acres of winter wheat or more had a disproportionately large share of the farm equipment of the county: nine of forty-nine tractors and five of ten combines. L. E. Trued, still a suitcase farmer, with four combines, and James Smid, with four tractors, must have done custom work for some of their neighbors. The nonresident wheat farmers, especially those who planted wheat extensively, were better equipped than local farmers, according to the assessor's figures.

It appears that the *Greeley County Republican* newspaper editor was at least as likely as the assessor to take note of the larger operations by nonresidents. Early large wheat operations by residents and absentees noted in the newspaper included the following: Fishman, most specifically for 1921; Frank Kucera, a Tribune businessman, 2,000 acres ready (May 11, 1922); the Wetzels, from Iowa, 1,200 acres planted (September 28, 1922); Anton Nelson and Wallin brothers, Saunders County, Nebraska, more than 5,000 acres; Frank Kucera, 2,000 acres; H. C. Smith, Tribune businessman, several thousand acres (July 5, 1923); O. H. Wetzel and sons, Iowa, "large wheat crop" (June 26, 1924); for 1925, the Trued brothers, about 2,000 acres; Tony Nelson, about 1,400 acres; O. H. Wetzel, 1,200 acres (December 25, 1924); Tribune Grain and Implement Company (Kucera), 1,600 acres (March 12, 1925). Of the larger early wheat farmers, Fishman, Nelson, the Trueds, the Wallins, and the Wetzels were suitcase farmers at the outset. By 1925 all but the Wetzels were listed as inhabitants of the county. While there can be no assurance that nonresidents were equally important among the rank and file of wheat growers, they were conspicuous among the larger early wheat farmers, who included a number of sidewalk, or town, farmers.

Table 2, based on the assessors' reports, shows the acreages or yields reported for the period 1920-25 for the larger local and suitcase farmers. Surprisingly, there were instances in which local as well as suitcase farmers were caught a year late, that is, shown with a wheat crop without having been recorded as sowing for the crop. If the farming reported by the assessor was representative, the suitcase farmers on the average carried on larger operations than local farmers.

A comparison of yields in those cases in which both acreages and bushels harvested were recorded is given in table 3. Although it would be dangerous to base any general conclusion on such a small sample, it is plain that for those included, farmers from a distance had the better of it on the average. Probably their know-how and equipment made the difference.

Although it is impossible to determine just how many suitcase farmers took part in making Greeley County into wheat country and how much of the wheat belonged to them, the assessor's reports leave no doubt of the small part played by long-time residents. New farmers were responsible. In two of the three townships of the county, most of those farming in 1920 (1921 in the case of Harrison Township, for which no record for 1920 was found) had given up by 1927. In all three townships a majority of the 1927 farmers were new in the township since 1920 (or 1921). Although a majority of the persisting farmers planted wheat for 1927, the new farmers planting wheat outnumbered them in all townships. The percentage of the wheat acreage belonging to newcomers by townships was Colony, 67.1; Tribune, 81.8; and Harrison, 93.3. Their leadership was due mainly to the large scale of operation by some of them. Overall, forty-eight of the new farmers were credited by the assessor with three hundred acres or more, but only eleven of the long-time residents had that many.[23] Table 17 summarizes the situation for the three townships of Greeley County and for others in western Kansas at the time that wheat was becoming important.

Understandably, the county agent of the Agricultural Extension Service was disturbed by the activity of absentee farmers because it interfered with the attainment of the primary goals of the extension service—the diversification of agriculture and establishment of stable communities. A statement of the agent in the 1930 annual report exemplified this feeling and distinguished sharply—perhaps too sharply—between suitcase and resident farming:

> With the Herd Law came the fences, the breaking of sod, and the "Suitcase Farmer." This type of farmer lives here only during the summer months. He plants his crop and comes back for harvest and another planting. Large scale production whether by individuals or corporation backing is too prevalent. Of the two hundred odd resident farmers (many of them old cattle men) nearly all are turning toward a more stable form of agriculture [cattle, hogs, feed crops, and wheat].[24]

The analysis of the records of the AAA applications for 1933 (included in the next section) indicates that local farmers were, in fact, following the example of suitcase farmers. Many resident farmers were also emphasizing wheat.

23. Assessors' reports, 1920, 1921, 1927, Library of Kansas State Historical Society.
24. Annual report of county agent, Greeley County, 1930. All the reports for Western Kansas cited were examined on microfilm at Kansas State University.

The Importance of Out-of-County Wheat Farmers, 1930-33

It is fairly clear that suitcase farmers dominated wheat growing for a few years, beginning with Fishman's early venture. Whether absentees were in a majority later or raised most of the wheat is uncertain. An analysis of the records of wheat farmers signing up for the AAA in 1933, checked against the lists of inhabitants in the county, suggests that out-of-county operators, largely suitcase farmers, rivaled but probably did not quite equal local farmers in numbers or total acreage in wheat.

The county agent, H. L. Murphy, in his 1933 report related at length the difficulties encountered in obtaining what were considered adequate allotments of wheat acres under the newly established AAA. He thought the failure to include absentee farming in the records first used to determine the allotment for the county was the chief reason for the very low figure (an average of 53,000 acres for the three years 1930, 1931, and 1932) given by the assessor. He noted that although the figures on which allotments were based were wrong for several reasons, "the main one was that our wheat is farmed by non-resident farmers who are never assessed here." He added that the county committee first determined the average acreage of wheat for the three previous years to be 134,544, then, after a recheck, changed it to 154,594, a figure subsequently adopted by the state and national committees with only small reductions. As summarized by the county agent, the acreages sown to wheat for the five preceding years were 1928, 45,000; 1929, 49,000; 1930, 99,000; 1931, 174,000; 1932, 191,000.[25] The sums of wheat sown that I obtained from the AAA applications, as published in the *Greeley County Republican* of September 21, 1933, were: 1930, 104,257 acres; 1931, 164,122 acres; 1932, 175,165 acres; average for the three years, 147,845 acres; and 1933, 169,140 acres.

Human nature being what it is, there doubtless were efforts made to claim too much—too many acres or too many bushels—in the AAA sign-ups. The publication in the county newspaper of total acreage and all production by operator and owner was a safeguard. Such information was available to all, including neighbors, who were in effect competitors for the allotments to be made for the AAA. Finally, locally elected committees had responsibility for the details of the allotments made.

The requirements for reporting were strict. The applications included names and addresses of owners and tenants, location and size of farm, acreages of wheat planted, and production figures. They were to be signed

25. Ibid., 1933.

by operators and owners. In addition, a sketch map of each farm, statement of disposal of wheat, and certificates of purchase by grain dealers or other evidence which the grower wished to present were required.[26] It is doubtful that proof of sale could be produced in most cases and unlikely that the local committees required it.

The applications for wheat allotments under the AAA included nearly all of the acreage of wheat sown.[27] Here, then, were data that permitted a fairly accurate determination of the farmers engaged in wheat farming. A check of the names of farmers signing up for the AAA against the lists of inhabitants should make it possible to distinguish between farmers living in the county and those living outside.[28] This check was made for all the farmers applying for allotments in the county. Table 4 shows the results.

An important source of uncertainty was the considerable number of farmers who were not listed as residents but who had the same family names as residents of the county. For convenience, I will call such farmers family name farmers. The assumption was made that family name farmers were actually members of families whose heads were recorded as inhabitants of the county. Table 4 was made on that basis. However, if any farmer was identified either in the newspaper or assessor's report as living somewhere else, he was classified as out-of-county.[29] If family name farm-

26. *Lakin Independent,* August 18, 1933.

27. Statements in eleven western Kansas county newspapers showed 85 to 99 percent of the land with wheat history included in applications for allotment as follows: Cheyenne County, 91 (*St. Francis Herald,* October 12, 1933); Finney County, 97 (*Garden City News,* October 19, 1933); Gove County, 96 (*Republican-Gazette,* October 19, 1933); Grant County, 94 (*Grant County Republican,* October 26, 1933); Hamilton County, 85 (*Syracuse Journal,* September 15, 1933); Haskell County, 99 (*Sublette Monitor,* September 21, 1933); Lane County, 95 (*Dighton Herald,* September 21, 1933); Pawnee County, 97 (*Tiller and Toiler,* Larned, September 14, 1933); Sherman County, 95 (*Goodland News-Republic,* September 20, 1933); Stanton County, 99 (*Johnson City Pioneer,* September 28, 1933); Wallace County, 95 (*Western Times,* Sharon Springs, September 28, 1933).

28. Farmers, acreage, and production from "Wheat Production and Acreage Statements of Members of the Wheat Production Association of Greeley County, State of Kansas," *Greeley County Republican,* September 21, 1933. List of inhabitants from Assessor's Report, 1933 for two townships and the towns of Tribune and Horace. Since there was no list of inhabitants for Colony Township in 1933, the 1932 list was used.

29. The Fisher Ranch was a case in point. For the first portion of the period covered in the AAA application, this 8,000-plus-acre farm qualified as resident-operated because the Fishers had moved onto the ranch in West-North Colony Township, building two houses, one for themselves and one for their employees, according to a letter from Lloyd E. Waldren, ASCS county executive director and long-time resident, May 18, 1970. However, as of May 26, 1932, the ranch was in receivership and the Fishers had moved back to Wichita (*Greeley County Republican,* May 26, 1932). The Fisher Ranch was therefore classed as operated out-of-county.

ers are counted as residents, resident farmers constituted 57.3 percent of the total. If family name farmers are ignored, the district by district count gives 197 out-of-county to 195 local farmers, and if all family name farmers are considered out-of-county, nonresidents had a majority of 80. Family name farmers, constituting one-sixth of those listed, were numerous enough to swing the lead either way, but it is more to the point to emphasize that regardless of how this group is placed, local and nonresident wheat farmers were fairly equal in numbers.

The most convincing evidence of the essential accuracy of the number of out-of-county farmers is that of contemporary statistics. For 1934, the year after the beginning of the AAA, it was reported that 47.33 percent of the land in the county was operated by nonresidents.[30] Table 5, which does not credit any of the family name farms to out-of-county farmers, shows the following percentages of the wheat acreage of the county for out-of-county farmers: 1931, 45.07; 1932, 46.24; and 1933, 43.92. The out-of-county farmers had 43.09 percent of the farm land in wheat farms. The difference between the 47.33 percent of farm land of 1934 and the derived figures above suggests an error of less than 10 percent. However, it may have been larger because suitcase farmers were mainly wheat farmers and not all the farmers in the county raised wheat. The 42.7 percent of wheat farmers shown living out of the county may need to be increased somewhat and, thus, their farm land and wheat acreages.

A name-by-name check of forty family name farmers led to the conclusion that most were residents. A community leader concerned directly with agriculture as superintendent of the Tribune Branch Agricultural Experiment Station for about forty years made the following classification of family name farmers listed in 1933 as operating wheat farms in the central part of the county (near the experiment farm): resident, 30; suitcase farmers, three; lived just over the county line, two; unknown, five.[31]

In addition, a test was made of the degree to which neighboring farmers crossed the county line. As shown in table 4, South Harrison, West South Colony, and East-South Colony townships, all adjacent to Hamilton County, ran high in the percentage of out-of-county wheat farmers. The names of all out-of-county farmers of these three districts, a total of eighty-four farmers, were checked against the lists of inhabitants as reported by the assessor in all the bordering townships of Hamilton County and in Syracuse, the county seat. Only one positive identification resulted: that of Christian Molz, a businessman of Syracuse. A large majority of

30. *Greeley County Republican,* October 17, 1940.
31. T. Bruce Stinson, interview, November 16, 1968.

out-of-county farmers came from farther, probably much farther.

Table 4 shows in the duplication of names that all groups included farmers who farmed in more than one community, but the areal spreading of farming endeavor involved only a small number of the farmers. It appears that not over 31 of 175 rural in-county, not over 22 of 45 sidewalk, and not over 33 of the 163 out-of-county operators farmed in more than one of the eight reporting districts in the county. A small amount of commuting from district to district was involved, but only sidewalk and out-of-county farmers typically commuted.

The sidewalk farmers of Tribune and Horace operated most in the nearest communities, South Tribune and North Harrison, but did some farming in all districts (tables 4 and 7) and more commonly than other groups farmed in more than one locality. Sidewalk farmers were a poor third behind rural residents of the county and out-of-county farmers but probably outnumbered farmers living in neighboring counties who had operations in Greeley County.

A Close-up of the Location of Wheat Farms in Colony Township

Overall, wheat growing was fairly evenly distributed over the county by 1933. However, Colony Township, at the west, had relatively less wheat land than other communities, except for the East-South division, and most of the land was still outside organized farms. Colony was then on the margin of wheat production and a large portion of it had little underground water. To the west in Kiowa County, Colorado, wheat was still of minor concern.

Figure 5 shows in detail the distribution of land in wheat farms in Colony Township as derived from AAA applications and the areas mapped officially as lacking an underground water table.[32] There is a general but irregular reduction in the percentage of land in wheat farms from east to west. The fractional townships (Range 43W) along the Colorado border at the extreme west contained few wheat farms, and the areas without a water table, especially in the big area in T17S, R41W, also lagged.

The distribution of land in wheat farms by residence of the operator is noteworthy. Farmers not resident in Colony Township, although common

32. The Greeley County newspaper listing of AAA applications, unlike other counties in the suitcase farming country, gave the locations within sections. Hence, precise mapping of land in wheat farms was possible. The areas with zero depth of saturated Pliocene and Pleistocene deposits are those shown by Glenn C. Prescott, John R. Branch, and Woodrow W. Wilson, in *Geology and Ground Water Resources of Wichita and Greeley Counties, Kansas,* State Geological Survey of Kansas Bulletin, no. 108, April 1954, fig. 12, p. 51.

throughout, dominated most areas that were without underground water. A count of quarter sections in wheat farms that were mainly within areas of no water shows the following results: operated by residents of the township 30.5; by residents of other townships of the county, 8.125; by town farmers, 25.25; and by out-of-county 98.5.[33] Residents of the township farmed fewer than one-fifth of such tracts. Town farmers accounted for almost as many and out-of-county farmers had almost 60 percent of the total. By comparison, in the remaining parts of Colony Township, those having a water table, the counts ran: residents of the township 126.25; residents of other townships, 12.25; town farmers, 25.25; and out-of-county residents, 157. As might be anticipated, resident farmers were relatively more important where underground water was available. Obviously, a well on the farm was more imperative for a farmer living on the land.

In Colony Township as a whole, the proportion of nonresidents, especially from out of the county, ran high. This was notably true at the western edge. The pioneering role of nonresident farmers is particularly evident in Range 43W, where there were only 12 quarter sections operated by wheat farmers resident in Colony Township in the nearly fifty square miles of this narrow strip. In contrast, two quarter sections were operated by rural farmers from townships other than Colony, town farmers operated 12.5, and out-of-county farmers had 37. Out-of-county farmers were far in the lead and town farmers were second. The demonstration of the pioneering role of suitcase farmers was anticipated, but that of town farmers was somewhat surprising. In their case, it seems especially likely that planting wheat on the frontier of wheat farming was a part-time speculative venture.

Land Use, Out-of-County and Resident

Summations of acreage and production figures for all the farms of Greeley County included in the 1933 AAA listing appear in tables 5 through 8. For the county as a whole, out-of-county farmers had 43 percent of the land (a small plurality over local rural farmers), and they outranked local rural farmers in both wheat acreage and production in each year except 1930. The local town farmers had approximately one-seventh of the land in wheat farms and about one-seventh of the wheat

33. Each separate tract of a quarter section or less was assigned entirely to either an area *with* or *without* a water table. If over one-half of the land unit was judged to be in an area without a water table, the entire unit was so classified. Thus, the classification of acreage is not exact although sustantially correct.

acreage and production for each year covered except 1932, when they contributed only a little more than one-twelfth of the total amount of wheat.

The question whether local and out-of-county farmers gave the same emphasis to wheat cannot be answered with certainty from an analysis of tables 5-8 because only farmers raising wheat were included in the 1933 data used. A comparison for Colony Township yielded nearly identical counts of 92 in-county farmers reported by the assessor in 1933 and 94 AAA applicants classed as in-county in this study.[34] It seems safe to say that by 1933 all or virtually all farmers in Colony Township, resident or not, were growing wheat. The same conclusion seems probable for Harrison Township because of similar evidence, but in Tribune Township over one-third of in-county farmers seem not to have been planting wheat. In effect, table 8 exaggerates somewhat the percentage of the farm land of local farmers sown to wheat because the non-wheat growers were excluded. (Table 8 shows the percentage of farm land sown to wheat for each of the three groups of farmers.) The acreage planted to wheat by each group increased each year except 1933, following the poor crop of 1932, as shown in tables 5, 6, and 7. In 1933 only local rural farmers expanded their acreage. Both out-of-county and in-county wheat farmers were sowing large acreages, averaging about 456 and 429 acres respectively. Local farmers had almost caught up with nonresidents in wheat acreage per farmer.

The generalization that suitcase farmers grew mainly wheat is supported for three of the four years. The first year, 1930, was the exception. The reason for the apparent failure of out-of-county farmers to outplant the others in that year is uncertain, but at least two explanations are plausible. One is that because wheat history went with the land, it was the responsibility of the operator to report how much wheat had been planted in previous years. Out-of-county operators, if not themselves the owners, were nearly always tenants on land owned by other absentees. In many cases the crop history may have been difficult for absentee tenants to obtain, while local residents, if new operators of absentee-owned land, might more readily get the information from their neighbors. A second possibility is that because a large part of the land operated by out-of-

34. The assessor showed one suitcase address, the only one listed for the county. Of course, this farmer was excluded from the count of in-county operators. Of twenty-six farmers shown as having post office addresses in Towner to the west and Weskan to the north, only one was found to actually live outside the county. The other twenty-five residents were included in the count of ninety-two resident farmers.

county farmers was located in the newer areas of the county, less wheat was actually planted. Tables 5-7 show that South Harrison district and all of Colony Township lagged behind the other portions of the county in the development of wheat farming and appear to have been undergoing wide-spread plow-up of grassland in the early 1930s. In South Harrison and each of the districts of Colony Township, the increase in the wheat acreage from 1930 to 1932 was substantially greater on farms being operated by out-of-county farmers in 1933 than on those farmed by residents of the county. Probably the concentration of the efforts of nonresidents on new areas was characteristic. At least there should have been more room for them there.

As a matter of fact, the census of 1935 indicates that more than one-half of the land in the entire county lay outside of farms. The 311 farms totaled only 232,838 acres of the 496,640 acres in the county. The 222,419 acres of land in wheat farms for which AAA applications were filed, as shown in tables 5 and 6, thus made up nearly all of the farm land of the county. Accordingly, it may be assumed that figure 5, in represent-ing wheat farms, also represented nearly all the farm land of the township.

Comparative Yields, Local and Out-of-County

Table 9 shows average yields on a planted acre basis for the three groups of farmers. These figures appear realistic. The publication of pro-duction statistics in the county newspaper virtually assured that exagger-ated claims would be discovered by the county committee. In fact, the average yields for the three years shown in table 9 were about two bushels per acre less than the county average of 11.1 bushels per acre for the five-year period 1928-32, prepared in advance by F. K. Reed, state statis-tician and allotment officer for Kansas.[35] Of course, if his estimate was on a harvested-acre basis, the figure was not comparable to those of table 9.

In each of the three years, the best results were obtained by out-of-county farmers. The town farmers had the poorest yields, although if the average yields by districts are compared, a few exceptions are found.

The apparent superiority of suitcase farmers as late as the early 1930s is somewhat unexpected, considering that they spent much less time in the county than the resident farmers and that local farmers were no longer novices in wheat farming. The results of the 1932 crop, in a crop year of severe drought and dust blowing, are especially surprising in view of the common judgment that absentee farmers were often unable to take ap-

35. *Lakin Independent*, July 21, 1933.

propriate measures to combat blowing dust in winter and spring, usually the most critical times, because they were rarely in the area. Moreover, there were doubtless short-term speculators among the absentee farmers who had no more experience in wheat farming than resident farmers. Probably the explanation is that many nonresidents continued to profit from longer experience in wheat farming and that neither resident nor nonresident farmers were prepared for Dust Bowl conditions.

An examination of yields tract by tract for the three years revealed, as expected, that results varied greatly from year to year, with only a few farmers showing even average yields for 1932. Also, while one farmer did well in a given year, another obtained poor results, and a given farmer might have high yields on one tract and low on another. As might be anticipated from the averages shown in table 9, high yields were obtained more often and poor yields suffered less frequently by out-of-county farmers than by in-county farmers. Table 10 summarizes the results for both poor and good crops. Yields in the middle range are not shown.[36]

Most of the abandonment of wheat (zero yield) was of the crop intended for harvest in 1932. However, out-of-county farmers reported 37 of their 184 total cases of zero yields in 1930 and 1931. Comparable figures for local town farmers were 8 of 63 and for local rural farmers 28 of 187. In this connection, the small number of low yields (one bushel or less in all three years and more than one but less than five in 1930 and 1931) harvested by out-of-county and sidewalk farmers, 19 and 6, respectively, as against 40 by local rural farmers, should be noted. The off-farm operators, suitcase and sidewalk, apparently preferred not to bother with the poorer crops, thus running up the abandonment figures. The presumably better informed sidewalk farmers were shown as harvesting only two tracts that produced less than one bushel per acre. Although out-of-county farmers ordinarily did not harvest their wheat when the crop was poor, their record of abandonment was no worse than that of local farmers. The farmers operating from distant bases produced more good crops than the locals. In short, the out-of-county farmers were, as a group, the best wheat farmers.

36. High and low yields were defined quite arbitrarily. In the rather good wheat years of 1930 and 1931, high was defined as twenty or more bushels per acre, poor as less than five, and very poor as one or less. In the poor year of 1932, five bushels or more was considered high and one or less as poor. The most common yields, except for 1932 (when the general result was zero) were between five and twenty bushels per acre.

Tenure of Local and Out-of-County Wheat Farmers

The listing of both owners and operators on applications submitted for AAA wheat allotments permitted determination of the tenure status of wheat farmers. Table 11 gives the results of the counts of tracts of the wheat farms in Colony Township, the largest of the three townships. In each case, the percentage of tenant operation was high, highest for local town farmers and lowest for out-of-county farmers. There is considerable question that Colony Township in 1933 was truly representative of the tenure status of out-of-county farmers because tenancy ran so much higher than determined then or later for other areas. For example, the percentage of operations by owners (including ownership within the family), among both absentee and local farmers in neighboring Wallace County, in which a one-fifth sample was run, was much higher at 64 and 46 percent respectively.

Table 12 shows that all groups of farmers used mainly land owned outside the county. Local rural farmers, accounting for 29 tracts owned by the operators and 9 locally owned tracts that were rented, were least dependent on land owned out of county. Even so, 77 of their 115 tracts used were so owned. For the local town farmers, the comparable figures were 34 of 53; for out-of-county farmers, 103 of 125. That out-of-county farmers were able to rent locally owned land is surprising, but some of the local owners were relatives of absentee renters and some of the absentees were former residents. There is also the possibility that some of the owners identified as local on the basis of family names were not residents.

The change from local owner-operation to absentee ownership and tenant operation in Colony Township had taken place rapidly. In 1920 the assessor had reported sixty-five owner-operators, three part owner-part renters, eleven renters, and four not classified. Of course, part of the change to tenant operation was undoubtedly due to the conversion to farms of unused land already owned by nonresidents.

Persistence of Suitcase and Local Wheat Farmers

It might be of some interest and relevance to inquire what became of the early suitcase farmers. A check was made of the later lists of inhabitants up to 1933 in order to learn how many of the suitcase farmers of the period 1921-27 identified from newspaper accounts became residents of the county. In addition, the list of wheat farmers in 1933 compiled for

AAA purposes, was checked to determine the number of suitcase farmers who were still operating as absentees in the county.

In summary, the results were these: eleven early suitcase farmers had become local residents and continued as wheat farmers in 1933; nine early suitcase farmers were still operating as absentee wheat farmers in 1933; five early suitcase farmers not operating wheat farms in 1933, but listed as absentee owners; and there was no record for twelve. The degree of persistence was high, especially for an agricultural frontier. By comparison, of thirty-one large or fairly large early local wheat farmers, not including suitcase farmers who had become local, twenty-three were growing wheat in the county in 1933. This was also a high rate of survival.

Conclusion

Greeley County, Kansas, in the forefront in the development of suitcase farming, offers many examples of how the conversion to wheat country was brought about. To a considerable degree it provides a cross section of men and events as a case study. The nonresidents were innovators, leading in the plow-up and extension of specialized wheat farming. As a promoter of land development, Simon Fishman, although unusual for the scale of his operation and earlier than most, was somewhat representative of a type, as will be pointed out later. The many newcomers, some who moved in and some who continued to farm wheat from homes farther east, seem typical for a larger region, although relatively more came to Greeley County from southeastern Nebraska than was generally true on the suitcase farming frontier. By 1933 local farmers were almost as committed to wheat as the nonresidents, but their yields were not yet as good.

CHAPTER THREE

The Early Suitcase Farming Frontier: Some Further Close-ups

Hamilton County

As the last county in Kansas to adopt a herd law, freeing farmers from the need to protect their crops by fencing, Hamilton was late in becoming wheat country. Like its neighbor, Greeley County, it is part of the driest portion of Kansas (fig. 1). Here the plow-up of prairie for wheat became important late in the 1920s and continued in the early 1930s. The year 1931 witnessed two related events: the establishment of herd law, and rail shipments of wheat equaling those of cattle for the first time.[1]

The development of suitcase farming in Hamilton County differed in some respects from that of Greeley County. It came somewhat later and was a little less important than in Greeley County; there appears not to have been a land developer comparable to Simon Fishman; and there were fewer Nebraskans and others from distant sources among the absentee farmers. Wheat-farming country some 75 to 150 miles to the east provided most of the nonresident operators.

The county assessor first reported wheat farming by absentees in 1925, showing one farmer from St. Louis, with 400 acres of wheat, and recording a harvest by a Nebraskan a year late. As far as the assessors' reports are concerned, the harvest of 8,200 bushels from 720 acres of wheat by A. E. Woodman of Omaha in 1924 was the earliest instance of suitcase farming

1. *Syracuse Journal,* January 9, February 20, and August 28, 1931.

in the county. It had been appropriately noted in the local newspaper nearly a year before the assessor reported it.[2] The largest acreages of winter wheat credited to local farmers in 1925 were 500, 300, and 280. The total for the county was only 7,893 acres.[3]

Woodman's 720 acres lay idle in 1925, but he reportedly sold 500 bushels as seed wheat to a suitcase farmer from Clinton, Missouri, who in September of 1924 was breaking land owned by another Missourian.[4] Although the farmer from Missouri got only his seed back in 1925, he tried again. The assessor reported 800 acres of wheat with a harvest of only 2,400 bushels for him in 1926. Another suitcase farmer, one from Boulder, Colorado, was credited with 800 acres of wheat and a harvest of 6,000 bushels. The largest planting by a local farmer in 1926 was given at 250 acres. Z. B. Zook, later identified as from Larned but erroneously given a local address by the assessor, was reported as sowing 1,100 acres for 1927.[5]

The Syracuse paper gave attention to a considerable plow-up in 1927 in Hamilton and Stanton counties and the next year identified six farmers by name in connection with the 1928 harvest. Three lived in the county; one, C. Molz was from neighboring Stanton County; and two, Woodman from Omaha and I. E. Martin from Wichita, were suitcase farmers by the definition used here. The previous autumn a farmer from Benkelman, Nebraska, was reported as sowing 800 acres of wheat, but he was not mentioned at harvest time.[6]

The newspaper took note of a number of large operators among the suitcase farmers, although the assessor usually missed them. One of these was Martin, who along with Woodman was later described as a pioneer wheat grower.[7] Martin was said to have harvested 30,000 bushels of wheat in the county in 1929. In 1931 his harvest of 150,000 bushels was produced by tenants, according to the editor. However, Martin himself was shown as the operator of a farm on the upland plain in the north of the county on the AAA applications in 1933.[8] Another large undertaking mentioned by the newspaper but not by the assessor was that of Mirt Newhouse of Pratt, Kansas, an experienced suitcase farmer who was reported to be extending his operations into Hamilton County in the spring

2. *Syracuse Journal*, July 18, 1924.
3. "Decennial Census and Statistical Rolls," Hamilton County, 1925, Library of Kansas State Historical Society.
4. *Syracuse Journal*, September 19, 1924; July 23, 1926.
5. "Statistical Lists, Agriculture," Hamilton County, 1926 and 1927.
6. *Syracuse Journal*, May 13, 1927; July 13, 1928; October 7, 1927.
7. Ibid., July 3, 1931.
8. Ibid., July 26, 1929; July 31, 1931; and September 15, 1933.

of 1929. Newhouse was said to have six tractors breaking land on some of the twenty-three quarter sections he had bought in the county after having taken "an active part in the agricultural growth of every county between Pratt and the Colorado line."[9] Not counting Pratt County, there are at the minimum six counties between Pratt and the Colorado line. Newhouse was not included in the Hamilton County AAA list of 1933.

The earliest mention found of corporation farming in the county was of the United Farms Corporation of Wichita in 1929, when it was stated that 3,000 additional acres of wheat and 10,000 more a year from then were planned. Fred E. Fisher, president of the corporation, was quoted as saying, "No one knows the exact way to farm out here yet . . . and my plans are to experiment until the best results are found." He recommended breaking ground in the fall, killing weeds in the spring, delaying planting wheat until the following fall, and summer fallowing. The editor added,

> For the present Mr. Fisher is trying several methods of management. Some of it is farmed by tenants, some work he is contracting, and he himself manages a large part of it. For a while Mr. Fisher plans to raise wheat entirely in Hamilton Co. but he does not advise this for the individual farmer.[10]

Three years later, at least the Greeley County part of the operation of the Fisher Ranch was in the hands of receivers, and the Fishers had moved back to Wichita.[11]

By the spring of 1930, the Sledd Farm Corporation of Lyons, Kansas, was breaking 2,800 acres of land purchased recently. It was represented by a manager.[12] In 1933, according to the AAA applications reported, the company held the same acreage in the northern part of the county, on which it had averaged 1,400 acres of planted wheat during 1930-32. On the same list, at least two Collingwoods (of Plains, Kansas), earlier said to be operators of large farms in southwestern Kansas, were shown as owners but not operators in the county.[13]

Although absentees triggered wheat farming in Hamilton County and commonly had the largest acreages, the assessors consistently found more local producers of wheat than outsiders. Some local farmers became large

9. Ibid., May 17, 1929.
10. Ibid., July 17, 1929.
11. *Greeley County Republican,* January 14 and May 26, 1932.
12. *Syracuse Journal,* May 16, 1930.
13. Ibid., September 15, 1933. The *Syracuse Journal* of September 21, 1928, referred to the Collingwoods' operation as probably the "largest wheat acreage under one management in the Middle West."

wheat growers even though additional investments in machinery, changes in mode of operation, and additional risks were involved. Among them was Christian Molz, an implement dealer in Syracuse, who had moved from Stanton County with his sons and was said to have a total of 114 quarter sections (18,240 acres) in wheat in the four-county area of Hamilton, Greeley, and Stanton counties, Kansas, and Baca County, Colorado, in 1931.[14] The AAA wheat lists showed 5,393 acres of farm land operated by Molz and Sons in Hamilton County in 1933, with 1,448 in wheat in 1930, increased to 5,061 in 1932. Molz traveled a shorter distance to his farms in Hamilton County than elsewhere. Only in Baca County, Colorado, would he have been a suitcase farmer by the definition used here.

A somewhat fanciful account of the making of a wheat farmer was reported by a neighboring county's newspaper in 1929:

> Wheat supplants steers—last year the steer gave way in this range country, according to Ike Martin, of Hamilton Co. who tried his best to keep the nesters from plowing up the sod and who swore this was grazing country and nothing else. Ike had 10,000 a. and he finally decided to put some of it in wheat.
>
> Last year he harvested 1,800 acres of wheat. It averaged between 25 and 30 bu. per acre, some of it making 38 bu. When Ike saw that pile of 54,000 bu. of wheat from his "experiment," he kicked his spurs and chaps into the clothes closet, hung up his lariat, and decided to call himself a wheat grower. He set aside $50,000 as a wheat fund to stake his venture. This year he has a better crop in sight than last.[15]

There is a good possibility that the rancher-become-farmer was a non-resident.[16]

In Hamilton, as in Greeley County, long-time resident farmers lagged in following the example of new farmers in wheat farming. Lamont Township, on the upland in the southeastern corner of Hamilton County, will serve as an example. Eleven of the forty farmers were shown as having planted a total of 517 acres of winter wheat for the 1920 harvest. The persisting farmers, including five new farmers of the same family name, numbered twenty-eight in 1927, only eleven of whom planted wheat, totaling only 891 acres. By comparison, thirteen of twenty-six farmers new since 1920 and not having family names of those farming in 1920 had

14. Ibid., July 31, 1931.
15. Ibid., July 17, 1929, quoting the *Lakin Independent.*
16. Martin was not listed by the Hamilton County assessor as farming nor was his name included among those of residents of the county.

a total of four thousand acres. The only farmers planting as much as three hundred acres were new, one a local farmer and one a suitcase farmer although he was mistakenly given a local address by the assessor. The old timers, including relatives of the same family name, were credited with only 18.2 percent of the wheat acreage in 1927.[17]

The first considerable number of out-of-county farmers found by the assessor was in Lamont Township in 1930, after he had been reprimanded by the state office for incomplete reporting. He reported five from a neighboring county and eight with suitcase addresses. Of the five from the next county (all at Ulysses in Grant County, just to the southeast), all sowed wheat, four of them over two hundred acres, but none over six hundred. All eight of the suitcase farmers listed grew wheat, seven of them over two hundred acres and three over six hundred. Only twenty-one, or less than one-third, of the seventy-six farmers having addresses in the county had two hundred or more acres of wheat; only forty-one local farmers grew any wheat at all. Of the three groups, suitcase farmers were most committed to the growing of wheat; farmers living in the county depended least on wheat.

As might be expected, resident farmers were least well equipped for extensive farming of wheat. In 1930, thirty-three of the seventy-six local farmers in Lamont Township had tractors, with a total of thirty-eight; ten had combines, for a total of ten. All five of the farmers from Grant County had tractors and two had combines assessed in Hamilton County. The assessor found four tractors and two combines belonging to the eight suitcase farmers. Back home, the several assessors reported the suitcase farmers who were listed by the assessor in Lamont Township as owners of three tractors and of one and one-half combines. One of the seven suitcase farmers from Kansas could not be found in the list of inhabitants of the county from which he was reported doing suitcase farming, and, of course, it was not possible to check in the Kansas records the machinery kept at home by A. E. Woodman of Omaha. Three of the seven Kansas suitcase farmers, but none of the farmers from the next county, proved to be towndwellers.

A more complete breakdown of the place of assessment of tractors of the suitcase farmers in Lamont Township in 1930 showed that three of the four town-dwelling suitcase farmers (including Woodman) left tractors in the township; the tractor of one who lived on a distant farm was assessed in his home county, and in two cases a tractor was assessed at home and another in Lamont Township. This suggests only a limited movement of

17. Assessor's reports for Lamont Township, Hamilton County, 1921 and 1927.

equipment back and forth.

In 1931 the assessors for Lamont Township reported eleven farmers having addresses more than one county away. It was the largest number found in a township anywhere in western Kansas prior to the AAA. In comparison, six were listed from neighboring counties, and seventy-nine had addresses in Hamilton County. The one-third sample of the AAA list of 1933 for the southeast community of the county yielded six of twenty-one as out-of-county wheat farmers, which indicates that most of the out-of-county farmers were identified in 1931. Of the suitcase farmers, all grew wheat, eight of the eleven at least six hundred acres each. Seven had a total of twelve tractors, and four had combines. All six farmers from neighboring counties grew wheat, four of them six hundred acres or more. Four had tractors, with a total of six, and three had a total of four combines. Fifty-two of the seventy-nine in-county farmers grew wheat; thirty-seven (less than one-half) had as many as two hundred acres. Forty-six of the in-county farmers had tractors, totalling sixty-one. Twenty-five had combines, with a total of twenty-eight. Local farmers had not caught up in wheat farming or in equipment for doing it.

Figure 6a shows the places from which suitcase farmers identified either from the newspaper or from the assessors' reports came to carry on their farming in Hamilton County in the years before the establishment of the AAA in 1933. The same pattern may have existed in 1933; for example, seven of the eight suitcase farmers on the assessor's list in Lamont Township in 1930 were on the Hamilton County AAA list for 1933. All seven Kansans recorded by the assessor, including the one who did not make application for the AAA in 1933, lived in an easterly direction at distances of 50 to 140 miles; another absentee who persisted was from Omaha.

The applications for initial AAA allotments made by the wheat farmers of Hamilton County were analyzed in the same way as for Greeley County except that in Hamilton a sample consisting of every third operator was run.[18] As in Greeley County, local residents, including farmers having the same family names as farmers listed as inhabitants, constituted a majority. If family name farmers are excluded from consideration, those plainly nonresident—not found as inhabitants and not having the same family names as resident heads of families—constituted a majority, as in Greeley County. Counting family-name farmers as residents, the sample showed sixty-eight on-farm operators, thirteen local town operators, and forty-seven out-of-county wheat farmers. Thus, out-of-county farmers numbered

18. As listed in the *Syracuse Journal,* September 15, 1933, and checked against the lists of inhabitants in the assessor's report of 1933.

about 38 percent of the wheat farmers of the county. Table 13 shows farm land, wheat acreage, and production for these three groups. Out-of-county farmers were in the majority in two communities of the seven communities, one of the two bordering Greeley County.

The average yield for the three-year period 1930-32 of 12.8 bushels per acre was in line with the official estimate of 13.2 bushels for the five-year period 1928-32.[19] The three groups of farmers ranked in the same order as in Greeley County in average yields obtained, with the out-of-county farmers first and the town farmers last. Average yields are shown in table 14. The explanation offered for the better results obtained by out-of-county farmers in Greeley County probably applies here also. More experience and better equipment paid off. However, the drought of 1932 seems to have been less damaging in Hamilton than in Greeley County.

The nonresidents' 32.5 percent of the county's total acreage for the 1936 wheat allotment sign-up[20] supports the general accuracy of the sample results. This figure was somewhat less than both the 40-odd percent which represented their share of the wheat acreage for 1930-33 and the 38 percent which out-of-county farmers constituted among the wheat growers.

Stanton County

Suitcase farmers were important in early wheat farming in Stanton County. Because the area was dry and western, the cattleman held on long there. The county agent pointed out in the annual report of 1933 that Stanton ranked 104th in population among the 105 counties of the state, that most of its land was owned by nonresidents, and that there were relatively few improved farms. In addition, he noted that there were 1,116 AAA wheat contracts, and that at least 75 percent of them had to be mailed for signing by nonresident owners. It does not seem farfetched that small population, nonresident ownership, wheat farming (especially by nonresidents), and a large proportion of unimproved farms were functionally related conditions.

Unlike its neighbors to the north, Stanton County had no early through

19. Five-year average prepared by F. K. Reed, state statistician and wheat allotment officer for Kansas. *Lakin Independent,* July 21, 1933.

20. The acreage signed up for the 1936 wheat allotment by November 15, 1935, was 132,320 acres operated by resident farmers and 63,680 by nonresidents, according to the *Syracuse Journal,* November 22, 1935.

railroad. Track was laid into the county in 1922, aiding, it was asserted, the more than 300 percent increase in cultivated area in Grant and Stanton counties shown in three years, although the free-range law then in effect in Stanton slowed the conversion of grassland to cultivation.[21]

A number of clear-cut instances of the retarding effect of free-range conditions were reported by the county newspaper, including the following:

> Mr. R. R. Wilson who owns a large ranch 5 miles north and 12 miles east of Johnson . . . has made a contract with some parties to break 2000 acres of his land in Grant County and the same parties will sow it to wheat this fall. He had also contracted the breaking of his Stanton County land but when he learned that he would have to have it fenced if planted to crop, he persuaded his renters to break land in Grant County instead.[22]

Despite the continuance of the open range until 1929,[23] wheat farming made substantial advances.

The plow-up for wheat in the middle and late 1920s followed a series of generally unsatisfactory wheat crops from very small acreages. A front-page story in the local paper summarized the county's previous experience as follows: 1917, the "first wheat sown in many years" was an entire failure; 1918, about five hundred acres, averaging about fifteen bushels; 1919, 2,000 acres, with yields of fifteen to thirty-five bushels per acre; increased plantings thereafter but 1922 an entire failure, with just enough wheat to provide seed; 1923, low yields; 1924, variable yields; 1925, largest acreage ever sown, good prospects for harvest.[24] The record showed wheat growing was a gamble. Long-established residents knew the results; the prominently displayed summary probably was read by most newcomers and by many nonresidents having land interests in the area.

As of 1925, the county assessor reported only 16,714 acres planted to wheat,[25] the largest acreages listed being 1,400, 900, and 800. Although no suitcase addresses were included, the largest wheat farmer in the county, E. Shore, then a resident, had been recorded by the assessor as doing suitcase farming in the county in 1922 and 1923. Shore, then from Coats in Pratt County, was credited with having 560 of 1,120 acres in wheat in 1922, the year the railroad came. In 1923 his wheat crop for the previous

21. *Johnson City Pioneer,* March 20, 1925.
22. Ibid.
23. Ibid., April 26, 1929.
24. Ibid., August 14, 1925.
25. "Decennial Census and Statistical Rolls," Stanton County, 1925.

year was given as 5,400 bushels and his 1923 acreage as 900 of the 1,440 acres in the farm. Other early suitcase wheat farmers listed by the assessor included a farmer from each of the following places: Pratt in 1921, 1922, 1927, and 1929; Washington, Illinois, in 1927; and Macksville in 1930.

The editor, not limiting himself to farmers present in early spring (as the assessor evidently did), took note of wheat farming by a number of the same and additional outsiders. In all probability more failed to come to his notice than did, but between 1925 and 1928 the newspaper mentioned absentees engaging in wheat farming from Hoopertown, Illinois (1925); McDonald, Kansas (1926); Satanta, Kansas (1927); Satanta, Pratt, Newton, and Cimarron, Kansas; and Cherokee, Oklahoma (all 1928).

The neighboring Syracuse paper noted other activity in Stanton County which apparently was not reported in the local paper. One example is:

> Garden City, July 21, 1926 — W. A. Baker, who bought 18 quarter sections in southeast Stanton County a few years ago and operated a cattle ranch for several years, is converting his land into a wheat farm, thereby following the example of many others in the county. Last year he put out 800 acres of wheat which is looking fine, and this year is putting the balance under cultivation.[26]

In Baker's case, the Stanton County assessor noted his operations in 1921, 1922, 1927, 1928, and 1929, giving his suitcase address as Pratt and his wheat acreages beginning in 1922 as 100, 1,100, not reported, and 440. Baker began trying out wheat by planting in 1920 because a 1921 crop of 600 bushels was reported in 1922.

Another story from Syracuse ran as follows: "Collingwood Bros. of Plains have purchased 27 more quarter sections of western Kansas land to be converted into wheat farms. The land is all in Stanton County. . . . The land will all be sown to wheat in the fall." The next spring, there was a follow-up story: "One of the biggest jobs of converting prairie into farmland ever witnessed in western Kansas is going on in Stanton County on land owned by Collingwood Bros. Last year 18,000 acres of sod were broken by these brothers, and this year 5,000 more acres have been broken." And again, "The largest wheat acreage under one management in the Middle West probably is that of the Collingwood Grain Co. which is preparing to seed this fall 18,000 acres."[27]

Although it would seem impossible to determine whether absentees planted or harvested more wheat than local farmers in any year or years in

---

26. *Syracuse Journal and Republican News,* July 23, 1926.
27. *Syracuse Journal,* May 13, 1927; May 18 and September 21, 1928.

the 1920s, it is clear that they were among those who pioneered wheat farming. The important part taken by absentees in the plow-up of Stanton County was, in effect, acknowledged and encouraged in true booster fashion by the local editor. In a story on real estate activity, he wrote, "We still have lots of room for the non-resident land owners if they care to come and improve their land and break part of it."[28] In Stanton County, as in other parts of the suitcase farming country, testimony by long-time residents credited suitcase farmers with the major portion of wheat farming in the early stages of the wheat boom. This was the assertion made by a former local farmer, Joe Kippes, who had come to the county as a boy in 1917, hired out to break land for others as wheat farming was introduced, and as a wheat farmer was elected to the county committee responsible for administering the control regulations of the AAA. He said that three-fourths of the early wheat farming was done by suitcase farmers.[29] The opinion is expressed here that not all the long-time residents identifying suitcase farmers as being responsible for most of the early wheat farming had faulty memories or were guilty of exaggeration.

Although it is impossible to determine accurately the role of absentee farmers in the making of the new wheat country, it is possible to determine the limited participation by long-time resident farmers, who, it can be assumed, were quite consistently found by the assessor on his rounds in the spring of the year. The essential facts for Stanton Township, centrally located in the county, are as follows: of the forty farmers in 1920, there were three with wheat, thirty-seven without, and the largest wheat acreage was 70 acres; of those farming in 1927, thirteen of the forty persisted, plus two relatives with the same family name, for a total of fifteen; of these fifteen persisters, eight were credited with the planting of wheat for a total of 1,740 acres in 1927. As reported by the assessor, newcomers who began farming after 1920, not including those with the same family names as farmers of 1920, numbered thirty-two, of whom ten were shown as growing wheat in 1927. The percentage of the newcomers growing wheat was smaller than that of long-time resident farmers, but their scale of operation was larger. The big wheat farmers, planting three hundred acres or more each, in 1927 consisted of one persister from 1920, who had begun growing wheat since 1920, one new rural resident, two new sidewalk farmers, and one new suitcase farmer (from Washington, Illinois). All the newcomers together were credited with 73.7 percent of the wheat acreage of the township in 1927. In this example from Stanton County, as in Greeley and Hamilton counties, it is plain that newcomers, suitcase and residents,

28. *Johnson City Pioneer,* November 16, 1928.
29. Joe Kippes, interview, November 19, 1968.

but not long-time residents, were responsible for the great increase in wheat farming in the mid-1920s.

Here, also, the big plow-up for wheat continued into the early 1930s. A sample of the wheat farms listed in applications for AAA contracts showed the wheat acreages claimed to have been sown for the four years 1930 through 1933 as 26,241, 31,842, 31,310, and 33,690, an apparent increase of 28 percent in the four-year period.[30]

The sample of every fifth name on the AAA applications of 1933 (excluding those covered up by the newspaper binding), checked against lists of inhabitants, showed 30 percent of the operators of wheat farms living out of the county. This figure may be somewhat low in light of the statement by the county agent in 1935 that there were then two hundred suitcase and 350 resident farmers in the county.[31] His figures give 36 percent for suitcase farmers.

Although the AAA sample appears to be representative of the relative number of out-of-county wheat farmers, it is doubtful that it is indicative of their scale of farming. Table 15 shows the out-of-county share of farm land at only 16.8 percent and wheat acreage and production at around 20 percent during the period. The inclusion of eleven (of a total of fifty-seven) local wheat farms of more than one thousand acres and only one (of twenty-four) out-of-county wheat farms of that size is not consistent either with previous conditions in the county or with the situation in Hamilton and Greeley counties, where the coverage was more complete. The large percentage of the farm land of the nonresidents in wheat may have been representative. The yields obtained by out-of-county farmers were very slightly below those of residents, the nonresidents being credited with 20.6 percent of the acreage and 20.5 percent of the production for the three years 1930-32.

Wheat country to the east continued to furnish most suitcase farmers. There were thirty farmers on the assessor's list of 1934 sufficiently distant to qualify as suitcase. Most names had been added by the county clerk. Twenty-eight had Kansas addresses between fifty and two hundred fifty miles to the east. The other two lived in Oklahoma adjacent to the Kansas border, in a generally southeastern direction.

Miscellaneous

Probably largely because Haskell County was located some distance to

30. *Johnson City Pioneer,* September 28, 1933, AAA applications, checked against lists of inhabitants, assessor report.

31. "Narrative and Statistical Reports from County Agents," Stanton County, Kansas, 1935.

the east of the counties already examined, wheat was the leading crop there before the suitcase era. However, it appears that with the arrival of nonresident farmers the emphasis on wheat and the scale of farming increased. According to the biennial reports of the state board of agriculture, the amount of winter wheat sown increased from 26,506 acres in 1920 to 144,979 in 1927, the number of tractors increased from forty-three to 314, and the number of combines (combined harvester-threshers) from thirty-seven in 1923 to 171 in 1927.[32]

Big wheat farming had begun in Haskell County by 1922. One of the newspapers in the county recognized two out-of-county and one resident farmer in a story about wheat as harvest time neared:

> James McAdams of Minneola is one of the large wheat raisers of Haskell Co. He has four thousand acres in the southeast part of the county, most of which is good. He will probably have 50,000 or 60,000 bushels of wheat this year.
>
> [The T. F. Hopkins outfit of Liberal] had just begun cutting it [1000 acre field] with a big Holt Harvester that cuts a swath 24 feet wide. They were also using a McCormick Combine . . . . Just across the road from this is a section of good wheat belonging to Fred Warner of Satanta. He is also at work in his field with a big 24 foot cut harvester.[33]

Later it was explained that the James McAdams wheat ranch was "leased and operated by H. C. Dunham [a resident], who has had charge of it for the past four years."[34] Thus, it appears that Hopkins, a nonresident farmer from Liberal, used both harvesters and a combine, while neither the McAdams-Dunham nor Warner farm was credited with a combine. In 1923, the assessor listed all three with both tractors and combines: Hopkins had two tractors and two combines; Dunham, three tractors and two combines; and Warner, two tractors and one combine. Dunham's wheat acreage was given at 4,160, Warner's 860, a close third among acreages reported. Although Hopkins was listed, no acreage was given.

Hopkins, at least, was recognized as an innovator, one whose success attracted attention, partly no doubt through the publicity he received in the newspapers. About five years after his first big sodbreaking in Haskell

32. *Twenty-second Biennial Report of the State Board of Agriculture, Kansas.* vol. 27, 1919-20, Topeka, 1921, pp. 480, 588; *Twenty-Fourth Biennial Report,* vol. 29, 1923-24, Topeka, 1923, p. 672; *Twenty-sixth Biennial Report,* vol. 31, 1927-28, pp. 480, 588.
33. *Sublette Monitor,* June 29, 1922.
34. Ibid., July 3, 1924.

County, it was reported:

> Mr. Hopkins has never paid over $20 an acre for his land and has never sowed a crop that the first crop didn't pay for the land. . . . The big wheat raiser has no doubt done as much as any man to advertise southwest Kansas and the productivity of its soil, for the story of his big crops of wheat has spread far and wide and many another has followed his example in breaking out sod and sowing large acreages.[35]

Locally, it was asserted that "50,000 acres of new sod was broken out and put in wheat" in the autumn of 1925 and that the population had increased 25 percent in the two years 1924 and 1925, largely because of "an influx of new settlers, most of whom moved in this county from their former homes in the territory between Hutchinson and Dodge City."[36]

The part of absentee farmers in the rapid development in Haskell County is uncertain because of the common underreporting of nonresidents by the assessors. However, the number from a distance identified went up sharply after the newspaper publicity given to the big wheat operations of McAdams and Dunham, Hopkins, and Warner in 1922. Excluding the county border town of Copeland, out-of-county addresses given by the assessor in 1922 numbered fifteen, with only one suitcase address for a wheat farmer. A good many of the fourteen having addresses in adjacent counties may have lived in Haskell County. In 1923, the suitcase addresses had increased from one to eight. Mention in the local newspapers of farming by absentees also became more frequent. Of the score of suitcase farming addresses given by the assessor and newspapers in the period 1923-26, a majority were in the belt to the east from which most of the new settlers were reported to have come. It is reasonable to assume that suitcase farmers in greater numbers than reported, as well as new residents, were attracted by the stories of quick profits in wheat.

A. D. Edwards's 1936 study of a portion of Haskell County is the earliest I have found of landownership and use in the area of the suitcase farming frontier. It provides circumstantial support of the important role of the suitcase farmer in the plow-up of the prairie.[37]

Since Edwards went to some trouble to map the use of land both in 1936 and earlier in the sample area of thirty-six-square miles in his study, it may be assumed that he intended that portion of Haskell County to

35. Ibid., July 1, 1926, quoting the *Liberal News*.
36. Ibid., January 21, 1926.
37. A. D. Edwards, *Influence of Drought and Depression on a Rural Community: A Case Study in Haskell County, Kansas,* Social Report, no. 7, Farm Security Admin. and USDA Bur. of Agr. Econ. (Washington, D.C.: G.P.O., January 1939).

illustrate its transformation by wheat farming. His pertinent generalizations include these:

> The practice [by resident stockmen] of using vacant acreage continued until the land was claimed by its owners when the wheat boom of the 1920's so greatly augmented its value. . . . From 1915 [when the railroad came] to 1924, the proportion of farmers raising wheat doubled and the average acreage planted in this grain rose from 113 to 230 acres. . . . Native pasture was broken out at a rapid rate between 1925 and 1927. As nonresident owners insisted upon having all available land planted to wheat, the demand for wheat land made it increasingly difficult for newcomers to obtain pasture or for the older resident operators to keep the land they rented from being plowed up. Owner-operators, *particularly those who resided upon their farms* [italics supplied] tended to reserve part of their land for pasture.[38]

In the account quoted above, the only statements which suggest the possibility of suitcase farming were those of absentee owners claiming their land and planting it to wheat and the implicit admission (italicized) that there were nonresident owner-operators about 1925-27 at the height of the plow-up. However, a check of the map of landownership in 1936 with the map of land use in 1925 suggests strongly that suitcase farmers had taken the lead in the plow-up of prairie and planting of wheat by 1925. Unfortunately, ownership of land in 1925 was not mapped, but a higher percentage of the land farmed by nonresidents in 1936 was in crops in 1925 than was true for other land. If nonresident and resident farmers operated the same land in 1925 as in 1936, the nonresidents had 57 percent in cultivation in 1925 as compared to 32 percent for resident farmers, including both that owned locally and by absentees. By 1936, all the land operated by nonresidents was mapped as cropland and all of this was shown as owned by nonresidents.[39] Table 16 is based on Edwards's maps. The evidence, although circumstantial, is supported by statements by Edwards that "mounting speculation and increased non-resident operation" led to the old settlers being "seized by the fever to plant more wheat on their own land."[40]

The first attempt I found by an assessor to summarize nonresident operation in any portion of western Kansas is in the 1927 report on Sherman County, two counties north of Greeley. The last entry for Smoky Township, following the list of individual farmers with farm acreages, is

38. Ibid., pp. 29, 46.
39. Ibid., pp. 35, 41.
40. Ibid., p. 98.

"Estimate of Non Residents: 20,000 acres winter wheat, 1,000 acres corn, 1000 acres barley, 10,000 acres native pasture." These figures, added to those itemized for the residents, gave the following totals for the township: winter wheat, 32,435 acres; corn, 2,960; barley, 2,590; and native pasture, 41,160. Thus, the assessor's estimate credited outsiders with a little over 60 percent of the wheat. Here was official recognition of the often repeated claim of long-time residents that absentee farmers dominated early wheat farming. The 10 percent sample of the wheat farmers who applied for AAA allotments in the township in 1933 showed eight rural residents, four living in Goodland (the county seat), and only two from out of the county. Apparently a big change had occurred between 1927 and 1933.

Notice of Fishman's 16,000 acres in Greeley County in 1921, discussed earlier, is the only other official recognition I found of the dominance of nonresident wheat farmers in western Kansas. One can only wonder how many more cases there were.

Although it is impossible to determine just how important suitcase farmers were in the development of wheat farming in west-central Kansas in the 1920s, it is certain that newcomers rather than long-time residents were responsible. This conclusion was reached for Greeley County and one township each in Hamilton and Stanton, as previously reported. The extension of the detailed study of assessors' reports to the next tier of counties to the east confirmed the results obtained in the counties on the Colorado border. The additional areas covered were a relatively isolated and little developed township in Logan County, one in Kearny County that ran high in the number of out-of-county farmers in 1933, and the large township in Grant County containing the county seat. The breakdown of essential information for all eight townships separately and combined appears in table 17. In summary, the table shows (1) few farmers growing wheat in 1920, (2) a big dropping out of farmers from 1920 to 1927, and (3) the dominance in wheat farming in 1927 by newcomers. Farmers new to these townships planted over 82 percent of the wheat on the average, with a range from 67.1 to 93.3 percent. This dominance was based largely on the large scale of operation of some of the newcomers.

Perhaps the following additional observations should be stressed again: (1) the importance of new farmers in wheat farming in 1927 is underrepresented because of the common failure of assessors to include absentee farmers and (2) many of the resident newcomers were former suitcase farmers.

Certainly, the old-timers were slow in becoming specialized wheat farmers, as the Greeley County agent generalized in his 1930 report.

There were, as noted earlier, some companies, including chartered corporations, engaged in wheat farming in western Kansas. In all, by May, 1933—actually probably by 10 March 1931, when a bill to prohibit the chartering of agricultural corporations for farming in Kansas became law—twenty corporations had been chartered since 1925 for general or wheat farming in the state.[41] Vance Johnson, without giving any authority or date, states that six corporations operated 100,000 acres or more in Kansas.[42]

The Wheat Farming Company, organized in 1927 with headquarters in Hays, was the largest, according to Emy K. Miller. It planted nearly 71,000 acres of wheat for 1931 in a ten-county block that consisted of a double row of five counties, separated from Nebraska by a single line of counties. Ellis County, whose county seat is Hays, was the southeasternmost in the block. Wallace County, bordering Colorado, was the most southwesterly and contained approximately 30,000 of the company's wheat acres. There were two concentrations in the county, one in the west and one in the east. Southern Thomas County had another concentration.[43] There were five blocks, or units, each run by a manager under centralized control from Hays.[44] The machinery of the company, including forty tractors and thirty combines, could be kept quite busy by trucking them around on a fleet of trucks belonging to the company. There were 25 permanent employees and about 150 workers at sowing and harvest. Such was the efficiency of operation that it was said the company made money at thirty cents a bushel, as in 1930.[45]

The Hays company, in the main, bought and broke prairie land, thus locally increasing cultivation notably. Miller states that this was especially true in Wallace County, where "only fourteen percent of the land was cultivated before organization of the Wheat Farming Company," adding that about thirty thousand acres had been brought under cultivation. The 23,520 acres of wheat credited to the Wallace Unit in 1931 was well over one-half of the 41,904 acres planted for that year in the entire county. Perhaps the Wallace Unit included land outside the county, but the Weskan Unit, presumably in Wallace County, had an additional 14,220 acres

41. Emy K. Miller, "Corporation Farming in Kansas" (Master's thesis, University of Wichita, 1933), pp. 12, 69.

42. Vance Johnson, *Heaven's Tableland: The Dust Bowl Story* (New York: Farrar, Straus and Co., 1947), p. 148.

43. Miller, "Corporation Farming," pp. 18 (map), 87.

44. *Sublette Monitor,* April 5, 1928, and Miller, "Corporation Farming," p. 87. Miller says seven units were in operation (p. 29) but the table showing company operation contains only five.

45. Miller, "Corporation Farming," pp. 37, 36, 61, 62, 35.

of wheat.[46]

Expert testimony credited the company with the introduction of scientific methods of farming:

> L. C. Aicher, superintendent of the Fort Hays Experiment Station, said that he had visited four of the units of the company and they carried on good farming methods which were more readily adopted by farmers living around them. Some farmers were not farming their land until they saw successful farming demonstrated by the company. The superintendent expressed the wish that all farmers would be as interested in scientific farming as the officers of the Wheat Farming Company.[47]

The company reportedly fallowed the land instead of planting wheat if the subsoil moisture tested less than 19 percent. Apparently this practice reduced the wheat acreage planted for 1932 to 29,890 from the 70,940 planted a year earlier.[48]

According to Miller, the Sledd Farm Corporation of Lyons, owners of 21,040 acres with 18,000 under cultivation in 1931, was the second largest wheat-farming corporation in Kansas. It held land in fourteen western counties, including over 2,000 acres each in Kearny, Lane, Sherman, Wallace, and Hamilton. The home county, Rice, just south of the center of the state, was the most eastern area of wheat farming by the company. Seventy-five percent of the land had been sod when the company acquired it.[49]

The Wheat Farming Company farmed along the northern edge of the main suitcase farming area, but the smaller, more scattered operations of the Sledd Farm Corporation were located largely in the chief region of farming by absentees. Lyons, its headquarters, was within the long-established major source area of suitcase farmers; Hays, headquarters of the larger company, lay near the northwestern edge of the main source area.

Summary

Resident farmers left the task of turning grassland into wheat fields

---

46. Ibid., pp. 62, 87; and *Twenty-eighth Biennial Report of the State Board of Agriculture, Kansas,* vol. 33, 1931-32, Topeka, 1933, p. 465.

Considering the 43,415 acres shown in the *Twenty-sixth Biennial Report* as planted for 1927, it is doubtful that the company pioneered wheat farming in the county.

47. Miller, "Corporation Farming," p. 63.

48. Ibid., pp. 52, 87.

49. Ibid., pp. 12, 24, 27.

primarily to newcomers. Many new farmers moved to the new wheat country, some after beginning wheat farming there as suitcase farmers. Other early nonresident wheat growers continued as absentee operators. In a few known instances—in Greeley County in 1921 and in Smoky Township in Sherman County in 1927—farmers from a distance were directly responsible for most of the plow-up for wheat. Other examples are claimed. There were numerous cases of outsiders outplanting the residents, and there is little reason to doubt their role as innovators. They brought a new emphasis on wheat, commonly were better equipped, and in some cases introduced new methods. The wheat farming frontier in the driest part of western Kansas in the 1920s and early 1930s was a suitcase farming frontier to a large degree. Farther east, where wheat had become the leading crop earlier, as in Haskell County, nonresidents did not pioneer wheat farming, but they were leaders in introducing wheat farming on a large scale.

CHAPTER FOUR

Early Suitcase Farming in Western Kansas: Summary and Interpretation

Geographical Distribution, 1933

Figure 7 shows the percentage of wheat farmers who lived out-of-county in 1933 for much of western Kansas. The method of determining in- or out-of-county residence has been explained for Greeley County. This procedure was extended through the block of counties in which improved land made up less than one-third of all land in 1920 (fig. 10) and beyond in the three directions possible—north, south, and east.[1] It was continued to the east as far as out-of-county wheat farmers constituted as high as 15 percent of the total. Thus, a region of high and fairly high incidence of out-of-county farmers was determined.

The incidence of nonresident operators as a percentage of wheat growers in 1933, as mapped, displays a rather coherent pattern. The regularity of distribution of high percentages is the more notable if the counties

1. The applications for AAA wheat allotments for 1933 were found in the following newspapers: Cheyenne County, *St. Francis Herald,* October 12; Finney County, the *Garden City News,* October 19; Ford County, *Dodge City Journal,* September .7 and October 5; Gove County, *Republican-Gazette* (Gove City), October 5, *Grinnell Record-Leader,* October 5, *Grainfield Cap Sheaf,* October 6; and *Gove County Advocate* (Quinter), October 5; Grant County, *Grant County Republican* (Ulysses),̄ September 21 and 28; Gray County, *Jacksonian and Gray County Record* (Cimarron), September 7 and October 12; Greeley County, *Greeley County Republican* (Tribune), September 21; Hamilton County, *Syracuse Journal,* September 15; Haskell County, *Sublette Monitor,* September 21 and 28; Kearny County, *Lakin Independent,* September 29; Lane County, *Dighton Herald,* September 14, 21, and

marked by asterisks are ignored. In counties so marked, there were substantial gaps in coverage, either in AAA applications or in lists of inhabitants, or both. The figures obtained for Thomas (25) on the north, Gray (35) and Ford (23) on the east, and Stevens (19) on the south are, therefore, judged unreliable—especially those for Thomas, Gray, and Ford. The only gap in information for Stevens County was the absence of a list of inhabitants for Hugoton, the county seat. Within the limitations of the method used, the results are most dependable for Greeley County, where the coverage was 100 percent. In adjacent Hamilton County, the sample was one in three, and in a number of other counties one in five. Elsewhere, the sample was one in ten (as shown on fig. 7).

Suitcase farming in western Kansas was near its peak in 1933 as the pioneering of wheat farming was ending. Somewhat arbitrarily, I have selected the figure of 20 percent for out-of-county wheat farmers as delimiting the major suitcase farming country. Most of this region deserves the name Kansas suitcase farming frontier. A considerable body of evidence has been presented to show that those from a distance pioneered wheat farming in the western border counties of Greeley, Hamilton, and Stanton. With increasing distance to the east, the title becomes less appropriate. However, in Haskell County, where wheat as the major crop antedated suitcase farming, the case for the innovation of large-scale wheat farming by absentees seems good. In Thomas, Gray, and Ford the high percentages of out-of-county farmers shown, if accurate, must be interpreted as a rapid filling of gaps left by resident farmers rather than as evidences of the suitcase farming frontier.

Perhaps it is in order to note that four counties in a row along the Colorado border—Wallace, Greeley, Hamilton, and Stanton—ran 30 percent or more on the 1933 map of percentage of out-of-county wheat farmers. These western-most counties of Kansas lay on the western margin of both important wheat farming and suitcase farming.[2] If indeed suitcase

---

28; Logan County, *Oakley Graphic,* September 22 and October 5; Morton County, *Elkhart Tri-State News,* September 28 and October 5; Pawnee County, *Tiller and Toiler* (Larned), September 14 and 21; Scott County, *News Chronicle* (Scott City), September 21 and 28; Seward County, *Southwest Tribune* (Liberal), September 14 and 28; Sheridan County, *Hoxie Sentinel,* October 5, and *Selden Independent,* October 5; Sherman County, *Goodland News-Republic,* September 20, 27, and October 4; Stanton County, *Johnson City Pioneer,* September 28; Stevens County, *Hugoton Hermes,* September 22; Thomas County, *Colby Free Press,* September 20; Wallace County, *Western Times* (Sharon Springs), September 28; Wichita County, *Leoti Standard,* September 21. In the case of Gray County, the records for two townships not included in the paper examined were inadvertently overlooked.

2. Wheat farming dropped off abruptly west of the core counties of suitcase

farmers took the lead in extending the wheat-farming country, they should have ranked especially high at the margin of advance. The detailed map of wheat farms in Colony Township of Greeley County (fig. 5) confirms close-up the pioneer role of nonresident farmers.

Accuracy of the Map

The question of the degree to which all wheat farms were represented by AAA applications is basic. All of the scattered statements that I found in contemporary newspapers show that a large majority of all wheat farms or acreages were included in the applications. The following percentages were reported locally by county: Cheyenne, 91 percent; Finney, 97 percent; Grant, 94 percent; Gove, 96 percent; Hamilton, 85 percent; Haskell, 99 percent; Lane, 95 percent; Pawnee, 97 percent; Sherman, 95 percent; Stanton, 99 percent; and Wallace, 95 percent.[3] In Greeley County the wheat farms for which applications were filed totaled 222,419 acres, according to my addition. The 1935 United States census reported only a slightly higher acreage for farms of all types—232,838 acres—which was an increase of more than 44,000 from 1930. The conclusion is that AAA applications were representative in that they included most of the wheat farmers and wheat acreage.

Empirical tests of the essential accuracy of the results obtained of the importance of suitcase farming have been cited for Greeley, Hamilton, and Stanton counties. Figure 7 shows 27 percent of wheat farms operated by nonresidents for Haskell County, where a contemporary study showed 32 percent out-of-county in 1936.[4] Another study indicates that 19 percent for Stevens County was approximately correct.

The figure of 19 percent of the wheat farmers in Stevens County in 1933 who were not found on the lists of inhabitants would have been reduced somewhat if there had been a list of residents of Hugoton, the county seat. A 1936 survey of land use in the county showed out-of-county and sidewalk farmers from the county towns of Hugoton and Moscow, together farming 22 percent of the farm land. On the silt loam, especially adapted to wheat, the percentage was 47, although it was explained that landowners had recently gotten rid of many tenants in order

---

farming in Kansas. Most wheat raising in Colorado was in the northeast—off to the northwest of the Kansas suitcase farming country. In addition, Baca County, to the southwest, had become important for wheat recently.

3. As cited in chapter 2, footnote 27.

4. Edwards, *Influence of Drought*, p. 50.

to keep from sharing AAA payments.[5] In 1936 the percentage of the wheat land of out-of-county farmers was probably somewhat higher than the 19 percent shown on the map.

To sum up, except perhaps for Thomas, Gray, and Ford counties, figure 7 is presented as a good approximation of the percentage of out-of-county wheat farmers in 1933.[6] Incidentally, it appears significant that the county agents in Greeley and Hamilton, as well as the county newspaper in Kearny County, in 1933 complained that the wheat acreages reported by the assessors, which the government proposed to use as the basis for allotment, were much too low.[7] In each case it was asserted that the failure to include most of the acreage of nonresident farmers was the main reason. These three counties have the first, second, and fourth highest percentages in figure 7.

Wheat Farmers as Percentage of All Farmers

As noted, figure 7 shows the percentage of wheat farmers who lived outside the counties where they were farming as absentees. Of course, to be representative of all farmers who were out-of-county, the percentages would have to be reduced to the degree that local farmers did not include wheat as a crop. By 1933 most farmers were growing wheat in the part of Kansas mapped, but the dependence on wheat varied considerably from one area to another.

Assuming that the assessor's reports of farmers resident in a county were relatively complete, a comparison of the number of in-county farm-

5. Detailed summary of Stevens County, Kansas, data, in "Land Survey of the Southern Great Plains Region, 1936, Progress Report," mimeographed (Resettlement Admin., Land Use Planning Division, Land Use Section, February 20, 1937), pp. 83-85.

6. In the case of Gray County, the raising of the AAA wheat allotment for the county may provide an approximation of the underrepresentation of the wheat history of the county resulting from the common failure of the assessors to report the farming operations of non-residents. At the time of the publication of the applications for wheat allotments, it was stated, "There are more acres of applications than the government expected, due to the fact that the nonresident wheat grower did not get his acreage on the assessor's books—and that is what the government based its figures on" (*Jacksonian and Gray County Record* [Cimarron], September 7, 1933). Shortly there was an adjustment in the allotment base, an increase from 297,000 to 342,000 acres. The increase of 45,000 acres amounted to about 13.4 percent of the adjusted acreage (*Montezuma Press,* October 5, 1933). This increase, presumably to recognize the acreage of nonresidents, was substantially less than the 35 percent shown for out-of-county operators in figure 7.

7. Annual reports of 1933 by the county agents of Greeley and Hamilton cited in chapters 2 and 3. The Kearny County newspaper was the *Lakin Independent* of July 7, 1933.

ers shown by the assessors with the number of in-county farmers among those making AAA wheat applications should indicate the degree to which local farmers were raising wheat. Table 18 attempts such an evaluation for eight counties in the suitcase farming area.

Possible sources of error in designating local farmers as growing wheat include the following. First, because the numbers of farmers making applications for wheat allotments by districts were added together to obtain county totals (except in Greeley County), there was some exaggeration of the actual number of individuals applying for allotments. Second, if family name farmers were in some cases not residents there was further exaggeration. A third cause of error, except in Greeley County, where all farmers were classified by residence, would exist if the samples used were not representative. The results in table 18 are plausible except in Stanton County, shown with more than 100 percent. It may be concluded that the percentage of in-county farmers raising wheat was very high in Stanton, Grant, and Kearny; high in Wichita and Greeley; over 50 percent in Hamilton; and fairly low in Logan and Wallace counties. Perhaps stock farmers and general farmers persisted to a greater degree along the draws of the Smoky Hill River in these counties than on the flatter lands farther south. Since all the out-of-county farmers represented in figure 7 were wheat farmers, it follows that the presence of this group in numbers tended to raise the percentage of wheat farmers among all farmers above the levels indicated in table 18.

Farmers from Adjacent Counties

Although in the 1930s farmers living in neighboring counties were commonly thought of as suitcase, the definition used in this study does not include them. The question of how many out-of-county farmers lived in adjacent counties is in order. Some evidence on this point will be presented here.

As mentioned in chapter 2, a check of the names of out-of-county farmers raising wheat in the southern part of Greeley County in 1933 against the lists of inhabitants of the northern townships and county seat of Hamilton County resulted in only one positive identification in eighty-four names. The suitcase residence of a large majority of out-of-county wheat farmers in the North Harrison part of Greeley County was also noted. In Stanton Township, centrally located in Stanton County, a test of the list of farmers in 1934 provided by the assessor, with additions by the county clerk, showed only a small number having addresses in neighboring Kansas counties. The total count of addresses was as follows: Stanton

County, 120; from neighboring counties, 4; suitcase farmers, 17; no addresses given, 5; total, 146. These several tests indicate that most out-of-county wheat farmers were actually suitcase farmers.

As a result of specific instructions to report absentee farmers in 1936, several county assessors reported unusually large numbers of nonresident operators in their annual reports of that year. A check was made of twelve townships having a considerable number of out-of-county addresses in order to determine the degree to which farmers from neighboring counties were included among out-of-county farmers. Such townships were selected deliberately on the thought that out-of-county farmers were reported more completely, therefore more accurately, than usual. In each of these townships the lists of inhabitants contained in the assessors' reports were checked in order to determine how many of those having post office addresses in neighboring counties were actually residents of the counties in which they were farming.

Table 19 shows that a large majority of those having post office addresses in neighboring counties really were residents. There was little farming from bordering counties. The results obtained reinforce those cited already for Greeley County and for central Stanton County. Most out-of-county farmers were, in fact, suitcase farmers. It can be claimed with some confidence that figure 7, which illustrates percentage of out-of-county wheat farmers, is a substantially correct representation of suitcase farmers, except for Thomas, Gray, and Ford counties.

Source Areas: Where Did They Come From?

True suitcase farming had begun in much of western Kansas by 1923, as shown on figure 3. Roughly one-half of those named by the county assessors as farming from a distance were emphasizing wheat. A reciprocal arrangement of long duration was being formed by two areas, the developing wheat country and the already developed wheat country, located mainly to the east. The farmers came various distances from scattered sources, but a portion of south-central Kansas stood out early as the chief source.

A similar pattern can be deduced from the listings of the county assessors for counties west of the one hundredth meridian for the years 1927, 1928, and 1929. Thirty-nine suitcase farmers (those coming from more than one county away) were reported growing wheat. Of these, seventeen traveled west from what might be recognized as a *core area* located to the south of the center of the state. The chief source area extended from

Dodge City, on the west, to McPherson, just east of the center of the state, a distance of about 125 miles. The north-south extent, of only a little over 100 miles, was from the Oklahoma border to the center of Kansas. Other sources for suitcase farmers were eastern Kansas, six; Colorado, including Boulder and Colorado Springs, three; Missouri, two; Arkansas, California, Florida, Nebraska, Texas (the northern panhandle), and Washington, one each; three came from Garden City, within the suitcase farming country, operating far enough away to qualify as suitcase farmers themselves; and three came from northwestern Kansas.

The addresses of the suitcase farmers reported by the county assessors for western Kansas in 1930 emphasized much the same source area somewhat south and west of the center of the state (fig. 8).

The pre-1933 sources of suitcase farmers in Greeley, Hamilton, and Stanton counties have been described. All three, especially Hamilton (fig. 6a) and Stanton, drew from wheat country to their east. As noted, successful real estate operations by men having Nebraska connections may have been responsible for the many Nebraskans among nonresident farmers in Greeley County (fig. 4). However, most farmers from southern Nebraska and Iowa had given up suitcase farming in Greeley County by 1940 (fig. 15a).

Figure 9 is based on about four hundred addresses, the largest number for suitcase farmers ever reported by the assessors in western Kansas. Even so, the record for those farming from farther than one county away was incomplete, except apparently for Wichita and Lane counties. Most of these nonresident farmers of 1936 lived in the old major source area to the east, but it had been extended eastward to include Wichita. The most common post office addresses were Dodge City, Wichita, Moundridge, and Hutchinson. Larned, Pratt, Great Bend, St. John, and Kansas City, Missouri, were important also. Eight of the nine leading centers were clustered, with intervening towns forming a concentrated source area.

In addition to central Kansas, the suitcase farming country itself and towns and cities along the Colorado Rockies were bases for absentee farming. Some of those from more distant places to the east, including southeastern Nebraska, seem to have given up suitcase farming. It must be assumed that most of those living at great distances utilized managers or hired men, or depended on custom farming. The Shanghai, China, address was the most remote found in the study.

There is substantial evidence that a considerable number of suitcase farmers were former residents, who continued to farm after they moved away. A check of new suitcase addresses reported by the assessors during the period 1923-36 showed this to be true. The count showed that thirteen of twenty-one with Wichita addresses and ten of twenty living in Colorado had been residents of the townships where they were reported as beginning suitcase farming in the years 1923-26. It is assumed from the consistency of the evidence that the sources of suitcase farmers in 1933 were similar to those of 1936.

The Making of the New Wheat Country

Considerable attention has been given in previous sections to the making of the wheat country. Here I propose to present generalizations about the processes of change, including, also, some pertinent details not yet noted.

The Scene in the 1920s

The scene where the action took place that changed a land of grazing and general farming into wheat country within a decade should be sketched for a better understanding of the transformation that occurred. Suitcase farming became important in a land that was mainly unbroken prairie, in part open range, the driest, least populous of which included Greeley, Hamilton, and Stanton counties. In 1920, according to the United States census, most of the land in these counties lay outside farms. Only 26.0, 41.6, and 29.1 percent, respectively, were classed as farm land. Three other counties were less than 50 percent in farms: Haskell, 34.7; Kearny, 37.8; and Morton, 48.0. No other county in Kansas had a figure as low as 50 percent, but Wallace at 57.0 and Grant at 59.7 percent were close. The percentage of improved land was only 3.7 in Greeley, 8.6 in Hamilton, and 6.8 in Stanton counties (fig. 10). Thus, even most farmland was unimproved pasture. Other western counties helping to form the block in which less than one-third of the land was classed as improved in 1920 were, in ascending order: Kearny, Haskell, Thomas, Wallace, Morton, Finney, Grant, Wichita, Sherman, and Scott. The only important suitcase farming county not in the list is Logan, for which the figure for improved land is well above one-third, but this is in doubt because of the very much lower percentage reported in crops in 1925. Truly, in the early twenties the land lay open.

The men who classified the land in western Kansas on the basis of field work done in 1926 and 1927 viewed the evolving wheat country in an early stage. They had seen enough farm and ranch country to be able to offer valid generalizations about the status of settlement. Their descriptions, sometimes with interpretations, pictured much of the area in the process of changing from nonuse or grazing to wheat farming.

Wheat farming tended to have a beadlike arrangement around the railroad towns. Wheat was grown mostly on the "hard" lands—silt loams and loams—and corn and grain sorghums were more characteristic of the less extensive sandy lands. Wheat was a risky crop, in Greeley called "speculative." Nonresident ownership was thought of as delaying the development of farms, since much land was only lightly used.[8] Of course, hard lands, railroads, towns, and wheat were all found mainly on the upland plains that are so extensive in west-central and southwestern Kansas. There was room for many additional farms either on slightly used land belonging to non-residents or on land that had been converted from ranches to farms as suitcase farming became important. As yet, the farming by local farmers was mainly by owner-operators,[9] and general rather than wheat farming was most common.

From Grass to Wheat

Some of the significant details of the attack on the prairie have been presented for Greeley, Hamilton, Stanton, and Haskell counties. Absentee farmers, large and small, were among the leaders in trying out the land for wheat. Some adopted a cautious, gradual approach; some plunged, risking much on the outcome.

A discriminating generalization made at the height of the big plow-up of the middle and late 1940s farther west seems equally apropos of the actors in the earlier development: "The drama of the land boom has a standard set of characters, the big operator, and the sidewalk and suitcase farmer."[10]

All three—the big operator, the sidewalk farmer, and the suitcase

8. J. Q. Peterson, R. E. Morgan, and E. R. Greenslet, "Land Classification of the Central Great Plains, Part 2, Western Kansas and Southwestern Nebraska," mimeograph no. 27749 United States Department of Interior, Geological Survey, 1928, pp. 20, 23, 27, 29, and 31.

The *Syracuse Journal,* June 19, 1931, several years later, reported a charge of one-fourth cent per bushel per mile for hauling wheat to the three markets in Hamilton County. In Hamilton and other counties along the Arkansas River, the railroad followed the valley rather than the upland.

9. Pertinent data for Colony Township in Greeley County for 1920 have been presented. The United States census for 1920 showed farm tenancy below 30 percent for the entire westernmost tier of counties. Three other western counties in the second tier ran below 30 percent—Wichita, Kearny, and Grant. Elsewhere west of the one hundredth meridian, the figures were above 30 percent but below 45.

10. John Bird, "Great Plains Hit the Jackpot," *Saturday Evening Post,* August 30, 1947, p. 16.

farmer—have been identified in preceding chapters as pioneers in wheat farming. The earliest of the big operators was Simon Fishman. He was a suitcase farmer at the outset. Likewise, the Trued aggregation, the Fisher Ranch, and several others who planted large acreages of wheat began growing wheat as nonresidents. The Wheat Farming Company of Hays and the Sledd Company of Lyons were examples of corporations that qualified as suitcase farmers. If the big farming on the McAdams wheat ranch in Haskell is credited to Dunham, the resident operator, an exception to the big operator being a suitcase farmer must be admitted, but usually the "standard set of characters" actually were only two—suitcase farmers, both large and small, and sidewalk farmers.

There were far more suitcase than sidewalk farmers. In 1933, after local businessmen in some numbers had gone into wheat farming, local towns provided 10 percent or more of those applying for wheat allotments in only three or four of the counties checked.[11] It appears that suitcase farmers were leaders in introducing specialized wheat farming. Within a few years some of the absentees became residents of the towns in the counties where they farmed and continued to raise wheat as sidewalk farmers. In addition, local businessmen, with the means or credit to equip themselves for wheat farming, followed the example of the outsiders. Frank Kucera of Tribune was an example. Local informants state that he was backed by Fishman. Fred Warner of Satanta, in Haskell County, was another sidewalk farmer who went into big wheat farming early.[12] As noted, town farmers were fairly numerous in the westernmost portion of Greeley County in 1933, when it was on the frontier of important wheat farming. Sidewalk farmers should be credited with an important supporting role in the drama of the wheat boom, but only a secondary one because the evidence shows that suitcase farmers had a much larger part in the expansion of wheat in western Kansas that preceded the great drought.

The farmers from a distance who began specialized wheat farming in west-central and southwestern Kansas in the period 1921-33, especially in the early years of the wheat boom, were innovators. Frequently the newspaper notices of their activities emphasized mechanization—a dependence

11. Greeley, Hamilton, Seward, and perhaps Stevens counties. Stevens County probably belonged in this group but the lack of a list of inhabitants for Hugoton, the county seat, prevented a determination of the figure. In 1936 it was stated, "Only a small percentage of the businessmen in the towns of Stevens County do not speculate in farming" ("Land Use Survey of the Southern Great Plains Region," p. 83). The assessor's report of 1935 for Moscow Township in that county listed 17 of the 129 farmers as residents of the small town of Moscow. Sixteen of the 17 planted wheat, 15 of them on well over one-half of their land.

12. *Sublette Monitor*, June 29, 1922.

on machinery that was still unusual west of the developed wheat country. In a number of cases, the practice of trucking equipment in and out was mentioned. Fishman's generalization, already cited, that corporations introduced machinery and methods which were then adopted by resident farmers,[13] needs two qualifications: (1) not only corporations but many nonresident individual farmers introduced machinery, new methods, and experience; and (2) long-resident farmers were slow to follow the example of mechanized specialized wheat farming. New resident farmers, some of them former absentees, took up specialized wheat farming more promptly than long-time residents.

Fishman's big venture in wheat farming in Greeley County, preparation of the land and sowing in 1920, and harvest in 1921, reported in some detail in chapter 2, is representative of the pioneering of outsiders in a number of ways—in its dependence on machinery, the emphasis on wheat, and his prior experience in earlier wheat country. It was exceptional in its earliness, its large scale, and the fact that his prior experience in wheat farming was near Sidney, Nebraska, and Burlington, Colorado, both located to the north of Greeley County. Fishman was also unusually effective in attracting both suitcase farmers and new residents into the area as wheat growers.

Only a few of the very early nonresident operations included over a thousand acres of wheat. But some of these were important in directing attention to the area and illustrating a way of using it. As noted, the two biggest wheat farming companies, headquartered in Lyons and Hays, were incorporated in 1925 and 1927 after suitcase farming was well begun.

Local farmers had caught up in wheat yields in Stanton County by 1933 although they lagged behind out-of-county farmers in Greeley and Hamilton. In Greeley, a complete count showed that the average out-of-county wheat farmers sowed 456 acres of wheat in that year; resident wheat farmers averaged 429 acres. In Hamilton County, a one-in-three sample gave averages of 370 and 320 acres, respectively.[14] By 1933 fairly large wheat acreages were planted by both groups. The example of absentee farmers had been followed.

Although absentee farmers outplanted local farmers in the early years of suitcase farming, many had only moderate acreages in wheat. The thirty-nine wheat acreages listed in the assessors' reports of suitcase farmers in western Kansas during the period 1921-27 broke down as follows:

13. *Syracuse Journal*, February 13, 1931.
14. These figures are based on the AAA applications of 1933 as reported in the *Greeley County Republican*, September 21, 1933, and the *Syracuse Journal*, September 15, 1933, and the lists of inhabitants contained in the assessors' reports.

100 acres or less, eight; 101-200, three; 201-400, eight; 401-600, nine; 601-1,200, eight; 1,201-16,000, three. Thus, the assessors took note of more small or moderate-size operations than of large ones. The county clerk wrote in wheat acreages planted in 1933 for seventeen suitcase farmers operating in Stanton Township in Stanton County, as follows: less than 100 acres, one; 100-200, one; 201-400, twelve; and 401-582, three.

Although the newspaper accounts frequently failed to specify the nature of arrangements under which early suitcase farming was carried on, they included owner-operation, custom farming, and tenant farming. Apparently owner-operation and custom farming were common, but only a few cases of tenant farming by absentees were noted. Among these were instances of Nebraska tenants leasing from an Iowan,[15] and a Missouri farmer who broke land belonging to a neighbor:

> James Spangler of Clinton, Missouri, has been at work for the past three weeks breaking land day and night, with a Wallis tractor in the northeast part of the county. The land is owned by R. L. Lindsey of Clinton, Missouri, and until this fall has been idle, or used for grazing purposes. Mr. Spangler says he intends to break out ten quarter sections, three of which are already broken and planted to wheat. . . . When planted to wheat it will be the biggest field of its kind in Hamilton County.[16]

It seems reasonable to suppose that contacts between acquaintances and the services of real estate dealers were the chief means by which absentee tenants were able to make arrangements for farming lands owned by other nonresidents. However, the advertisement of a would-be suitcase farmer from Cimarron, Kansas, represented another approach. The potential farmer expected to be paid for plowing the sod and to receive three-fourths of the crop.[17]

James C. Malin, a Kansas historian who witnessed the development of wheat farming in western Kansas fairly close-up, classified suitcase farmers as (1) ephemeral "drugstore cowboys," largely youths; (2) large operators like Simon Fishman; and (3) corporations.[18] It is assumed that Malin took for granted those farmers who added to their operations by expanding into the new wheat country. Another type that may have been fairly common

15. *Greeley County Republican,* April 13, 1922. "While here from Iowa last week, R. S. Beall leased three sections of his Wichita County land to parties from Haigler, Nebraska, for a term of five years crop rent."

16. *Syracuse Journal,* September 19, 1924.

17. *Greeley County Republican,* March 6, 1930.

18. Letter from James C. Malin, Lawrence, Kansas, July 16, 1963.

was the distant town dweller who took a long-term interest in part-time wheat farming.

Actually, suitcase farmers were a most varied group, including lifelong real dirt farmers; town dwellers, some with prior farming experience, some without; developers from the outside, some who farmed, some who directed farm operations; and farming companies, including corporations. Banks, oil companies, and insurance companies were included. Probably some firms were involved against their wishes because of foreclosures made during the hard times on the farms in the twenties and thirties. The individual suitcase farmers had many different occupations. An undetermined number of full-time farmers were prominent among absentee wheat growers. Real estate men, land investors, and speculators were prominent, as were business and professional men, including owners of grain elevators, merchants, lawyers, teachers, preachers, and doctors. High school and college boys and a few women carried on suitcase farming.

The occupations of out-of-county farmers in a thirty-six-square-mile area in Haskell County in 1936 may well have been representative:

> Eleven of the 51 farmers in the area studied intensively lived outside the county. Some of them were former residents who continued to farm in the county even after they had changed their domicile. The majority had never lived in the county, but had begun suit-case farming recently because of the chance for quick profits. One farmer, who owned a large place in Sumner County, Kansas [to the east], had acquired this additional land when his sons grew up and became his partners. Another operator who had lost his position with an oil company was planning to continue working land in western Kansas. All but one of the 11 nonresident operators had other work. Five farmed elsewhere, two sold farm implements, and the others included a general contractor, an auto mechanic, and a farm laborer.[19]

The generalization that "with the wheat boom of the twenties, a new population of young men came to the wheat country with the machine-mindedness of their generation—glad to use tractors,"[20] while probably sound, had exceptions. The newspaper references to father-and-son teams of suitcase farmers suggest the spread of ages. Among early father-and-son suitcase farmers were O. H. Wetzel and sons from Manila, Iowa, and Rev. F. A. Searcy and sons from Oskaloosa, Iowa, in Greeley County in 1924, and A. E. Woodman and son, Omaha, Nebraska, in Hamilton County in

19. Edwards, *Influence of Drought,* p. 51.
20. Bell, *Contemporary Rural Community,* p. 48.

1924.[21] There was later newspaper recognition of the farming efforts of all three of these families. E. Shore of Coats, Kansas, who was listed by the assessor as growing wheat in Stanton County in 1922 and 1923, was then in his sixty-eighth and sixty-ninth years, judging from the fact that the Stanton County assessor listed him as a seventy-one-year-old resident in 1925.

Of course, youth was represented in father-son combinations, too. As mentioned, Malin considered the "drugstore" variety of suitcase farmers as mainly young. A high school instructor and college boy teamed up to carry on suitcase farming in Hamilton County in 1928, and Macksville, Kansas, boys still in high school raised wheat as suitcase farmers.[22]

It is a safe assumption that many farmers from the outside took a long-term interest in their western farming operations. As cited already, only twelve of thirty-seven Greeley County suitcase farmers identified in the period 1921-27 had disappeared by 1933. Nine were still suitcase farmers, eleven had become resident and continued as wheat farmers, and five were nonresident owners of wheat land. A similar inquiry into the degree of persistence of thirty-five suitcase farmers in Hamilton County identified by the local newspaper during the years 1927-30 yielded the following results: persisting as suitcase farmers in 1933, ten; had become resident wheat farmers, five; were nonresident owners of wheat land, seven; and had disappeared, thirteen. Of the eight wheat farmers with suitcase addresses reported by the assessor in Lamont Township, Hamilton County, in 1930, seven were listed among those filing applications for AAA wheat allotments in 1933. These examples suggest that many early absentee wheat farmers in western Kansas had interests that extended beyond skimming off the profits of a fleeting gamble.

Factors in the Development of Suitcase Farming

Although numerous examples of how suitcase farmers boomed wheat farming have been related and some generalizations have been given, contemporary appraisals of factors involved in the development of the early suitcase farming frontier seem to be very scarce. However, it may be assumed that the *how* and *where* throw light on the *why*.

The closest thing to an analysis of the development of early suitcase

21. *Greeley County Republican,* June 26 and September 13, 1924; *Syracuse Journal,* July 18, 1924.
22. Ibid., July 27, 1928; *Lakin Independent,* October 7, 1933, referring to earlier years.

farming in western Kansas known to me was formulated following a study of Haskell County made by Earl H. Bell in 1940:

> An unusual combination of factors—a one-cash-crop system which required only a little labor and that at particular seasons, rapid and easy transportation, power machinery which enables one or two men to do a great amount of work, and an abundance of unfarmed land—permitted the development of a new phenomenon in American agriculture—the suitcase farmer.[23]

Although Bell was writing about a single county within the suitcase farming country, the considerations stated seem to have had general application. Bell does not seem to have been aware, however, of the mutual relationships between suitcase farming country and source areas. Neither did his assessment include absentee ownership as a factor in the development of absentee farming. The 1920s witnessed both a drastic reduction in the labor requirements for wheat farming[24] and the rise of suitcase farming to importance in part of western Kansas. Bell's recognition of mechanization as a factor of importance was well founded, but by itself more efficient farm machinery could not determine either the source area or destination of suitcase farmers.

Spatial Relationships

The chief area of suitcase farming (fig. 7) and the chief source area for suitcase farmers (fig. 9) lay side by side, one in west-central and southwestern Kansas, the other directly to the east. This convenient arrangement depended on marked differences in development between the two areas.

The late plow-up of the grassland in the suitcase farming country has been related earlier in this chapter. At the beginning of suitcase farming, the area was nearly empty, in strong contrast to the country to the east. The gradient in percentage of improved land was steep. In 1920 the percentage of improved land declined from 67 percent in Lane County, the third county east of Greeley and about seventy miles distant (fig. 10), to 4 percent in Greeley County. The percentage of cropland in wheat also decreased toward the west, as recorded in 1924, the first year in which the census reported cropland. From Rush County, the fifth east of Greeley,

---

23. Bell, *Contemporary Rural Community*, p. 11.
24. L. P. Reitz and E. G. Heyne give the man-hour labor per acre of wheat as follows: 1909, 6.1; 1919, 5.6; 1929, 2.6; and 1936, 2.2, in "Wheat Planting and Wheat Improvement in Kansas," *Twenty-third Biennial Report of the Kansas State Board of Agriculture, 1941 and 1942* (Topeka, 1924), p. 170.

the portion of the cropland in wheat fell from 80 percent to less than one-half that figure in Greeley (fig. 11). Both east-to-west declines were much the same for every row of counties ending in the suitcase farming country. Figure 11 shows that the commitment to wheat was greater in the Kansas wheat country than anywhere else in the central Great Plains. Nowhere else was the contrast as sharp as between this developed wheat country and the nearly empty land just to its west.

Early in the 1920s, many of the farmers of the specialized wheat region of Kansas had new power machinery. Such machines were fewer to the west. In the east-to-west cross section between Rush and Greeley counties, the density of tractors in 1922 declined from one per 2.8 square miles to one in 27.3 square miles (fig. 12). The percentage of farmers having trac-east of Greeley. Sixteen percent of Greeley County farmers had tractors. Other border counties included Stanton 12 percent and Hamilton and Wallace with 9 percent each.[25] It seems clear that many farmers in central Kansas were equipped to enlarge their wheat farming but that little land was available there. The nearly empty land some thirty to two hundred miles away offered a chance to expand by farming both at home and as suitcase farmers to the west. As nonresident farmers the operators from the central part of the state emphasized wheat and commonly introduced the new equipment coming into use at home.

A comparison of figures 7 and 10 shows that suitcase farming became concentrated primarily in the parts of western Kansas in which less than one-third of the land was shown as improved in the census of 1920. Discrepancies are few and would be fewer if, as suspected, the amount of improved land in Logan County was exaggerated, and if the percentages of out-of-county wheat farmers in Gray and Ford counties shown were actually too high.

Level Land

The new wheat country was physically well suited to large-scale farming by machinery. Such an appraisal was made for Greeley and Wichita counties at the beginning of suitcase farming in 1921: "It is a level prairie as far as the eye can reach. It is the tractor's paradise for there is no end to acres of land as level as a table, and any kind of heavy modern machinery can be operated with the greatest degree of efficiency."[26] Level land is common

25. Based on the assessors' reports (of Greeley, Hamilton, Lane, Ness, Scott, Stanton, Wallace, and Wichita counties) of 1922.
26. "Narrative Report of the Wichita-Greeley Counties Farm Bureau, December 1, 1920 to November 15, 1921," Microfilmed, Kansas State University.

throughout the Kansas suitcase farming country, especially on the inter-fluves to the north and the south of the Arkansas River (fig. 13). Greeley and Wichita counties are to the north, Stanton and Haskell to the south. Of course, mechanized wheat farming is possible on slopes much greater than 2 percent, but figure 13 suggests that most of the suitcase farming country was and is a "tractor's paradise."

Absentee Ownership

The little-farmed level grassland lying almost next door to the farmers of the specialized wheat country of Kansas would not have been available to their tractors and other machinery had the land been owned by residents. The situation in Colony Township of Greeley County in 1933, already reported, showed that out-of-county farmers were fairly completely limited to land owned by absentees. A sample of the AAA applications in neighboring Wallace County gives similar results.[27] In the thirty-six-square-mile area in Haskell County studied by Edwards in 1936, all of the land farmed by out-of-county operators was owned by absentees.[28] Absentee ownership was a prerequisite for suitcase farming.

Nonresident ownership of land was common as suitcase farming began and probably was common much earlier. It is likely that the reversion to the county of 61 of 104 privately owned quarter sections in a thirty-six-square-mile area of Haskell County between 1895 and 1900 and subsequent sale for back taxes[29] was representative of the loss by early owners. Persons from outside the stricken pioneer area were undoubtedly most able to buy. Local stock raisers as well as farmers suffered heavy losses.[30]

In 1921 the district agent for the Farm Bureau who described Greeley and Wichita counties as a tractor's paradise prefaced his remarks with the statement that "in many localities there are thousands of acres of idle land owned by non-resident owners." Those classifying the land in western Kansas for the United States Geological Survey in the late 1920s called attention to nonresident ownership in several instances, as in Morton and Scott counties;[31] and local newspapers made sporadic references to the

27. The Wallace County sample of AAA applications by out-of-county operators showed owner-operators, seven; tenants of absentee owners, two; farming partly locally owned land and land of another absentee, one; and farming locally owned land, one.

28. Edwards, *Influence of Drought,* pp. 35, 41.

29. Ibid., p. 38.

30. The winter of 1918-19, for example, had "proved disastrous for a large proportion of cattlemen," according to the 1919 "Annual Report of the Tribune Branch Experiment Station," Kansas State University.

31. Peterson, Morgan, and Greenslet, "Land Classification," pp. 23, 26.

buying or selling of land by absentees in the 1920s. According to an account in a national journal, buyers from farther east "swarmed out" to buy western land between 1922 and 1930.[32] Doubtless, distress sales during the agricultural depression of the 1920s and in the 1930s resulted in increased absentee ownership. In 1934 it was stated that 60 percent of the land in Greeley County was owned by out-of-county residents.[33] Hamilton and Stanton county agents emphasized nonresident ownership in their 1933 annual reports; there was mention of absentee ownership in the 1933 report for Wichita County; and in 1935 the county agent of Stanton County reported that 66 percent of the land was owned by persons living outside the county. The sample of tenure arrangements in Wallace County in 1933 indicated nearly 50 percent ownership by out-of-county residents. Absentee ownership increased during the period of early suitcase farming.

The only comprehensive survey known to me of the amount of absentee-owned land in the general region was for the year 1936.[34] It covered a substantial part of the Dust Bowl in New Mexico, Texas, Oklahoma, Colorado, and Kansas. Figure 14 represents nonresident ownership in fourteen counties in southwestern Kansas and others in southeastern and east-central Colorado. Generally, the greatest concentration of absentee ownership was in Kansas, with more than 50 percent of the land owned by nonresidents in nine of the fourteen counties. Greeley County, with 73.8 percent, was the highest in the Kansas-Colorado area, and was exceeded in the general region only by Moore County, in northern Texas, with 80.9 percent. Actually, the percentages given on figure 14 may be too low because land owned by corporations was classified separately, not as owned by absentees. In Kansas the percentages owned by corporations ranged from 6.6 in Morton County, 5.8 in Stanton, and 5.5 in Finney, down to 0.5 in Haskell. It would appear that most of the corporations were headquartered outside the several counties. Probably their land had been acquired recently through foreclosures on mortgages. Local residents owned more than one-half of the land in only two of the fourteen Kansas counties: Meade and Seward.

The distribution of out-of-county wheat farmers in 1933 (fig. 7) and that of nonresident ownership (fig. 14) were similar. For example, Greeley County ranked highest and Hamilton second in both, and percentages on both maps decrease at the south and toward the east. Only Kearny and Gray counties ran notably higher and Morton notably lower in out-of-

32. Avis D. Carlson, "Dust Blowing," *Harper's Magazine,* July 1935, p. 156.
33. *Greeley County Republican,* January 11, 1934.
34. "Land Use Survey of the Southern Great Plains Region," pp. 73, 74.

county wheat farmers than might have been predicted from the map of absentee ownership. For the thirteen counties for which data of both types are available, a reasonably good correlation (Pearson product moment) of +.6769 was obtained.

In effect, Edwards recognized the dependence of absentees on land owned by nonresidents in Haskell County in 1936 when he wrote, "The non-resident ownership of land became associated, to some extent, with a system of non-resident operation known as 'suit-case farming.' "[35] There is no mystery about the nature of the association. Some nonresident owners, as noted, claimed their land for their own use as mechanized wheat farming developed, ousting those who had used it for pasture. Other outsiders, needing land on which to utilize their new machinery, bought at low prices. Still others sought out unused land owned by other nonresidents for rental. By 1933, much of the retarding effect of nonresident ownership on farming had disappeared.

Well Water

The lack of well water was a factor of some local importance in helping to explain the distribution of early suitcase farming. In 1933 the largest area in which out-of-county operators formed 50 percent or more of the wheat farmers consisted of four contiguous districts, three in Greeley and one in Hamilton County. The shortage of water may be inferred as important for this distribution.

The three largest areas mapped as being without a continuous water table in the fifteen southwestern counties, whose northwestern and northeastern counties are Greeley and Lane, are in northern and southern Hamilton County, in both cases extending eastward into Kearny County; and northeastern Finney County, extending northward into Lane County. Another map used the legend "water table is generally absent" for the same areas.[36] On both maps, an especially large area in which the depth to water was more than 150 feet included most of Haskell County and extends into Grant, Seward, and Meade counties. The depth to water is also great in parts of Kearny, Stanton, and Greeley. As noted in the chapter on Greeley County, parts of western and southern Greeley are without a water table.

Although the local newspaper referred on occasion to pioneer settlers

35. Edwards, *Influence of Drought*, p. 50.
36. Richard Pfister, "Water Resources and Irrigation," *Economic Development of Southwestern Kansas*, part 4. Bureau of Business Research, University of Kansas (Lawrence, 1955), p. 11; V. C. Fischel, "Ground Water Resources of Kansas," *Transactions, Kansas Academy of Science* 50, no. 2 (September 1947): 108.

giving up their homesteads in the western part of Greeley County because of the lack of well water, the Tribune paper took little note of the existence of an area without water. In 1941, however, the Greeley County planning committee of the United Agricultural Program concluded that nearly 132-square miles in the southwestern and south-central part of the county were "not suitable for the permanent establishment of homes due to the fact that, in general, water cannot be obtained. Therefore, the land in the area will either be farmed by non-residents; or farmed by residents [elsewhere in the county], who in most cases, will have other land better suited to cultivation which they will work first." It was added that only eight families were living in the region specified and that residents owned only 5,200 acres of the total of 84,480.[37] The problem area included major parts of three of the four communities in the county dominated by out-of-county wheat farmers in 1933.

The Hamilton County agent, in his annual report for 1945, acknowledged somewhat belatedly the existence of a water problem thus, "The water supply in some rural parts of the county presents a problem because of the depth to water. This is especially serious in the northwestern part of the county." There is some circumstantial evidence that the lack of well water in northeastern Finney County had the effect of leaving an opening for suitcase farmers. In Garfield Township, which occupies that part of the county, 35 percent of the wheat farmers were from out of the county in 1933, in contrast to 19 percent for the county as a whole.

An exact relationship between a depth to ground water of more than 150 feet and suitcase farming is uncertain, but at most the depth to ground water and the absence of a ground water table had only local importance for the distribution of suitcase farming.

Other Considerations

The Dust Bowl is a high-risk area. Failures there have been many and repeated. Table 20 summarizes the abandonment of wheat in west-central and southwestern Kansas over a long period. Perhaps neither residents nor newcomers were acquainted with these figures, but the apparently objective year-by-year summary given in the Stanton County paper as the wheat boom began, noted earlier, should have discouraged all but the

37. Greeley County United Agricultural Program Progress Report (Prepared by J. E. Taylor, Chairman, Greeley County Planning Committee, after meeting, March 1941), manuscript (Greeley County agent's office, Tribune, Kansas), pp. 7, 6.

boldest readers. Probably resident farmers knew the odds against success; possibly nonresidents did not.

It is likely that farmers from more humid areas did not realize how damaging drought could be. Several nonresidents receiving special recognition in the local papers came from considerable distances—Wetzel from Manila, Iowa; the aggregation from Ceresco, Nebraska; and Spangler from Clinton, Missouri, for example. Figures 4 and 6a indicate that farmers from several hundred miles to the east were common. Even the more numerous farmers from central Kansas came from less droughty country than the new land in which they were experimenting. The characterization of the suitcase farmers of western Kansas as "all optimists" in a national magazine in 1932[38] suggests that many outsiders did not view their prospects realistically. More recently, farmers with the least experience in the central Great Plains were found to perceive the drought hazard least accurately.[39]

Many of the nonresident farmers seemingly knew that wheat farming in the new land was hazardous but hoped through luck or foresight to get in on a good thing at an opportune time. They may have thought that men with machines could succeed where men with horses had failed. Many claimed that one crop paid for the land. The turnover of suitcase farmers was high. Perhaps many got out in time with a profit. Probably many did not.

Among those who were aware of the hazards, apparently a considerable number thought that they could take the risks of raising wheat in western Kansas as a side line. It was claimed in a national journal that "men of this type are not essentially farmers. . . . They are capitalists, doctors, lawyers, bankers, merchants and plumbers who, seeing a few years ago that there was good money in wheat, bought cheap land, paid for it with a couple of good harvests and are now operating it as a side line to their other endeavors."[40] In one case, Rhoda Johnson, from Winfield, was described as raising wheat as a hobby.[41] Probably many of the former residents who continued farming in western Kansas did so as a side line, perhaps when they were semiretired.

Many farmers were part-time suitcase farmers in western Kansas and

38. Owen P. White, "Wheat's Here to Stay," *Collier's*, January 2, 1932, p. 11.
39. Thomas Frederick Saarinen, *Perception of the Drought Hazard on the Great Plains*, University of Chicago, Department of Geography Research Paper, no. 106 (Chicago, 1966), pp. 70, 76.
40. White, "Wheat's Here to Stay," p. 11.
41. *Syracuse Journal*, January 11, 1929.

part-time resident farmers farther east. This sort of farmer could raise wheat in both places, often with the same machinery. Even if they sustained losses in suitcase farming, they might stay solvent because of the surer returns from the home farm. Now and then they might hit the jackpot with good crops in both places.

The wheat-farming corporations hoped to realize profits from the economies of scale and, at least in some cases, from the spreading of the risk over several geographical areas. Fishman, who managed the first big venture into wheat farming for New York interests, knew the country, including the risk of failure, since he had gone broke in an earlier effort in Cheyenne County, Nebraska.[42] Probably some farmers, both resident and nonresident, took the long view—that the profits of the good years would tide them over the poor years.

The fact that many suitcase farmers were experienced in wheat farming and were equipped with machinery gave them initial advantages—in yields and scale of operation. They also commonly had the important advantage of being able to move in promptly to begin or expand their suitcase farming at times they thought opportune. It is probable that they could cut back on their nonresident operation or get out entirely more readily than residents. To some degree they could reap the bounty of good crops while escaping the full penalty of recurrent failure.

Summary

The development of suitcase farming in the part of Kansas shortly to become Dust Bowl is comprehensible as a product of a given place and time. The place was one of recurrent drought and crop failure. It was fairly empty of crops as suitcase farming began. The suitcase farmers came largely from the adjacent specialized wheat-farming region of central Kansas. Absentees owned much of the land immediately to the west of this specialized wheat area. With the great mechanization of wheat farming in Kansas in the 1920s, many wheat farmers there were able to extend their operations to the west. Thus suitcase farming became important.

42. Henry L. Carey, "The Rise of Simon Fishman," p. 274. He was forced to sell his 3,000 acres in the Nebraska panhandle at ruinous prices, but later, "near Burlington, Colorado, he acquired and planted 40,000 acres." Greeley County, although not quite as far west as Cheyenne County, Nebraska, and Burlington, Colorado, is a little drier than either.

Within the suitcase farming country, the western margin ran especially high in the percentage of nonresident operation. The prominence of farmers from a distance in an area very recently important in wheat farming suggests the role of suitcase farmers as innovators. The distributional pattern itself suggests that the name suitcase farming frontier was deserved.

CHAPTER FIVE

The Early Colorado Scene

Baca County, in the extreme southeastern corner of the state, appears to have been the only area in Colorado in which suitcase farming was important at the time when the Kansas suitcase farming frontier took form. This was the only clear case of a major early extension westward beyond Kansas. In northeastern Colorado, the earlier close settlement including wheat as an important crop,[1] left little room for nonresident farming. Kit Carson County, which adjoined the Kansas suitcase farming country on the northwest, lay at the southern margin of the developed dry-farming country of northeastern Colorado in 1920.[2] Southward along the Kansas border wheat was not yet a major crop;[3] only near the southern end of that border did suitcase farmers from Kansas cross in significant numbers before the great drought of the 1930s.

1. In 1920 five counties in northeastern Colorado harvested more than 80,000 acres of unirrigated winter wheat: Logan, 166,392; Washington, 164,306; Yuma, 138,781; Weld, 87,235; and Phillips, 87,141, according to the *Crop Report for Colorado,* Bulletin no. 17, Colorado Dept. of Agr. with the USDA (Denver, September 1920).

2. A summary of agricultural development in Kit Carson County contained in the 1935 annual report of the county agent began with a figure of 126,000 acres planted in wheat in 1920. The crop must have been very poor since only 26,253 acres were harvested, according to the *Crop Report for Colorado,* Bulletin, no. 17. Three years later, the harvest was given at 136,155 acres in *Crop Report for Colorado,* Bulletin no. 53, Colorado Dept. of Agr. with the USDA (Denver, December 1923).

3. According to the official crop reports, the unirrigated winter wheat acreages harvested for the following border counties to the south in 1920 and 1923 were: Cheyenne, 1,945 and 24,199; Kiowa, 2,079 and 12,933; Prowers, 4,928 and 24,045; and Baca, 14,748 and 26,563.

Northeastern Colorado was not an area of specialized wheat farming. Wheat and corn were frequently grown together, either in general or cash grain farming. Wheat and corn were often grown in rotation, with wheat usually planted between widely spaced rows of as yet unharvested corn. This practice was mapped as common in 1919 in an extensive area that included not only northeastern Colorado but also parts of Kansas, Nebraska, Wyoming, and South Dakota:

> In the western part of the Great Plains corn is grown very largely with the end in view of preparing a seed bed for wheat. The cultivation of the corn serves practically the same purpose as summer fallow. The average yields are somewhat less than under the strictly summer fallow method, but not enough less when considering the value of the corn crop to make the summer fallow the more profitable practice.[4]

However, in much of the wheat-growing country, corn was the more valuable crop. In 1923, for example, only in Adams County in eastern Colorado was wheat more valuable than corn. In the late 1920s, corn and wheat were still customarily grown in rotation, especially on less sandy land, the practice being reported as the rule in northern Lincoln, Logan, Morgan, Phillip, Sedgwick, and Washington counties.[5]

Most early suitcase farmers in Colorado were probably from Kansas. Even as far north as central Washington County, the suitcase farmers were identified as Kansans and characterized as innovators. Between 1931 and 1933, it is reported that they broke sod, using bigger tractors than the residents, and introduced duckfoot (sweep) cultivators and combines, while local wheat farmers were still using horses, without combines, in threshing.[6] In effect, Kansans were credited with introducing modern wheat farming into this part of northeastern Colorado. An official report confirmed the introduction of the one-way disc, or wheatland plow, from Kansas.[7]

4. G. H. Arnold, "Farm Practices in Growing Wheat," *USDA Yearbook,* 1919, pp. 135, 140.

5. Depue Falck, E. R. Greenslet, and R. E. Morgan, "Land Classification of the Central Great Plains, Parts 4 and 5, Eastern Colorado," mimeograph no. 56284, U.S. Dept. of Interior, Geological Survey (Washington, D.C., 1931), pp. 82, 85, 87, 92, 102, 105.

6. Interview with Robert K. Dansdill, assistant state soil scientist, SCS, Denver, August 27, 1965, and letter of February 26, 1971. Dansdill grew up in Washington County and worked with threshing crews there.

7. Akron Dryland Field Station, "General Report," 1927. Examined in office of C. L. Fly, Colorado State University.

It should not be assumed that suitcase farmers were ever numerous in northeastern Colorado despite reference to them in Washington County in the early 1930s. It will be shown later that nonresidents participated more actively in the big plow-up of the post-World War II period in the southern portion of Washington County than elsewhere in the northeast. Perhaps the same was true earlier. The following generalization made by a Colorado agricultural economist is probably valid: "Of course, northeastern Colorado was not farmed by suitcase farmers, but by local people breaking out additional lands for cultivation."[8]

Suitcase farmers appear not to have been numerous in east central Colorado in the twenties or thirties. In a fairly detailed report of 1935 that identified suitcase farming in the southeastern corner of the state, there was no reference to nonresident farming in Kit Carson County, in spite of its having experienced a big plow-up in the twenties and the prevalence of cash grain farming of wheat and corn.[9] Although the county agent took notice of the hazards of nonresident ownership, there was no specific reference to suitcase farming in the contemporary reports for Kit Carson County.[10] According to some long-time residents, however, the real estate operations of Simon Fishman around 1920, including the breaking of a large acreage, planting of wheat, and fencing, resulted in some farming by nonresidents from areas to the east.[11] According to another long-time resident acquainted with the western portion of the county, suitcase farmers began farming in Kit Carson County about 1922 and were most numerous before the mid-1930s, when they were credited with planting 4 or 5 percent of the wheat.[12] The eastern portion of the county, located closer both to the Kansas suitcase farming country and to the major source areas, may have run higher in numbers of nonresident farmers, but probably not high enough to constitute a suitcase farming frontier.

In the dry grassland adjacent to and a short distance north of the Arkansas River next to the Kansas border, both wheat and suitcase farm-

8. Letter from Harry G. Sitler, agricultural economist, Economic Research Division, USDA, Colorado State University, Fort Collins, May 22, 1963.

9. Bryon Hunter et al., *Type of Farming Areas in Colorado,* Colo. Agr. Exper. Sta. Bull., no. 418 (Fort Collins, September 1935).

10. The county agent of Kit Carson County in 1935 referred to the mining of the soil on farms owned by nonresidents and in both 1935 and 1936 he reported that nonresident ownership contributed to the hazard of soil blowing. All reports of the Colorado county agents cited were examined in the Extension Division, Colorado State University, Fort Collins.

11. Letter from Avis Bader, Burlington, Colorado, June 21, 1969; she reported that this opinion was held by old-timers.

12. Letter from Arthur E. Gaines, Flagler, Colorado, June 26, 1969.

ing came late. In Cheyenne County, located just to the south of Kit Carson County, a government-sponsored report of 1938 stated that only 1 percent of the farms were operated by nonresident owners in 1935 and that few farmers grew wheat.[13] Since suitcase farmers were commonly owners, it is almost certain that suitcase farmers were few. In Kiowa County, located just south of Cheyenne County and bordering Greeley County, Kansas, the amount of wheat farming was also very small during the 1920s and 1930s, much less than across the border in Kansas, although there was some extension of absentee farming into this part of Colorado. As reported by a long-time resident in the Towner area, close to Greeley County,

> Very little wheat was raised here in 1925, 26 and 27 due to dry years. Conditions improved in 1928. Then the Real Estate Agents got busy about 29 and 30 and by the spring of 1930 we had some new residents that came to make their home here but there were many suitcase farmers that plowed up land with no intention of ever living here. Then with the depression of the 30's and dry years much of this new farm land went back to grass. A few of the non-resident farmers continued to operate here.[14]

According to a contemporary on-the-spot check, the few suitcase farmers who continued to try to farm in Kiowa County during the mid-1930s were considered too many. A study of southeastern Colorado indicated that one of the major prevailing attitudes was that " 'suitcase farmers' are the largest menace in the 'dustbowl.' "[15]

The extension of wheat farming from Greeley County, Kansas, into Kiowa County, Colorado, was on a small scale. In Kiowa County the AAA authorities in 1933 accepted a three-year average production of 140,747 *bushels* of wheat for the county,[16] while much smaller Greeley County had that many *acres* of wheat. As noted, the number of applications for AAA

13. R. S. Kifer and H. L. Stewart, *Farming Hazards in the Drought Area,* WPA, Division of Social Research, monograph 16 (Washington, D.C.: GPO, 1938), pp. 170, 61.

14. Letter from C. L. McFarland, county commissioner of Kiowa County, May 6, 1969.

15. "Annual Report" of James E. Morrison, Assistant Director of the Colorado College Extension Service, 1936, citing James C. Foster, land specialist. The report includes a detailed survey of four townships in Kiowa County, with field note. Report stored with Annual Reports of county agents, Extension Division, Colorado State University, Fort Collins.

16. "1933 Annual Report," County Agent, Kiowa County. Stored with Annual Reports of county agents, Agricultural Extension Service, Colorado State University, Fort Collins.

wheat allotments in Greeley County was 439; the count in Kiowa County was 75.[17] Since no lists of inhabitants of Kiowa or other counties of Colorado were discovered, it was not possible to determine how many wheat farmers were absentees. A search of the county newspaper for mention of suitcase farming from June 20, 1930, to November, 1933, uncovered references to a man from Denver and brothers from Stafford, Kansas, who were suitcase farming. One of the brothers was listed as the operator of a wheat farm on the list of AAA applications of 1933.

Suitcase farmers had an important part in the rapid breaking of sod for wheat planting in the late twenties and early thirties in Baca County. Although some wheat was grown by both resident farmers and absentees before 1928, wheat was not listed among the six important sources of farm income that supplemented broomcorn as the chief producer of dollars in 1927.[18] The county newspaper took note of a substantial amount of plow-up of the prairie in 1928 and again in 1929, when a rail line was built westward to Pritchett, most of the way across the county. In 1927, however, soon after what was called "the longest drouth in the history of the west" broke, many were described as ready to plant wheat,[19] partly on the newly plowed prairie.

According to the official report of the state agricultural statisticians, the increase in the acreage of unirrigated winter wheat harvested from 1925 to 1929 in Baca County was greater than in any other county in eastern Colorado, advancing it into sixth place in the state. The year-by-year figures in thousands of acres harvested were 7.2, 38.1, 26.1, 14.0, and 73.4. The acreages planted were probably substantially larger than those harvested because state-wide abandonment figures of 441,000, 302,000, 410,000, and 452,000 acres, and 20 percent, respectively, were reported. For Baca the harvested acre yields ran from four bushels in 1927 to fifteen in 1929. In 1931 it was claimed locally that Baca County had 400,000 acres of wheat, the largest acreage of any county in the state;[20] officially, 245,050 acres of winter wheat were listed as planted.[21] The acreage planted for 1932, officially reported as 355,100, was the highest until

17. Ibid.; *Kiowa County Press,* October 13, 1933. According to the county agent, the seventy-five contracts represented 85 percent of the wheat growers.
18. *Democrat-Herald,* December 23, 1927.
19. Ibid., May 11 and 25, June 22, 1928; May 24 and August 2, 1929; June 17, July 29, August 5, 12, and 26, 1927.
20. Ibid., June 4, 1931.
21. Unpublished acreages obtained from the USDA, Field Crops Statistics Branch, Agr. Estimates, Agr. Marketing Service (Washington, D.C.).
22. *Democrat-Herald,* December 7, 1928.

1947, well along in the second wheat boom. The plow-up for wheat in the late 1920s and first years of the 1930s had been big.

The absence of the year-by-year record of individual farms and lists of inhabitants, such as the assessors in Kansas used in reporting farm statistics, prevents determination of the relative importance of old-timers and newcomers in making Baca County important wheat country. Nevertheless, the general statement made in 1928—"Those old settlers didn't believe that God intended this country for agricultural purposes, never experimented along those lines and making good money out of stock, they gave no thought to anything else"[22]—may be substantially true, as it was in several counties of western Kansas. Certainly, both resident and suitcase newcomers were acknowledged by the local newspaper as leaders in the development of wheat farming.

The list of places from which suitcase farmers came to grow wheat—in some cases other crops as well—reads a good deal like those from neighboring Stanton County, Kansas. A check of the *Democrat-Herald* from 1927 to 1932 showed the following addresses of suitcase farmers: Liberal, Pratt, Sublette, Copeland, Jetmore, Great Bend, Bucklin, and Fowler. Liberal, in Seward County, Kansas, was clearly the most important base of early suitcase farmers, and several came from Pratt and Sublette. Perhaps it is not surprising that all the addresses given are in the southwestern quarter of Kansas. One reference was made to "a couple of young men from Kansas,"[23] whose address was, of course, uncertain.

Among those from Liberal engaged in suitcase farming were J. W. Baughman, later the owner of a vast acreage in Kansas and Colorado, Tom S. Hopkins, and Fred Prater.[24] Hopkins, it has been noted, was an early nonresident wheat farmer in Haskell County, Kansas. The importance of Hopkins and Prater was acknowledged locally and outside. In retrospect, the *Denver Post* reported that "wheat raising began in Baca County in 1928, when Tom Hopkins, then the 'wheat king' in southwestern Kansas, proved wheat could be raised in the area on summer fallow soil and little moisture." He was said to have taken 130,000 bushels off his five thousand-acre tract in five days, using twenty-six combines and fifty trucks.[25] Locally, it was reported, "It has been learned that Mr. Fred Prater of Liberal, Kansas, is to farm 3000 acres entirely of wheat in Baca County next year. This makes him the new 'King of wheat growers,' replacing Tom Hopkins." Included was the following revealing analysis:

23. Ibid., September 9, 1927.
24. Ibid., July 1, 1927, August 2, 1929.
25. *Denver Post,* August 27, 1942.

"Modern pioneers such as Fred Prater and Tom Hopkins have convinced hundreds that Baca Co. is a wheat producer. That's the reason we see scores of trucks, laden with tractors and other machinery headed toward the setting sun."[26]

It is understandable that not all the residents of the county approved the influx of Kansas wheat farmers. Prophetically, in an open letter to "Mrs. Newcomer," a local housewife warned, "It is regrettably true that two or three droughts would break some of our Kansas friends who are showing us how to farm."[27]

As in Kansas, some who came to engage in suitcase farming became resident farmers:

> Mr. Cook and family formerly lived at Fowler, Kansas, [and] have moved into their farm in the Wonder District. . . . [He] came to Baca county and bought a large acreage and has been raising good crops of wheat and so successful has been his venture that he has decided to move his family out here. . . . Mr. Cook has out about one thousand acres of wheat in Baca county northeast of Two Buttes.[28]

Another Baca County farmer who identified himself as starting as a nonresident gave this explanation:

> Many young farmers were crowded out from where we came. . . . I was called a suitcase farmer because we came out here and bought land, broke the sod, planted a crop and went back to Kansas. In my case that winter we built a farmstead out here and moved the next spring [1930].[29]

The greater incidence of suitcase farming in Baca County than elsewhere in Colorado in the early 1930s is suggested by the fact that a study of types of farming areas of the state published in 1935 specifically recognized suitcase farming only in a region consisting mainly of Baca County. The area called the Cimarron River High Plains, centers on Baca and extends into southeastern Prowers County on the northeast and westward into a small part of Las Animas County. The pertinent statement read thus:

---

26. *Democrat-Herald,* August 2, 1929; September 20, 1929, from the *Kiowa Clipper.*
27. *Democrat-Herald,* June 28, 1929.
28. Ibid., February 26, 1931.
29. Letter from Vance L. M. Novinger, Route 2, Springfield, Colorado, February 26, 1964.

It may be said that the area has suffered from the development of absentee or so-called "suitcase" farming. The operators of some of the large wheat farms spend a few weeks within the area during summer and autumn, harvesting one crop of wheat and seeding another. The balance of the year they live elsewhere.[30]

Since, unlike western Kansas, there seemed no way in which the number of out-of-county farmers could be determined from the AAA applications, a number of long-resident farmers, whose names were suggested by the ASCS county office manager, were asked to estimate the percentage of the wheat that was planted by early suitcase farmers. Those who ventured percentages gave the following figures: 20, 20, 25, 60, and 75 percent. One respondent wrote, "Not very many." Even if absentees in the late 1920s or early 1930s numbered only 20 percent of the farmers, this figure must be judged higher than elsewhere in Colorado at the time and near the average for western Kansas.

Several of the farmers who were asked to estimate the number of suitcase farmers in Baca County stated that most had given up farming as Dust Bowl conditions developed. This judgment is sustained by the small number of references to nonresident farming in the local newspaper during that period. Suitcase farmers from the following places were reported: 1934, St. John and Montezuma, Kansas; 1935, Liberal and Halstead, Kansas; 1937, Oklahoma. The 1937 note is especially interesting since it said, "An Oklahoma man was around on the flats Tuesday to see if his land had blown away. He was unable to find any wheat he had sown."[31] But some absentee farming continued; a neighboring Prowers County paper of 1939 mentions the good wheat prospects on farms operated by or for three Kansans.[32]

The only contemporary quantitative data found on suitcase farming in any part of Colorado prior to the ASCS wheat lists of 1954 are some derived from a government survey of Baca County made in 1936, after several years of Dust Bowl conditions. In a study in which it was stated that all operators were interviewed and all land use mapped, abandoned cropland exceeded the acreage then in actual use in four of the six land-use areas recognized.[33] By putting together data from two different sources, a

30. Hunter, *Type of Farming Areas in Colorado*, pp. 122, 123, 62. In this area, 69 percent of the land was in farms in 1929, of which 35 percent was in crops. Cash grains occupied 41 percent of the cropland and feed grains 32 percent.
31. *Democrat-Herald*, May 13, 1937.
32. *Lamar Daily News*, June 8, 1939.
33. "Land Use in Baca County, Colorado, Based on a Field Survey," Mimeo-

derived figure of 85 nonresident farmers was obtained: 1,045 farm operators in the county minus 960 resident-operated farms equals 85. Elsewhere in the study there were said to be 946 occupied houses at the time of the survey,[34] indicating 99 off-farm operations. Farms without residences were most numerous in the northeastern and north-central parts of the county, the same localities which had experienced the greatest abandonment of cropland.

Whether there were 85 or 99 nonresident farmers, apparently including local town farmers, nonresidents numbered less than 10 percent of all farmers. Hence, the actual number of suitcase farmers may well have been much below even that percentage. Many suitcase farmers had given up what looked like a hopeless struggle sooner than most local farmers, who had no place to which they could retreat readily; however, 782 abandoned farm houses, of which 414 had been abandoned recently,[35] were mute signs of the greater tragedy suffered by many former resident farmers.

Not all the suitcase farmers in Colorado were from Kansas. According to the former county agent of Adams County, nonresident farmers from predominantly irrigated country to the northwest were among the wheat farmers. The addresses of out-of-county farmers included Milliken and Johnstown in Weld County, and Loveland in Larimer County. Farmers from Larimer lived far enough away to qualify as suitcase farmers under the definition used in this study. The county agent was reluctant to call them suitcase farmers, explaining that they were among the best farmers operating there in the late 1920s and early 1930s. Since he estimated that out-of-county farmers ran about 10 percent of the total, those from far enough away to be suitcase farmers made up a substantially lower percentage. The falling out of nonresidents interested in temporary profits had reduced the number farming from a distance by 1933, although there was greater persistence among those employing summer fallowing.[36]

Insofar as I have been able to determine the circumstances and significance of early suitcase farming in Colorado, the results validate the findings reported for western Kansas: Kansans were innovators, extending wheat farming into less developed country to the west. Only in Baca County was there a substantial overlapping of nonresident wheat farming from Kansas.

---

graphed (Land Utilization Program, USDA Bureau of Land Economics April 1, 1938), pp. 16, 17, 18.

34. Ibid., Appendix, pp. 35, 4, 25.

35. Ibid., p. 26.

36. Interview with Herman Sandhouse, county agent of Adams County, 1929-44, Fort Collins, August 25, 1965.

CHAPTER SIX

Pause and Retreat

Introduction

The big expansion of wheat farming, in large part spearheaded by suitcase farmers, began to slow with the poor wheat years of 1932 and 1933. As drought continued, both planted and harvested acres decreased and the number farming went down. In at least some areas, the number of suitcase farmers dropped out relatively faster than that of local farmers. The oft-asserted generalization that drought and bad years reduce the number of nonresidents, who are relatively foot-loose, doubtless applied. It was asserted at the time that nonresidents were the first to abandon their farms.[1]

The degree to which the wheat crop was abandoned should be a significant measure of the discouragement of wheat farmers. On this basis, Baca County, Colorado, was greatest at an average abandonment of 79.7 percent for the period 1932-40. Other parts of the suitcase farming country in order of percentage of abandonment were by counties: Morton, Hamilton, Greeley, Kearny, Grant, Stanton, Haskell, all well above 60 percent; and Stevens, Wallace, Logan, Seward, Wichita, and Scott. Of those listed, only Scott County at 47.7 percent was below 50 percent.[2] Records

---

1. C. W. Thornthwaite, "The Great Plains," p. 241.

2. Calculated from *Colorado Agricultural Statistics,* Colorado Dept. of Agr., with the USDA (Denver, 1932-38); statistics for 1939-40, Floyd K. Reed, "Winter Wheat, Total Acres Planted, 1939-1956," mimeographed; and unpublished statistics for planted acres of winter wheat in Colorado for 1938, furnished by the USDA, Field Crops Statistics Branch, Agr. Estimates, Agr. Marketing Service (Washington, D.C.); and *Biennial Reports of the State Board of Agriculture, Kansas,* Topeka, 1931-40.

of per capita relief payments, another measure of distress, are readily available only for the years 1933-36; surprisingly, they emphasize not the western part, but a block of counties in and adjacent to the southern portion of the suitcase farming country. Haskell had an average of $609 per capita in federal aid. Other per capita payments were $532 in Stanton, $446 in Grant, $446 in Hodgeman, and $420 in Gray. Greeley County, farther north, had $417. Only two other counties in the entire Plains region reached the $400 level—one in the Indian country of South Dakota and the other in the extreme north of the Texas Panhandle.[3] Baca was the only county in Colorado with a payment above $200. Perhaps both lack of urban development and major dependence on wheat were indicated in high per capita relief payments in western Kansas.

Greeley County

Greeley County, where suitcase farming had been especially important, provides an example of the pause and retreat that occurred after the big plow-up of the 1920s and early 1930s. Here the decline in suitcase farming was sharp, probably more so than in most of western Kansas. Certain local factors unfavorable to suitcase farming, in addition to those operating more generally, contributed to the especially notable decline. The documentation of trends and causes and of the amount of suitcase farming is unusually good.

In Greeley County, despite the devastating drought, the acreage planted to wheat did not drop sharply until the autumn of 1937, when the wheat intended for harvest in 1938 was sown. At that time the acreage fell to pre-1930 levels. As noted in chapter 3, the acreages reported on the AAA applications of 1933 ran approximately 104,000, 123,000, 175,000, and 167,000, respectively, for the years 1930-33. The local newspaper, basing its information on the records of the AAA committee, which I confirmed

3. Francis D. Cronin and Howard W. Beers, *Droughts: Areas of Intense Drought Distress, 1930-1936,* WPA, Division of Social Research, Research Bulletin, series 5, no. 1, USDA Agr. Econ. Bur. and Resettlement Admin. (Washington, D.C.: GPO, January 1937), pp. 41-54.

4. *Greeley County Republican,* October 19, 1939, and October 17, 1940. The statistics compiled by the AAA committees are judged to be authentic despite the 111,467 acres planted to wheat reported for 1938 by the assessor, and the estimate of 115,000 prepared by the state agricultural statistician. Records for Greeley County in the Kansas City Federal Records Center contained in a file for 1939-40 validated the figures given in the newspaper for the years 1936-39 to the acre. The forms were Summary Sheets WR-402 and WR-504.

by records in the Kansas City Federal Records Center, gave acreages planted for the crop years 1936-40, as follows: 133,987; 163,299; 53,383; 69,166; and 42,390.[4]

At first, the decline in nonresident farming was not large. As noted in chapter 2, out-of-county farmers reduced their wheat acreage a little after the poor crop year of 1932, while resident farmers were seeding larger acreages. In the autumn of 1934 there was considerable competition for wheat land, one real estate agent saying, "The number wanting land on which to seed wheat is the largest of any year since I have been here." In the autumn of 1935 it was reported that more land was to be under AAA contracts than earlier. In 1936 the AAA committee admitted that the county could not "control the number of tillable acres in the county due to the fact that so much of this land is owned and operated by nonresident men." At least one suitcase farmer, L. E. Keeton of Salina, expanded his operation greatly. The 1933 AAA application showed that he seeded 1,070 acres of wheat for the 1932 crop, the most credited to him in the four years recorded; however, in the summer of 1936 it was noted that "he has 14 tractors, fully equipped, going in this county and expects to sow 12,000 acres of wheat next year."[5] On the apparently complete list of farmers reported by the assessor in 1940, the name of Keeton did not appear. It appears that he had decided not to buck the tide any longer.

Although the Tribune newspaper noted activity by a number of suitcase farmers during the summer and autumn of 1937, the county agent reported after seeding time, "Those who have been in the habit of coming to Greeley County and scratching in their wheat, then leaving it to blow away, did not visit us in very large numbers this fall."[6] As noted already, the acreage planted in the county for 1938 was less than one-third of that sown for 1937. Although the general failure of suitcase farmers to visit Greeley County in the autumn of 1937 cannot account for all of the decrease, the nonparticipation of most nonresidents must have been an important factor. It should be recalled that in 1934 out-of-county farmers operated over 47 percent of the land in the county.[7]

The decline in suitcase farming probably was influenced strongly by the heavy abandonment of the 1937 crop—83 percent on a county-wide basis, as reported by the state statistician. In addition, after the Agricultural

5. Ibid., September 13, 1934; November 28, 1935; January 16, June 25, 1936.

6. "Annual Report," Greeley County Agent, 1937, microfilm, Kansas State University, Manhattan.

7. *Greeley County Republican,* October 17, 1940. In the context of crop farming, with specific reference to wheat.

Adjustment Administration Act was declared unconstitutional, qualifying for the replacement payments for soil conservation proved difficult for non-residents. In the early years, under the AAA the major part of payments went out of the county,[8] but now they went mainly to residents of the county. If absentees owned most of the land and farmed about as much as local farmers, out-of-county payments should have been larger, with the tenant's share being three-fourths and the owner's one-fourth. However, it was reported that of the $200,000 to be distributed for compliance with the 1937 soil conservation program, "the greater portion . . . will be paid to local men."[9] A follow-up newspaper report indicated how small the portion going out of the county was. The payments received up to that time consisted of $61,279.51 on February 11, 1938, and $80,043.63 on February 16, totaling $141,323.14. It was added that the county agent, Mr. Brewer, "estimated that $115,000 of the payments to date would be received by local operators." If such payments constituted the "wheat harvest," as newspaper editors and others referred to the payments made by the government, the 1937 harvest of suitcase farmers was small indeed, since the 20 percent for out-of-county men must have gone mainly to the absentee landlords of local tenants who qualified. It appears that under conditions prevailing in 1937, suitcase farmers were much less successful than residents in farming the government. Small wonder that suitcase farmers stopped coming out to sow wheat.

Perhaps it is in order to emphasize further the importance of government payments in the period of high failure of the wheat crop. In 1936 the Stanton County agent in his annual report included the following statement: "During the past year, as in the two years previous, AAA benefit payments have been the only source of income of many families." Similarly, the county agent of Hamilton County wrote in his report for 1937, "The major income in 1937 as in the past will be from AAA payments." Under the heading "What the AAA Program Meant in 1935," a Colby newspaper compared income from the wheat harvested with AAA payments for five counties in northwestern Kansas. In only one, Cheyenne in the extreme northwestern corner of the state, less affected by drought than the others, was the income from wheat appreciable.[10] Table 21 shows the comparison. It should be added that if many farms in Logan and ·Wallace counties in 1935, as in 1933, had no wheat sown on them and if

8. Interview with Marie Holland, former AAA office manager, Tribune, August 21, 1961; letter from T. Bruce Stinson, April 3, 1963.

9. *Greeley County Republican,* December 30, 1937.

10. *Colby Free Press-Tribune,* January 1, 1937.

the AAA payments referred to were mainly or entirely for wheat, the payments per wheat farm were higher than shown in table 21. In Greeley County, AAA payments for the three years ending in 1936 amounted to $445,299.95 for wheat and $47,825.12 for the corn-hog program.[11]

There were several reasons for reduced payments to absentees. Only the absentees most willing to work at suitcase farming would be present long enough and go to the trouble or expense of the additional operations in order to qualify for payments for summer fallowing. And for the same reasons, absentees would not generally take part in emergency tillage to control soil drifting (blow damage). The soil-drifting payments for 1937, it was noted, "may be almost as large as those for soil conservation."[12] Other handicaps of absentees were that the sign-up dates for the soil conservation program were announced in the county newspaper only a few days ahead;[13] costs of emergency tillage by the county to prevent soil drifting were added to taxes and soil conservation payments on such lands were denied; the requirement was made that payments for summer fallowing would not be made under the soil conservation program unless protected by strips of small grain stubble or strips of a row crop. Also, nonresidents were not eligible for summer fallow loans.[14]

The requirement that wheat be planted in narrow strips, begun in 1937 and in effect in Greeley County through the harvest of 1942,[15] had the desired effects of squeezing most suitcase farmers out and reducing the damage from soil drifting. It seems clear that local agricultural committees, probably with the control of soil blowing as the primary objective, fashioned rules that were intended both to reduce soil drifting and to cut down on suitcase farming. In his annual report of 1935, the county agent for Greeley County asserted, "The many non-resident operators in many instances made no attempt to control soil blowing." In his report for 1936, he added, "For those non-resident operators who do not get into the county to do their work at the proper time we should have some

11. *Greeley County Republican,* July 30, 1936.
12. Ibid., December 30, 1937.
13. Ibid., May 12, 1938. "Those operators and owners who expect to comply with the 1938 Soil Conservation Program are asked to call at the Farm Bureau office according to this schedule: Colony township, Monday, May 16, Tribune township, Tuesday, May 17, and Harrison township, Wednesday, May 18."
14. Ibid., August 5, 1937; March 24, 1938; March 26, 1936.
15. Ibid., March 5, 1942. "Strip cropping loses 82 to 39. . . . This county is the only place in this section of the country that has had compulsory strip crop farming during the last four years." By 1942, with the return of better crop years, local farmers were no longer so greatly dependent on government payments nor greatly concerned about soil blowing.

provision for them to work to stop wind erosion of their soil, in order to protect the farmer who farms his ground at the proper time." After the administrative requirements already noted were put into effect, a Greeley county farmer was quoted as follows:

> There were less than 200 of us in the county. There were 270,000 acres of cropland to be handled. Almost three-fourths of the land was owned by persons outside the county, persons who had bought quarter sections of wheat land as an investment, or "suitcase farmers" who came out here to put in a crop and come again only to harvest it.
>
> We had to figure out some way to get blowing stopped on their land as well as our own. So we worked out a program that would do the job. There are today less than 5,000 acres subject to blowing.

He went on that strip cropping was the heart of the program.[16] There is evidence that local farmers partly had in mind discouraging the suitcase farmer when they voted to retain strip cropping for an additional year. "By vote of 76 to 75, Greeley Co. farmers voted to continue the practice of compulsory strip cropping for those desiring to get Triple A soil conservation payments. . . . Strip cropping has a tendency to hold the fellow out who made it blow in the first place. The problem of not being able to farm this land while living one or two hundred miles away was mentioned."[17]

The decline in the number of suitcase farmers in Greeley County, from 1937 through 1940, reflected the general wheat failure and coincided with the substantial increases in summer fallowing and strip cropping. Table 22 gives data on summer fallowing and strip cropping for the years in which suitcase farming declined greatly.

As pointed out in chapter 2, out-of-county wheat farmers in Greeley County numbered about 164 in 1933, not duplicating names of operators within the eight reporting districts. These out-of-county operators farmed about 43 percent of the land, and in 1932 seeded over 46 percent of the wheat and harvested nearly 55 percent of the wheat crop of the county. They were reported to have operated 47.33 percent of the land in the county in 1934. In the seven years from 1933 to 1940 the number of out-of-county operators was cut by more than four-fifths. The newspaper

16. *Kansas City Star,* November 19, 1939.
17. *Greeley County Republican,* March 13, 1941. Note that the vote was taken early in the spring, before the arrival of suitcase farmers.

report was first "less than 25," then 26 nonresident farmers in 1940.[18]

The statistical rolls (assessor's reports) for 1940 showed suitcase addresses in three different ways: a few on the regular rolls were sandwiched in among resident farmers, some were on the regular rolls but set off under the heading of "absentees," and some were listed on special absentee rolls. There was considerable duplication between the different listings. Only the forms for regular farms provided for the breakdowns of acreages by use. Thus, there was no provision for listing acreages for various crops, pasture, fallow, or failure the previous year for the thirty-eight entries made only on the absentee rolls. There were forty-four entries for farmers with suitcase addresses on the regular rolls, mainly under the heading of absentees, for whom the details of their land use were set down. Of these forty-four farms, fourteen consisted entirely of pasture or were idle in 1940, leaving thirty active suitcase farms. Since these thirty active suitcase farms included five that appeared among those of resident farmers, it was determined that the twenty-five not included probably constituted the twenty-six nonresident farmers reported by the local newspaper. Detailed information for such uses as wheat and fallow was available in the county offices of government agencies. It is assumed here that the land-use records were obtained from such agencies and that the record of absentee farming was complete. Detailed records for six operators from adjacent counties were included among those for the absentee operators set apart on the regular lists. Adding these six to the thirty gives a total of thirty-six out-of-county operators with detailed land-use records.

If the assumptions made above are correct, the out-of-county farmers had declined from about 164 to 36 from 1933 to 1940, and their wheat acreage from about 81,000 in 1932 to 7,992 in 1940. Farmers from adjacent counties were credited with only 145 acres of wheat in 1940. The 30 suitcase farmers of 1940 constituted 14 percent of the total 214 farmers. Suitcase farmers had declined from nearly 164 to 30 in seven years, and in their share of all farmers they dropped from nearly 43 to 14 percent. The acreage of wheat planted by them had fallen to about one-tenth of that of 1932. Even if many of the 38 listed as absentees from a distance but without detailed land-use records actually farmed, the decline in suitcase farming from the early 1930s had been great, greatest probably between 1937 and 1938. Most of those continuing as suitcase farmers lived fairly close in the specialized wheat country of Kansas. A comparison of figures 4 and 15a shows that most nonresidents from greater distances had given up.

18. Ibid., October 17, 1940; March 5, 1942.

Elsewhere in Western Kansas

Most of the factors working to reduce suitcase farming in Greeley County in the late 1930s operated in the suitcase farming country generally. High wheat failure, the difficulty of earning conservation payments because of the inability to control blowing, ineligibility for certain loans, and the small degree of attachment to the locality where they were farming combined to discourage many suitcase farmers from continuing absentee farming in western Kansas and adjacent parts of Colorado. Perhaps the requirement of strip cropping, in effect only in Greeley County, was an especially effective deterrent to suitcase farming. On the other hand, absentee ownership of land probably increased as outsiders less hard hit financially bought land at distress sales.

It appears from fragmentary evidence that suitcase farming in Stanton County declined during the same time as in Greeley. As noted in chapter 3, the percentage of suitcase farmers was greater there in 1935 than in 1933. The apparent increase from 30 percent in 1933 to 36 percent in 1935 could be either evidence of an actual increase or an indication that the methods used in sampling and determining the classification of farmers from the AAA applications gave results that were too low. In at least two counties nearby it was charged that owners were becoming operators by eliminating their tenants.[19] A few years later, however, a resident farmer, in recalling circumstances of the Dust Bowl era, gave the following account of the events:

> G. E. Winger farms 22 quarter sections in the N. E. corner of Stanton County and has 1800 acres of wheat. . . . 1927, he says, was the big year when most of the virgin pasture was broken and put under cultivation. There was too much "suitcase farming" the next few years. One good thing about the drouth and dust years, as Winger sees it, is "that we got rid of those guys." . . . As the hard times struck, the "suitcase farmers" and the less competent farmers struck out.[20]

The sense of relief of local farmers at the reduction of suitcase farming in Stanton County seems to have been premature, however:

19. In the "Land Use Survey of the Southern Great Plains Region, 1936," p. 85, there is a specific reference to Stevens County, as cited in chapter 4. The *Syracuse Journal*, February 8, 1935, reported a meeting of farmers to "protect the tenant wheat farmers in the distribution of allotment money in Hamilton County."

20. *Lamar Daily News*, March 18, 1939.

Prospects of a return of good crops have reversed the landlord-operator problem. In recent years landlords advertised and sought men to rent their land while this spring operators looked for land to lease until County Agent H. O. Wales said Monday most of the land in the county has been leased with practically only the undesirable left.

Local operators have taken up more ground and farmers have come from the eastern part of the state seeking land to work. . . . A few young men have come out and leased land with the intention of staying but most of them want to be suitcase farmers.[21]

Apparently it didn't require much encouragement to bring the absentees back onto Stanton County farms.

Perhaps it is in order to point out that the Collingwood Land Company had lost its suitcase status in shifting its base of operation from Plains, Kansas, from which suitcase farming had been conducted in Stanton County, to Johnson, the county seat of Stanton. Government benefit payments of $27,137 to the company were the largest made in Kansas in 1940.[22] It appears that far more suitcase operators stopped coming out to farm wheat than became local. The Collingwoods were probably exceptions. There seems to have been a reduction in suitcase farming in the late 1930s in Stanton County.

As noted in the case of the suitcase farmer from Salina who extended his wheat farming between 1933 and 1936, not all absentees agreed that the time for caution had arrived with the drought. Although such claims seem not to have been common, the old story of land paying for itself in one year reappeared:

Guy Humes of Dodge City, who owns a number of quarters of Grant County land, advised this office that last June he purchased a half section of land in east Grant and immediately put some of his tractors to working the soil preparing a bed for the seed wheat last fall and he is now harvesting a crop which will pay for the land. Considering the drouth which this county has suffered since planting time last fall the harvesting of a crop of this kind is indeed a tribute to good farming. Mr. Humes also stated that while his wheat was not turning out as well as he had anticipated it would still yield him a crop of around 25,000 bushels.[23]

21. *Johnson City Pioneer,* March 16, 1939.
22. *Greeley County Republican,* March 21, 1940.
23. *Grant County Republican,* July 5, 1934.

Haskell County, well southeast in the major suitcase farming country, was one of several in which out-of-county wheat farmers apparently were relatively more important in 1936 than 1933, although there is the alternative interpretation that the method used to determine the percentage in 1933 gave too low a figure. The results were that suitcase farmers accounted for 32 percent in 1936 and 27 percent in 1933.[24] By 1940, there had been little or no decline in the percentage of out-of-county farmers. The 1940 breakdown of nonresidents operating in Haskell County is as follows: farmers from bordering counties (excluding those with post office addresses in the town of Copeland), 11.1 percent; farmers from more than one county away, 18.7 percent. The number of out-of-county farmers was 164 of a total of 550,[25] or a combined percentage of 29.8. This suggests that there may have been no reduction of nonresident operators from 1936 to 1940.

Another example of relative constancy in the importance of suitcase farming is afforded by Wichita County. The one-in-five sample district by district of the AAA applications of 1933 gave 21 percent of farmers as out-of-county. A count of those actually farming in 1940 gave 19 percent with home addresses far enough away to qualify as suitcase farmers.[26]

Wichita, bordering Greeley County on its east, experienced a somewhat lower percentage of abandonment of wheat during the period 1932-40, with an unweighted average of 51.1 percent as compared to 63.7 percent for Greeley, as determined from the reports of the state agricultural statistician. The biggest differences were for the years 1936, 1937, and 1938, with the 83 percent abandonment in Greeley in 1937 contrasting sharply with the 23 percent in Wichita County in the same year.

In Wichita County, as in a much larger area, local citizens and agricultural officials were painfully aware of absentee farming as a cause of blowing dust. The county agricultural agent for Wichita, like his counterparts elsewhere in the Dust Bowl, made a report to headquarters at Kansas State College, Manhattan, on the degree of land blowing on farms operated by resident and nonresident operators in 1935, probably the worst year for soil drifting.[27] The location of this report is not known, but Roy E. Gwin, the county agent, then a thirty-one-year county resident and wheat farmer, summarized that resident farmers were much more effective than

24. Edwards, *Influence of Drought*, p. 50, gives 32 percent for 1936.
25. Bell, *Contemporary Rural Community*, p. 31.
26. "Statistical Rolls," Wichita County, 1940, microfilm, library of Kansas State Historical Society, Topeka.
27. "Narrative and Statistical Reports from County Agents," Wichita County, 1935. (Annual report.)

absentees in controlling the blowing of dust. Despite the disadvantage of greater blow damage and probable inability to qualify for some soil conservation practice payments, the nonresidents persisted and may even have become relatively more numerous during the 1930s. The following explanation was also offered by Gwin:

> Farmers were having a hard time staying in business, with the poor crops, the low prices, and with all the other problems of the 1930's. Many farms changed hands during this period—there were forced sales, many farms were broken up, and during this period I am inclined to think that our percentage of "suit case" farmers increased, because many farmers from farther east came out here and either purchased farms or parts of farms, and then came out here to operate them. Eventually, some of these people moved out here and improved their holdings, but I am inclined to say there was an increase in our non-resident operation in those days.

He continued by explaining that since the German-Russians of the Marienthal community in the eastern portion of the county, who were grouped near their Roman Catholic church, in the main owned their own farms and apparently retained them, there was little nonresident-owned land available, preventing much non-resident land operation there.[28]

An analysis of the distribution of nonresident wheat farmers in 1933, 1936, and 1940 in Wichita County showed the greatest relative importance of this group in the southernmost of the reporting districts: Lydia community had 44 percent out-of-county farmers in 1933; Whitewoman Township had 21 percent suitcase in 1936 and 34 percent in 1940. The data are not strictly comparable because Whitewoman Township was a larger area and had more farmers than the Lydia community. A difficult water supply and the distance from the major highway and railroads may have favored nonresident farming.

The assessors' reports of both 1936 and 1940 are here considered representative, having complete or nearly complete listings of farmers in Wichita County. In both cases, farms were counted only if some cropland use was reported for the year in question. Thus, entries showing all cropland idle or farms consisting entirely of pasture were omitted. About 94 of about 450 farms were operated by out-of-county farmers in 1933. Farms of suitcase operators, not counting farmers from adjacent counties, numbered 59 of a total of 444 Wichita County farms in 1936 and 103 of a total of 532 in 1940.

28. Letters from Roy E. Gwin, August 24, 1965, and November 10, 1966.

Land Use of Suitcase and Local Farmers

A comparison of farm land and acreage planted to wheat for the 1936 crop in Wichita County shows that suitcase and local farmers sowed comparable acreages but had quite different percentages of their farm land in wheat. The average figures were: suitcase farmers, 400.4 acres planted to wheat of 563.2 acres of farm land; local farmers, 412.1 acres in wheat of 802.1 acres of farm land.[29] The percentages of farm land in wheat were 73 for the suitcase farmers and a much lower 51 for local farmers. It is obvious that summer fallowing was not yet an important part of wheat farming.

A similar treatment of the records of the fourteen suitcase farmers (obviously an incomplete record of suitcase farmers) and fourteen matching local farmers in Grant County for 1936, as included in the assessor's report for that year, showed that suitcase farmers averaged 485.7 acres of wheat sown on an average farm of 643.2 acres, while local farmers averaged 483.9 acres of wheat on 824.3 acres of farm land. Percentages in wheat were 76 and 59, respectively. In both Wichita and Grant counties, if the less complete report from Grant County is representative, suitcase farmers emphasized wheat substantially more than local farmers. The emphasis of the suitcase farmers on wheat was consistent, whereas local farmers varied from growing wheat predominantly to growing none.

The apparently complete reporting of absentee farmers in the assessors' reports in 1940 in both Greeley and Wichita counties permits a meaningful comparison of suitcase and local farming. Table 23 shows averages for land use in 1940 and 1939 for eighteen suitcase farmers and eighteen matching local farmers of Whitewoman Township of Wichita County. The eighteen suitcase farmers were the only ones of the township for whom the record appeared to be complete or fairly complete. Considering that the local farmers on the average had much larger farms, the two groups gave about the same emphasis to wheat in 1940 (about 20 percent of their acreage). The acreage harvested in 1939 amounted to about 13 percent of the farm land of the suitcase farmers and 16 percent for the local farmers. Both groups made extensive use of summer fallow. Suitcase farmers had more

29. Based on the forty-three suitcase farms and on forty-two local farms in the townships of Edwards, Leoti, and Whitewoman as shown in the assessor's report of 1936. Only Beaver Township in the northwestern part of the county was omitted. The local farms selected were those that followed the suitcase farms most directly in the lists, a procedure which should have ensured a fairly random sample. Inadvertently, the matching locals numbered forty-two instead of forty-three.

idle land and suffered a relatively greater crop failure in 1939. Surprisingly, the suitcase farmers planted more grain sorghum.

The assessor's report showed that nine of the eighteen suitcase farmers planted wheat for 1940, the largest acreage being 600 acres; twelve harvested wheat and thirteen fallowed in 1939. For the local farmers, sixteen sowed wheat for 1940, the largest acreage being 1,600 acres; fourteen harvested wheat and sixteen fallowed in 1939. It appears that one-half of the absentees thought it not worthwhile to plant for 1940, thus lowering the average per suitcase farmer.

As pointed out, the thirty suitcase farmers for whom the Greeley County assessor reported farming operations in 1940 were probably the only absentees from a distance. The same report showed 33 farming in 1939. The operations of the sixty-eight local farmers of Colony Township and matching farmers from the other two townships were compiled for comparison. Table 24 represents the averages obtained.

As might be expected of full-time farmers, the local operators had larger farms; also, they gave more emphasis to crops other than wheat, had more land in fallow, had less idle land, and suffered relatively less crop failure. The suitcase farmers stood out for their emphasis on wheat. A larger fraction of the suitcase farmers sowed winter wheat for 1940—twenty-seven of thirty—in contrast to fifty-one of ninety-five local farmers; but the assessor's report showed comparable percentages of the farmers harvesting wheat in 1939: fourteen of thirty-three suitcase and forty-six of ninety-four local farmers. The largest acreage planted for 1940 by a suitcase farmer was 1,440 acres; the largest by a local farmer was 2,560; the largest acreage of winter wheat harvested by a suitcase farmer in 1939 was 1,780 acres; and the largest by any local farmer covered in the table was 1,900 acres.

Most local farmers and some, but not a majority, of the suitcase farmers were carrying on diversified cropping. Of the ninety-five local farmers in 1940, sixty-four planted barley, eighty-four planted grain sorghum, and eighty-five put in crops other than these and winter wheat. In comparison, of the 30 suitcase farmers, seven planted barley, seventeen grain sorghum, and fourteen crops other than these and winter wheat. In 1939, eighty of ninety-four local farmers were reported as harvesting crops other than winter wheat and seventy-six as summer fallowing. Of the thirty-three suitcase farmers, only seven were reported as harvesting crops other than winter wheat and seventeen as summer fallowing. It appears, however, that they had incorporated crops other than wheat into their operations and that summer fallow had become important to them. In order to survive drought and because of the need to comply with government agricultural control programs, many of the suitcase farmers were farming in much the same way as local farmers so far as cropland was concerned.

The government payments for 1940 suggest larger-scale operations by local than by suitcase farmers. Of the more than fifty checks in excess of $1,000 paid to Greeley County farmers, only one went to an address outside the area, a payment of $3,654 to George E. Gano of Hutchinson.[30] It would appear that most of the payment represented his share as a landowner rather than as a farm operator because the assessor's report of 1940 showed Gano farming only 1,320 acres, probably through a custom-farming arrangement, on which 660 acres had been sown to wheat and 640 planted to grain sorghum for 1940. For 1939 the assessor's record showed that Gano harvested 660 acres of winter wheat and had 660 acres of crop failure.

Summary

The generalization that bad years brought a reduction in suitcase farming is exemplified in Greeley County in the late 1930s. The experience was shared elsewhere, as in Baca County, Colorado, and perhaps in Stanton County, Kansas. However, a sharp all-over decline does not seem to have occurred. For example, in both Haskell and Wichita counties there was little change. Although suitcase farmers continued to depend more on wheat than local farmers, by 1940 many of the absentees had adopted more diversified cropping systems than were characteristic earlier, and many nonresidents, like the resident farmers, had included summer fallowing. Both the diversification in crops and summer fallowing required more traveling by the absentees, longer periods of residency, or increased dependence on custom farming.

30. *Greeley County Republican,* March 21, 1940.

CHAPTER SEVEN

A Renewal of Suitcase Farming

Introduction

With the increased precipitation and higher prices for wheat during and just after World War II came renewed interest in wheat farming on the suitcase farming frontier of western Kansas and in adjacent parts of Colorado. The appeal to patriotism—wheat for the war effort—added a sense of duty. The response of absentee farmers, however motivated, was especially strong. In Colorado the big increase came after the war's end. The increase in cropland in Kansas, indicative of the emphasis on wheat, was relatively greatest in Greeley and Hamilton counties. The transformation was especially great in Colorado, as shown in the percentage increase in cropland (fig. 16).

New Activity in Greeley County

Greeley County, Kansas, where the decline of wheat farming and non-resident operation in the late 1930s had been marked, offers a made-to-order setting in which to examine the revival of wheat farming and the return of the suitcase farmer. The local AAA committee made it clear that it wished to prevent another big plow-up as the long period of high wheat failure came to an end. A release from the Farm Bureau office read:

> Penalty of contributing to Defeat of Conservation Program stressed—It is construed by this regulation that anyone who is a

cooperator and, for example, breaks out sod whether as an operator
or hires out with his machinery to break sod for anyone in the
county or allows his machinery to be used by anyone who breaks
sod in the county will be subject to a penalty, and such penalty will
be charged against him or his application for payment for 1941
performance.[1]

Absentees, who owned most of the land and usually had less to lose
than local farmers if they miscalculated their chances and were not forced
to live among the blowing fields if Dust Bowl conditions returned, took
the lead in breaking grassland. The revival of wheat farming was signaled
by the return of nonresident farmers; the county agent reported an increase in their number from twenty-six in 1940 to sixty-eight in 1941.[2]
The increase took place despite the requirement of strip cropping for
conservation program payments. Apparently farmers from the outside
were again ready to take their chances on wheat, pass up government
payments, and thus avoid the penalties for plowing sod. In 1942 the
requirement of strip cropping was voted out. Between 1940 and the beginning of 1947, the plow-up was great, resulting in an increase of cultivated
land from about 208,000 to over 350,000 acres.[3] The 1947 harvest was
estimated at 5,000,000 bushels and officially reported as 4,546,000
bushels.[4]

The Greeley County newspaper in 1944 noted the activity of several
non-residents in extending crop farming. The county gasoline rationing
board (a wartime agency) plainly shared the view of the county agent and
soil conservation board that a rapid extension of crop farming was unwise,
turning down requests for gasoline to be used for sod breaking. A series of
newspaper stories identified the principals in one instance and, in effect,
contrasted what was claimed to be the anti-sod-breaking sentiment of the
local farmers with that of outsiders. At the time of year at which residents
a few years earlier had experienced Dust Bowl conditions, a picture of a
dust storm appeared in the local paper, with the caption: "Seen above is
one reason why most local residents are not in favor of plowing up more
sod . . . . Winds of the past week indicated graphically that storms such as

1. *Greeley County Republican,* March 21, 1940, and April 10, 1941. The issue of
October 17, 1940, had given figures of 208,696 acres of cultivated land and 208,400
acres of pasture in the county.
2. Ibid., March 5, 1942.
3. Ibid., October 17, 1940, and January 30, 1947. The 1947 figure was given by
T. Bruce Stinson, superintendent of the Tribune branch agricultural station.
4. Ibid., August 7, 1947. Estimate by T. Bruce Stinson; Ibid., August 14, 1947.
The State Board of Agriculture figure was 4,546,000 bushels (*Thirty-sixth Biennial
Report,* vol. 41, 1947-48, p. 414).

pictured above can return." Then followed a story entitled "AAA Coercion Here Denied," in which it was said:

> But local board is turning down applications for gas to plow sod. Why break up more sod, when the government is paying $5 an acre to seed cultivated land back to sod, and when there are thousands of acres of broken ground in the county not farmed, [a member of farm transportation committee] continued. . . . Few farmers living in the county appear to desire to plow sod, except perhaps an isolated patch or two. In one instance (according to a Topeka daily) . . . an extensive Kansas wheat grower [George E. Gano of Hutchinson] wanted to break land in Greeley county, sow it to grass and plant it to wheat later in the year. The board denied him gasoline for machinery to prepare the soil for the much needed wheat production to come later.

A week later, the local rationing board was overruled, apparently as the result of the intervention of the governor of the state:

> In reference to a rationing appeal of George E. Gano requesting 600 gallons for breaking out 2,170 acres of sod, which was rejected by the local boards on March 7, [1944,] H. O. Davis, district director of Wichita, said, "No provision is inserted which authorized the rejection of non-highway gasoline for any occupational purposes," but the local board is continuing to deny gasoline for breaking of sod.[5]

Gano got the gasoline.[6] Despite wartime shortages of farm machinery, the stage was set for a return of wheat farming.

Following the overruling of the local rationing board and a rainy spring in which over seven inches fell in April, an unsurprising headline appeared: "Wave of Sodbusting Is Expected in Greeley County This Spring." Aaron Sell, a large landowner and suitcase farmer from Stafford, predicted that about 80,000 acres, or approximately one-sixth of the area of the county, would be broken during the spring. He added, "They shouldn't discourage people from coming here by telling them they can't get water and only raise a crop once in ten years." Of the several men with him from Belpre, Cullison, Maxwell, Hill City, Sylvia, and Garden City, Sell said, "Most of them are taking five-year leases and will locate here if they can find improvements (places to live)." The article stated, "There aren't many improved places for rent in the county, nor vacant houses in Tribune. Some men still prefer to speculate mainly on wheat and to buy farms

5. *Greeley County Republican*, March 30 and April 6, 1944.
6. Ibid., April 13, 1944.

without improvements."[7]

Gano of Hutchinson; Sell of Stafford, with forty-two quarters, or 6,720 acres, and R. H. Garvey of Wichita (identified elsewhere as from Colby), fifteen quarters, or 2,400 acres, were major figures in the plow-up. These three nonresidents were apparently responsible for more than one-half of the sod broken in the county in 1944,[8] which was only about one-fourth as large as the amount Sell had predicted.

As the season for the plowing of pasture arrived in 1945, it was said that the county AAA committee had received applications to break out ninety-one quarter sections without penalty. Permission was granted if the slope of the land was 2 percent or less with the proviso that the penalty of three dollars per acre would be applied if the land were to become a wind erosion hazard.[9] Many acres were broken without permission.

Some information is available on arrangements made for farming the land of the three leaders in the new surge of wheat growing. Gano, a big landowner and operator of a chain of elevators, who in 1940 farmed in Greeley County, may be presumed to have relied then as later on tenants and those doing custom farming.[10] Aaron Sell, listed as a farm operator in some earlier assessors' reports, seems to have relied heavily on farmers from farther east who rented land from him. Garvey shifted early from renting to local farmers to dependence on roving crews operating under the control of a manager. The report of a former employee included the following information:

> I was in the employment of Garvey from 1943 until 1959. Garvey came from college to Colby as an attorney. He soon became a real estate dealer, dropping the practise of law. He acquired some land. For a few years he leased land to farmers living near by. During the 30's he began to farm the land himself using roving crews to get the job done. John Kriss was his foreman, until 1943 when E. M. Fogelman took over. It was in 1941-42-43 that he added substantially to his Kansas holdings. In 1945 John Kriss returned as manager for two years. . . . I was responsible for the preparation and seeding of the Kansas 1947 wheat in the amount of very near 12,500 acres.[11]

Understandably, it was not just the big land buyers and sod breakers who were attracted to Greeley County by the promise of good wheat

7. Ibid., May 4, 1944.

8. Ibid., May 18, 1944, and April 12, 1945. "Our records show that in the neighborhood of 125 to 140 quarters of sod were broken out in Greeley county during 1944," the AAA committee reported.

9. Ibid., April 12, 1945.

10. Interviews with T. Bruce Stinson, July 11, 1966, and November 16, 1968.

years. As was the case some fifteen to twenty years earlier, "Farmers in central and eastern Kansas who have found their chances for expansion limited are coming west." [12] The Greeley County paper noted that "Sell maintained more would come to live in Greeley County permanently, if they could find places to stay," and added, "There is a definite housing shortage in Greeley County." The housing shortage, at least partly a result of wartime priorities, was doubtless a factor in preventing new or returning suitcase farmers from becoming residents.

Many of the suitcase farmers operating in Greeley County in the late 1940s did not follow the practice of summer fallowing, which had become standard in the county and adjacent country in the late 1930s. [13] Similar disregard for summer fallowing in moist years is well documented elsewhere in the semiarid wheat country at this time. It may be assumed that both the chance of a quick profit and experience in a somewhat more humid setting farther east were reasons for the continuous cropping of wheat carried on by nonresidents at this time.

Hamilton County, Kansas

Although the record does not provide as detailed information for Hamilton County as for Greeley County, it is plain that the revival of suitcase farming in the mid-1940s described for Greeley also took place in this area.

The county newspaper took note of land purchases by nonresidents, and buyers from Winfield, Hutchinson, Dodge City, and Tribune were specifically identified, though Dodge City was the address given most often. During the period of land purchase, described as at record levels for part of the time, nonresidents were found to own 75 percent of the land in the county, [14] up from 68 percent in 1936.

The return of better weather brought forth a warning editorial entitled "No Time for Plows," which read in part,

> The suggestion that the former dustbowl again be stirred up to overcome a temporary food shortage should be ignored by its land owners and farmers who live in it. . . . To suggest that this area be

11. Letter from O. A. Snell, Carson City, Nevada, April 16, 1970.
12. *Greeley County Republican,* May 10, 1945, citing Clement Wilson, Tribune real estate operator.
13. Letter from T. Bruce Stinson, July 25, 1969.
14. *Syracuse Journal,* July 16, 1943; June 30, 1944; January 12 and 26, February 2, 1945; and June 30, 1944. By mid-1944, nonresident ownership was reported at 75 percent.

planted to crop and farmed in spare time suggests a great ignorance of recent conditions here on the part of those who suggest it. It was part time farming of non-resident farmers who appeared to plant their crop and returned to harvest it if any, half-way farming by inexperienced resident farmers who were over-expanded, and unprecedented drouth which caused the dust bowl in the first place. . . . Encouraging unwise expansion now is doing the reclaimed area a great disfavor.[15]

It was later acknowledged that conditions were right for another plow-up by absentees:

While resident farmers know the conditions here and will stick to the best farming practices, much land in the area has passed into the hands of persons from higher rainfall regions and persons unfamiliar with conditions here. Many such persons will be tempted to forsake good farming practices for increased acreage.

One "suitcase farmer," after hearing of the lifting of restrictions [on wheat acreage], made the statement that he intended to "one way" every acre of land, stubble and all, and put every foot of it to wheat this fall to help the war effort.[16]

The county agent was quoted in the same issue as expressing concern that the ending of government acreage restrictions would cause an increase of poor farming practices.

During this second wheat boom in which absentees played a major role, self-propelled combines were reported as being used in the county for the first time.[17] The fact that wartime restrictions made the purchase of farm machinery very difficult and that the newspaper account credited *one* of the combines to a local owner leads to the inference that most of these new machines were introduced by suitcase farmers.

In his official report for 1944, the county agent confirmed the newspaper accounts of events that led to a major reentry of nonresident farmers.

These four successive years of unusually good crops have resulted in much Hamilton County land being purchased by non-residents. It has also resulted in the immigration of many farmers into Hamilton County from counties farther east in Kansas and from other states . . . . These new landowners and new operators for the most part *live* [in] or *migrated* [italics supplied] from regions of higher

15. Ibid., May 28, 1943.
16. Ibid., July 16, 1943.
17. Ibid., July 21, 1944.

rainfall. Their concepts of what are good farming practices too frequently do not fit western Kansas. They do not realize the importance of the conservation of moisture in the production of crops. As a result too many of these new owners and operators, spurred by the memory of the recent big crops and motivated by a get-rich-quick idea, have been insisting on "plowin' her up and puttin' every foot of it back to wheat to help the war effort." Very few resident farmers have followed in their footsteps. [18]

In the next year's report, the county agent restated the importance of suitcase farming, including some further explanation:

> The population of Hamilton County is approximately 2,000 and is increasing. This increase has caused a severe housing shortage both in rural and urban areas. Much of the increase is due to the excellent crops of the past five years. The good crops have resulted in a high turnover in real estate at highly increased prices, and we find many land buyers, notably from the area east of here, coming into the county to farm their newly acquired land. Some are residing here, while others farm by "remote control."

Acknowledged in the same report but not identified as a factor contributing to nonresident operation was the difficulty in obtaining well water: "The water supply in some rural parts of the county presents a problem because of the depth to water."

Confirmation of a substantial plow-up and appraisal of the quality of the land by the regional conservationist are contained in a contemporary report. As of 1947, slightly over 70,000 acres more had been plowed than up to 1936, but only 47 percent of the increased acreage was judged of sufficient quality that it could "stay in cultivation." [19] Considering that a large amount of cropland had reverted to grass during the late 1930s, the actual plow-up was probably much greater than 70,000 acres.

Land speculation, the attraction of high prices for good crops, the possibility of farming by remote control by those to the east who had insufficient land at home seem to be the basic reasons for the comeback of suitcase farming in western Kansas. A shortage of housing and building materials, as well as difficulties in obtaining domestic water in some places, probably reduced the attractions of the area as a place to live, confirming the advantages of suitcase farming.

18. Annual report of county agent for Hamilton County, 1944.
19. H. H. Finnell, "How Much of the New Plow Up Is Good," *Minutes,* Great Plains Agricultural Council, Southern Division (Amarillo, January 5, 6, 7, 1948), p. 56.

Eastern Colorado

Introduction

The resumption of absentee farming of wheat in Greeley and Hamilton counties in western Kansas was followed shortly by an influx of nonresidents into drier country to the west. This was the first big invasion by suitcase farmers in much of east-central Colorado. Here a new suitcase farming frontier was formed rapidly. As in much of western Kansas some two decades earlier, outsiders led the way in the plowing of the grassland and wheat planting.

It was authoritatively estimated that four million acres of grassland, mostly in eastern Colorado, were broken for cropping in a period of ten years. As stated at the time,

> The greater portion of the increase in land used for crops took place in eastern Colorado especially in the counties of Cheyenne, Kiowa, Elbert, Lincoln, and Washington. . . . Although specific information is lacking, the evidence available indicates that probably three million or more acres of virgin land were broken out and cropped during the 10 years following 1939. In addition probably one million acres of land broken out and cropped during the late 1920's and early 1930's, but which had been permitted to go back to grass, was brought into cultivation.[20]

Figure 16 shows Kiowa County, located just to the west of Greeley County, Kansas, as affected most. According to the United States census, cropland (acreage harvested, failure, in fallow, and idle) in Kiowa County amounted to 129,002 acres in 1939, 117,086 in 1944, 423,548 in 1949, and 551,790 in 1954. In 1964 the figure was 442,444 acres. By far the biggest plow-up was between 1944 and 1949. As late as January, 1945, the Kiowa County abstract of assessment gave the amount of dry farm land as only 182,873 acres of a total of 1,050,838 acres assessed in the county. Thus, the cropland amounted to only slightly more than 18 percent of the land area assessed. Perhaps more important was the low appraisal given cropland as compared to grazing land. The assessed value per acre ($3.90) was only twice that of the poorest grazing land (Class B, $1.95), and less than one-half above that of the better grazing land (Class A, $2.79).[21] By May, 1949, a little over four years later, it was stated that 48 percent of

20. *Colorado Agricultural Statistics, 1948 and 1949,* Colorado Department of Agriculture, with the USDA (Denver), p. 3.
21. As reported in the *Kiowa County Press,* January 26, 1945.

the land in the county was cropland. The inclusion of 47,000 acres of land plowed for the first time in 1949 indicated that sod breakers were still active.[22] Later in the year, the county agent in his annual report stated that altogether 51,000 acres had been broken during the year.

The increase in cropland in Kiowa County was primarily for wheat. The acreage planted in winter wheat, as reported by the state agricultural statistician, remained essentially static until 1943; then, after a small decline in 1944, wheat acreage went up tremendously. For the crop years 1939, 1940, and 1941, less than 5,000 acres were planted. Then 8,530 acres were planted for 1943 and 20,930 acres in 1945. There were still greater increases in the following years: 55,560 acres were planted to wheat for 1946; 104,900 acres for 1947; in 1948 there were 220,900 acres; in 1949, 268,320 acres; 335,510 acres for 1951; and in 1953, 347,540 acres were sown. The high point was reached in 1953, when approximately seventy times as much wheat was planted as in 1940.[23]

In Crowley, the next county to the west, the state agricultural statistician in the same unofficial report showed less than a thousand acres of unirrigated wheat planted until 2,240 were planted for 1946. Relatively large increases took place for the crop year 1949, in which planted acres in wheat expanded to 14,100 acres from 1,500 in 1948; 1950 showed an increase to 27,300 acres; and the peak came in 1951 with 35,860 acres in wheat.

Into and Through Kiowa County

In an effort to reconstruct the essential features of the big surge of wheat farming in Colorado and to determine the processes at work and the forces behind the transformation of a grassland into wheat country, special attention will be given to the major thrust through Kiowa County, the county which acquired the most suitcase farmers and experienced the greatest increase in wheat acreage. A number of critical details will be noted that help present a close-up view of the changing scene. These, in addition to some general appraisals made at the time, should aid in understanding the role of the suitcase farmer, who was again an innovator.

22. Ibid., May 6, 1949. The breakdown, based on an aerial survey of the county, was listed as growing wheat, 229,760 acres; summer fallow, 254,850 acres; new breaking (1949), 47,000 acres; and grassland, 575,600 acres. Probably the summer fallow as reported was actually partly land intended for summer crops, such as grain sorghums. Over 71,000 acres of grain sorghum were planted, according to the state agricultural statistician.
23. Floyd K. Reed, "Winter Wheat, Total Acres Planted, 1939-1956." Mimeographed, Denver.

It is fortunate that the spread of wheat farming was unusually well reported in the newspapers of the area. A column of local news of the Haswell locality (in western Kiowa County), contained in a neighboring weekly constitutes an exceptionally complete chronicle of the activities of nonresidents. The county agent noted and interpreted major trends, and occasionally regional and national media gave attention to the more spectacular events.

Wheat growing took only a few years to become important throughout the nearly eighty-mile length of Kiowa County and some 10 miles beyond into Crowley County on physically suited land. Skipping over the most sandy parts, this penetration into the driest part of southeastern Colorado was also the deepest nearly continuous extension of important suitcase farming into the state. As of 1945, only the two most eastern communities of Kiowa County were producing substantial crops. Towner produced 150,000 bushels of wheat, Sheridan Lake, next to the west, about 45,000 bushels, or about 25 cars, and Eads and Galatea, in the central area of long-established general farming, 4,000 bushels. In addition, the J. D. Infield Grain Company, also in the county, was expected to ship about 15,000 bushels of wheat.[24] In 1946 the wheat harvest at Brandon, the third community west in the county, was the subject of a major story, with a shipment of 133 cars, about 232,000 bushels, reported. In 1948, the wheat harvest at Haswell, in the western part of the county, was estimated at more than half a million bushels. The shipment in 1949 from Arlington, the westernmost rail point in the county, was given as 56 cars, or nearly 100,000 bushels.[25] In the previous year, 1948, wheat was harvested from "thousands of acres" in eastern Crowley County, still farther west.[26] Wheat farming had extended to Horse Creek, west as far as the loess-mantled plains extend. In this especially dry part of eastern Colorado, annual precipitation averages less than twelve inches.

As noted earlier, a small amount of wheat raising, partly by nonresidents, had continued in the eastern part of the Kiowa County during the bad years of the 1930s. Farther west, it appears that newly arrived suitcase farmers introduced specialized wheat farming. The well-publicized harvest in the Brandon area in 1946 on the Garvey-Kriss farms seems to have been a pioneer venture. Garvey, who had been engaged in nonresident wheat raising in western Kansas, led the way in the big extension of suitcase farming. The featured news story appearing at harvest in the county seat

24. *Kiowa County Press,* August 10, 1945.
25. Ibid., July 12 and August 16, 1946, July 23, 1948, and August 12, 1949.
26. *Ordway New Era,* July 16, 1948.

paper reported the integrated nature and large scope of their operation, as well as the widespread notice it received.

> The little town of Brandon, in Kiowa County, has attracted a lot of attention the past few days as a result of the huge wheat crop that is being harvested on the Garvey-Kriss farms near that village. Pictures have appeared in a Denver paper, and photographers from several large magazines have been there taking pictures for their publications. Fox Movietone also sent a representative to get information and photos for their news reels.
>
> Roy Huston of Dodge City, Kansas, is in complete charge of the harvesting, combining, and delivery operations. Lester Cravens is auditor and weighman for the harvest period at Brandon.
>
> Tuesday evening only three of seven available grain cars had been loaded on the Missouri Pacific, and the balance of approximately 125,000 bushels of wheat was piled in windrows on a vacant lot, making a beautiful sight. At that time 7 out of 16 sections had been harvested, which represented the best wheat, with an estimated yield of from 20 to 50 bushels per acre by machine measure.
>
> Mr. Huston was high in his praise of the efficiency and cooperation of the men operating the 35 combines hired for the harvest. They came from wheat fields in Texas, Oklahoma, Kansas, and Missouri, and one from Washington. . . . Seventy trucks were also in use. Our informants were high in their praise of John Kriss of Colby, Kansas, who is general manager of the Garvey-Kriss farming operations, for the success of the Brandon project. They stated that Mr. Kriss has had much experience in dry land farming, and believes the summer fallow practice has proven very practical. *His experience in wheat production at Colby is being extended to Kiowa County* [italics supplied].[27]

If one can rely upon mention in the press and local opinion, the first sizable venture in wheat farming near Haswell, on beyond the long-established general farming area near Eads in the central part of the county, was on the Blakemore ranch. From the neighboring *Bent County Democrat,* the following general description of the Haswell locality at the beginning of the year 1946 seems significant: "The surrounding country is composed of cattle ranches and sheep ranches and some farming is done. The large Blakemore ranch of 3,000 acres raises extensive crops of grain and ships to market. Also several small farms have produced grain to ship

27. *Kiowa County Press,* July 12, 1946.

in the last few years." Blakemore of Liberal, Kansas, with Jim Carpenter as manager, also raised cattle.[28] The "Haswell News" section of the same paper in its July 25, 1947, account of the wheat harvest identified the Blakemore farms, Glen Dixon of Oklahoma, and the Garvey farms as harvesting wheat. By the definition used here, these operations qualified as suitcase farms.

That they were not alone is indicated by the statement in the same account that land buyers and sod-breaking people were in town "every day." The following spring, the same local reporter stated, "Farming activities are being resumed at Haswell lately, with large equipment and people moving in daily. Numerous trailer houses are making their appearance over the country as people are locating temporarily to break sod and plant wheat."[29]

With the 1948 harvest, it became apparent that the big name in wheat farming at Haswell was Garvey, as it was two years earlier at Brandon. Under a three-column headline about the harvest, a newspaper story began with the statement "The 1948 'gold rush' is on in the Haswell country north of Las Animas." It continued with reference to the bumper crop being harvested on the forty thousand acres of land owned and operated by Ray H. Garvey, here identified as from Wichita. The foreman was from Wichita, the field manager from Dodge City, the plow foreman from Eads, the county seat. There were seventy combines, only one belonging to Garvey, and one hundred trucks at work. Both the foreman and field manager maintained offices in Eads.[30] The home-county newspaper specified that 178,381 bushels of wheat had been shipped from Haswell by July 19 and that there were 249,426 bushels of Garvey wheat piled on the ground. The total harvest of the locality was estimated at 554,807 bushels, including about 100,000 bushels not yet hauled to the elevator.[31] Garvey's share reportedly amounted to more than three-fourths.

Farther from the scene, the *Denver Post* recognized that a big change had occurred in western and central Kiowa County and the adjoining area:

> Best estimates are that one million bushels of wheat were produced this year within a thirty-five mile radius of Haswell. The same area produced only 25,000 bushels in 1947, when cattle were still the main crop.
>
> The coming of a million bushel wheat crop to Haswell and Eads largely was the work of R. H. Garvey of Wichita, Kansas, wealthy

28. *Bent County Democrat,* January 4 and September 22, 1946.
29. Ibid., April 9, 1948.
30. Ibid., July 9, 1948.
31. *Kiowa County Press,* July 23, 1948.

wheat operator who turned 40,000 acres of sod around Haswell last fall and planted it to wheat.... Some 25,000 acres harvested this summer will be left fallow and around 10,000 acres of new sod will be broken [by Garvey].[32]

The thirty-five-mile radius from Haswell credited with 40,000 acres of Garvey wheat and a total harvest of one million bushels included the western portion of Kiowa County, part of central Kiowa County (Eads area), eastern Crowley County, southeastern Lincoln County, and northern Bent County, as well.

For the eastern part of Crowley County, long-time local residents consider Pete Franzman as the pioneer wheat farmer in the plow-up of the 1940s. Although the Ordway paper carried earlier mentions of wheat, as well as barley and beans, from the northwestern part of the county, the first big sowing specifically credited to an individual was that of Franzman in the autumn of 1947:

Pete Franzman of Leoti, Kansas, with Orville Hugh of Leoti assisting him, have sowed several sections of land on the Sugar City and La Junta road in wheat and it is up and worth driving out to see. This spring they have plowed sections out by Lake Henry, north of Sugar City, and this will be sowed to wheat.[33]

Although Franzman was a suitcase operator for somewhat over a year, he apparently became a local town farmer in the summer of 1948.[34]

Franzman must have had company in land preparation and wheat sowing in 1947 because it was reported in the spring of 1948 that

large tracts of land east of Horse Creek in Crowley County, and on to the east and north in Kiowa and Lincoln counties were seeded to wheat last fall on summer fallowed land. There may soon be more land plowed up for wheat in Eastern Colorado than there are acres of grama grass pasture land.

The ensuing harvest was estimated as yielding ten to thirty bushels per acre, "sufficiently good to encourage *wheat growers who have invested in farms* [italics supplied] in this area and to the east in Kiowa and adjacent

32. *Denver Post,* August 12, 1948. In all probability, the plowing of the grassland took place in the spring rather than the fall of the year. In fact, the *Ordway New Era* of May 28 and July 16, 1948, specifically mentioned "summer fallowing" of the newly plowed land.
33. *Ordway New Era,* April 2, 1948.
34. Ibid., May 14, 1948. The Franzmans were scheduled to move at the end of the school term to the town property that he had bought.

counties."[35] At that time, men from Carmen, Oklahoma, were plowing for wheat and others from Haskell, Texas, were reported to have bought land with the intention of sowing wheat.[36]

During the next few years, the Ordway paper identified other nonresident wheat farmers, including men from Wichita, Arkansas City, and Gueda Springs, Kansas. Garvey extended operations into the county. Gano, who has been mentioned previously, was a partner in the grain elevator built in Ordway in 1949 and bought a large acreage in the eastern part of Crowley County in 1950.[37]

But the best wheat years were past. In mid-1950, the formation of a rain-making organization received front-page coverage and in 1951 the precipitation for the first half of the year was reported as 6.44 inches.[38] In the words of an unsympathetic rancher, Gano "got his seed back one year in twenty" in his custom farming operation in Crowley County. Shortly, even those who had tried to grow wheat agreed that an average rainfall of about twelve inches per year was not enough, especially in the years when precipitation fell below that amount.

Part of southeastern Lincoln County is included within the thirty-five-mile radius of Haswell credited with the million-bushel harvest of 1948. Here a local resident claims the role of pioneer wheat farmer. According to him, he and his neighbors "hadn't thought" of growing wheat until he planted thirty acres in 1942, expanding to three hundred acres the next year. He had grown both barley and dry beans as dryland crops in addition to ranching.

The first year he used his bean combine to harvest wheat. However, the local innovator credited most of the plow-up for wheat to newcomers—largely suitcase farmers—from Kansas, Texas, and farther south in Colorado. Among them were Garvey and the Baughman Land Company of Liberal, Kansas, as a land owner.[39] Although the local farmer and several neighbors were growing some wheat prior to the arrival of the suitcase farmers, the essential conditions under which wheat farming developed seem to have been much the same as in Kiowa County.

Summary View of Kiowa County

During the 1948 harvest, after most of the conversion of grassland to

35. Ibid., May 28 and July 16, 1948.
36. Ibid., April 2 and 30, 1948.
37. Ibid., August 12, 1949, and October 27, 1950.
38. Ibid., June 30, 1950, and July 6, 1951.
39. Interview with Warren Leonard, Karval, county commissioner of Lincoln County, June 11, 1966.

wheat farms had taken place, James LaVelle, the editor of the *Kiowa County Press* took stock of the situation as follows:

> In driving around the county these days one is more or less surprised when he meets a person he is acquainted with, or an auto with a license 45 license plate among the influx of persons and vehicles from Texas, Oklahoma, and Kansas. Wheat harvest is more than half over. ... The bumper wheat crop in Kiowa County has prompted many more persons to expand operations and look to the county as a place for investments. The big program was introduced here this time by large operators such as R. H. Garvey, who own vast tracts of fertile land and successfully produce lots of wheat; others have followed on a much smaller scale, but in great numbers, thus making the over all program one of gigantic proportions. It has been so very successful that even old timers who failed years past are now taking advantage of new methods and modern machinery to produce wheat, and lots of it. ... The gold rush to the mountains in the early days has nothing on the 1948 edition in Kiowa County.[40]

The editor's summary account emphasizes farmers from neighboring states, although he does not use the terms *suitcase, absentee,* or *nonresident.* A week earlier, however, LaVelle had complained that "the new program has displaced so many families and so much personal property that there is inadequate valuation in many of our school districts to raise enough money on a 20 mill levy to maintain the schools. With so much money being syphoned out of the county and the state the question of tax adjustment has become of major importance." A year later, he lamented, "Eastern Colorado is one of the last frontiers open for development by people of moderate means. More should take advantage of opportunities that exist and make this their home. Why should they live in other places and exploit our resources without giving anything in return when this is a better place to live anyway?" In the same issue, reference was made to a man from Oklahoma who, with a crew of twenty-eight men, was operating ten combines for Garvey near Galatea, northwest of Eads.[41] Clearly, the editor was describing suitcase farming.

The percentage of wheat land farmed by non-residents must have run very high in the Brandon and Haswell localities when the huge crops harvested by Garvey attracted national attention. A resident who worked for Garvey before he went into farming for himself estimated that 90 percent of the wheat land in the Haswell locality in the late 1940s was operated by suitcase farmers.[42] The long-time county commissioner from

40. *Kiowa County Press,* July 16, 1948.
41. Ibid., July 22, 1949.

the district independently estimated that suitcase farmers planted 90 percent of the wheat at the start.[43]

In the eastern end of Kiowa County, where a few suitcase farmers had entered before the disastrous thirties and a little growing of wheat had continued, it was reported authoritatively that nonresidents had had a smaller part in the big revival of wheat growing.[44] The county commissioner for that area, a long-time resident, generalized:

> Conditions improved by 1940 but the war started soon after that. We had some good years during the war but with a shortage of men and machinery there wasn't much more plowed up. Then in 1946 with good crops, good prices, men coming out of the service and more machinery available, the boom began. The farms got larger and many non-residents came to the county. . . . A large percent of the land here was plowed up in the late 1940's.[45]

As might be expected, the Kiowa County agent did not approve of the general trend of land use and living taking place there. He included in his annual report of 1946 the statement "There has not been much interest in reseeding range here, in fact the breaking of sod has been the greatest activity." In 1947 he stated that 200,000 more acres were in cultivation than in the 1930s. He continued, possibly with some exaggeration, "Farmers and ranchers who have been in the county for some time are interested in soil conservation; the newcomers do not seem to be concerned," and added, "Summer fallowing, an accepted practice in wheat production, was abandoned for the most part when time came for seeding the 1948 crop. The heavy crop of straw produced in 1947 was burned on many acres by farmers who came into the county during the past year." He also said, "Many farmers who were here in 1945 have sold out and moved away simply because land they knew was unfit for crop production was broken out."

The analysis was in much the same vein in 1949:

> Almost all the cropland owned by non-residents is planted to wheat. Most of them have started to follow a wheat summer fallow wheat rotation. The reseeding of grass to drier land is the farthest thing

42. Interview with John O. Stavely, Haswell, June 10, 1966.

43. Interview with P. L. Reed, Haswell, county commissioner, June 10, 1966.

44. Interview with Kathlyn Forster, Kiowa County ASCS office manager, Eads, interview, July 11, 1966. Mrs. Forster went to work for the Kiowa County ASC office in 1951.

45. Letter from C. L. McFarlane, Towner, Colorado, Kiowa County commissioner, May 6, 1969.

from their mind. The "get rich quick" on wheat view has encouraged even more absentee ownership the past year in spite of the controlled wheat acreage program. Sod is still being broken out but on a lesser extent than has been done in the previous five years. 51,000 acres were broken out this year.

He conceded that "some of the resident owners have followed the practice of the 'sod busting' non-residents."[46] He might have added "after watching suitcase farmers for about five years." Probably their point of view was expressed accurately by the reporter for the Haswell locality, who used the expression "trying their luck" in referring to wheat planting by resident farmers.[47]

Notes from Other Areas

Cheyenne County, just to the north of Kiowa County and bordering on Kansas, also underwent major changes at the hands of suitcase farmers. Here, also, the major increase in wheat acreage occurred as nonresidents became numerous in the late 1940s. The percentage increase in cropland from 1939 to 1954 was exceeded in the general region only by that of Kiowa County (fig. 16).

Unlike Kiowa and Crowley counties, most of the better farm land in this county was included in the soil conservation district that contained restrictions against the plowing up of grassland and the cropping of abandoned land.[48] The change in wheat acreage paralleled that of Kiowa, however, up substantially first in 1946, with the greatest increase between 1947 and 1948. The privately published acreages of winter wheat sown prepared by the state agricultural statistician for the years 1944 through 1949 were 16,370, 33,530, 59,930, 100,200, 166,900, and 204,910 acres. The peak year was 1951, with 255,000 acres.[49] It must be concluded therefore that the anti-sod-breaking ordinance that was in effect until voted out in the summer of 1945[50] had but little influence in the timing of the plow-up for wheat in Cheyenne County.

46. The annual reports of the county agent of Kiowa County for 1946, 1947, and 1949.

47. *Bent County Democrat,* July 23, 1948.

48. Stanley W. Voelker, *Land-Use Ordinances of Soil Conservation Districts in Colorado,* Great Plains Council Publication, no. 5, Colorado Experiment Station (Fort Collins, March 1952). The part of the county having an anti-sod-breaking ordinance is shown in figure 25.

49. Reed, "Winter Wheat, total acres planted, 1939-1956."

50. Voelker, *Land-Use Ordinances,* p. 46; The *Cheyenne County News,* July 12, 1945.

It seems significant that in less than a month after the defeat of the sod ordinance the attorney who had served as secretary of the group which organized the proxy opposition to the regulation advertised that he wanted to hire "tractors, discs, oneways, drills to do work between Cheyenne Wells [the county seat] and Sheridan Lake [Kiowa County] on fine level belt of wheat land."[51] According to a local informant, much of the land plowed up and planted to wheat was sold to a suitcase farmer from Oklahoma.

Less than a year after the defeat of the sod ordinance "a representative from the Cheyenne district, Neil Hawthorne, told the radio audience (KLZ) that much of the plowing up going on at present is the work of so-called 'suitcase' farmers, fellows coming in with camp wagons and plows, bent on making a killing with a few crops."[52] At the same time, the state conservationist for the Soil Conservation Service said that 25,000 acres of grassland had been plowed up near Cheyenne Wells.[53]

Some indication of where the nonresidents were from is provided by the list of delinquent personal property taxes for 1946, showing amounts from $20.15 to $197.65 due, probably on farm equipment. Addresses given were Adams, Dumas (two listings), and Pecos, Texas; Scott City, Kansas; and Marne, Iowa.[54] Similarly, the lists of subscribers to the newspaper may well indicate home bases of suitcase farmers. Two such listings for 1948 included the following addresses: Denver (5), Florissant, Fort Collins, Golden, Lamar, and Orchard, Colorado; Ashland, Bazine, Collyer, Frankfort, Fort Dodge, Great Bend, Kiowa, and Wichita, Kansas; Alva, Forgan, and Oklahoma City, Oklahoma; Hildreth and Omaha, Nebraska; Laramie, Wyoming; Lancaster, California; and Iowa City, Iowa.[55]

Apparently there was no pioneer suitcase farming venture in Cheyenne equal to those of Garvey in Kiowa County. However, a writer reporting in a nationally circulated magazine in 1947 was impressed by the scale of a nonresident's operation:

> In Cheyenne County, Colorado, I watched the world's largest plow crawl toward me across what shortly before had been level grazing

51. *Cheyenne County News,* August 2, 1945. The group, calling itself the Cheyenne County Improvement Association, was identified in the same issue of June 7, 1945, as consisting of three real estate men, an abstractor, three implement dealers, the manager of the elevator, a lumber dealer, a restaurant operator, an attorney, a druggist, and a physician.

52. Ibid., June 13, 1946.

53. *Bent County Democrat,* June 21, 1946, quoting an Associated Press release from Denver.

54. *Cheyenne County News,* September 26, 1947.

55. Ibid., April 1 and June 3, 1948.

land. Although this monster pulled by a powerful tractor, was eating up a forty-two-foot strip of ground, turning under 16 acres every hour, it was still no more than a small yellow beetle in the spacious landscape.

He added, "Currently he has several thousand acres of fine wheatland in [the panhandle of] Texas and is taking a side bet on the high edge of the Plains with the 3,300-acre plot I saw the big plow working."[56] Monroe Terrell, the man doing the plowing, was then a suitcase farmer operating from a Texas base, but he soon became a resident.[57] Although he kept some himself, Terrell reportedly sold land largely to suitcase farmers, part of it with growing wheat.

At the same time a regional farm magazine described Cheyenne as a county "divided like an amoeba—grass on one side of the scale and wheat on the other. This usually represents the resident land owners (mostly stockmen) and the non-resident 'sod busting' wheat farmer." To the writer, the contrast was sharp, although he admitted that there were "resident owned wheat farms," adding, "Long time residents do not want to make the same blunder and mistakes as before and be caught in a backwash of dust storms." He blamed the defeat of the sod ordinance on nonresidents.[58] A continuation of the sod ordinance in eastern Cheyenne County beyond 1945 would have restricted the invasion of suitcase farmers and the plowing of grassland for wheat, but without such an ordinance, "non-resident operators moved into the Cheyenne District in large numbers."[59]

Bent County, located south of the western part of Kiowa County, was on the dry western margin of suitcase farming after nonresidents pushed westward in the 1940s. As late as January, 1947, the abstract of assessment for the county showed only 38,314 acres of dry cropland, 53,267 acres of irrigated land, and 690,168 acres of grazing land. The valuation of combines was given at only $1,570. By 1953 the abstract of assessment showed 84,801 acres of dry farm cropland, more than double the figure of January, 1947.[60] The acreage of unirrigated wheat planted on the uplands above the Arkansas lowland went up from 2,130 in 1944 to 32,220 in 1949 and reached a peak of 50,400 in 1951, according to the state agricul-

56. John Bird, "The Great Plains," p. 88.
57. According to an in-law interviewed.
58. Phil Patterson, "Cheyenne, Eastern Colorado County of Wheat, Cattle, and Opportunity," *Western Farm Life* (Denver), as quoted in the *Cheyenne County News*, October 16, 1947.
59. Voelker, *Land-Use Ordinances*, p. 47.
60. *Bent County Democrat*, January 17, 1947, and January 9, 1953.

tural statistician.[61] The ASCS wheat lists for 1954 showed a total of 82,340 acres of wheat, including some irrigated, planted in the county in 1951.[62]

An area of high drought risk and without large blocks of loess-covered plains, Bent County offered only a limited opportunity to dryland farmers, but absentees in moderate numbers made it a forward part of the second suitcase farming frontier. Apparently the biggest planting of wheat was that of a Texan in 1949, whose wheat fields later became a source of dust. The county paper reported that they criticized the farmer "for coming up from Texas six years ago and buying 6,300 acres. At that time only about 300 acres of the farm had been plowed up. But in the first year, [he] plowed up the whole place," noting further that he had planted wheat every year "but has gotten a crop to speak of only once."[63] The ASCS wheat lists of 1954 showed his 6,809 acres planted to wheat in 1951 on a farm of 7,002 acres, the largest wheat acreage in the big upland district south of the Arkansas. In 1954, probably after the dominance of absentees in wheat farming had been reduced by local farmers following their example, the county Soil Conservation Service head reported that 86 of the 147 county dryland farms were being operated by men living outside the county, forty-three of them from out of state. The out-of-county farmers were operating about 66 percent of the dryland acreage.[64]

General Considerations

After several years of good rainfall, high prices, and the ending of wartime restrictions on farm machinery and travel, the time was ripe for another movement onto the grassland, beyond the earlier wheat country. Men were again willing to take a chance on wheat. The advance involved mainly newcomers at first. The wheat boom's "standard set of characters, the big operator, the sidewalk and suitcase farmer," were active, especially the suitcase farmer, sometimes as a large operator. Local newspaper accounts leave no doubt that suitcase farmers, both large and small, pioneered; as earlier, some of the absentees became residents.

The numerous nonresident farmers who did not establish residence in the new wheat country were, in effect, accused of being irresponsible

61. Reed, "Winter Wheat, Total Acres Planted, 1939-1956."
62. Agricultural Stabilization and Conservation Service wheat listing sheets for Bent County and other parts of eastern Colorado were examined in the Federal Records Center, Denver.
63. *Bent County Democrat,* April 22, 1955.
64. Ibid., March 5, 1954.

exploiters. Secretary of Agriculture Clinton P. Anderson put it plainly:

> Spearheading the plow-up drive has been the suitcase farmer. . . . If the past drought was an indication, we at least know that the suitcase farmers aren't going to worry about that land if it gets in trouble. The last time, they simply abandoned that land as soon as it ceased to pay dividends. The resident farmers took the dust.[65]

H. H. Finnell of the Soil Conservation Service went further, predicting a new Dust Bowl.

> The next Dust Bowl will be bigger and better. The plow-up after World War I was mainly on good land; this time it is on thin hardlands and the loose sandy soils along the western edge of the Plains. . . . There will be general abandonment by speculators and absentee owners.[66]

In general, the conditions under which suitcase farmers pushed westward into Colorado in the middle and late 1940s were basically the same as in Kansas some twenty years earlier. Movement into a drier area to the west, the plowing of cheap grassland owned or bought by absentees, and major dependence on power machinery were characteristics common to both advances. Some of the names were familiar, those men who, after beginning in Kansas, pushed on into Colorado. Among them were Baughman, Garvey, Gano, and Kriss, as landowners, real estate dealers, and farmers.[67] Baughman, at least, had participated in the earlier wheat boom in Baca County, Colorado, as noted in chapter 5.

Although it is probably impossible to spell out the ways in which suitcase farmers were innovators on the second suitcase farming frontier, it is apparent that they introduced changes of basic importance. Among these were the large scale of operation, the major emphasis on wheat, and probably greater mechanization. Experience was acknowledged to be important, as in the recognition that John Kriss's experience in wheat farming at Colby, Kansas, was being extended to Kiowa County in the Garvey-Kriss operation at Brandon. Of course, the experience of many from the older wheat country included working with wheat-farming machinery and a knowledge of methods. The judgment, cited earlier, of

65. Clinton P. Anderson, "Soil Murder on the Plains," *Country Gentleman,* September 1947, pp. 85, 88.
66. Bird, "The Great Plains," p. 90.
67. The earliest notice of John W. Baughman of Liberal, Kansas, was in newspaper advertisements of 1925, in which he said, "Will give sod crop for breaking land in Haskell, Grant, Stanton, or Morton Counties" (*Sublette Monitor,* March 12, 1925). Something of the operations of Garvey and Gano, operating separately, was described for Greeley County. Kriss was identified as a foreman for Garvey in Greeley County.

the editor of the Kiowa County paper that "even old timers, who failed years past, are now taking advantage of new methods and modern machinery to produce wheat" was probably a valid generalization that recognized suitcase farmers as innovators.

Differences between the first and second great invasions by suitcase farmers included the larger scale and probably more speculative character of the second. After events of the Dust Bowl era, everyone must have realized something of the nature and extent of the disaster that had occurred. Most nonresidents surely realized that they were gambling. The awareness of residents that they might suffer from a new Dust Bowl resulted in considerable concern and probably hostility toward the sodbreakers from the outside. "Development" was not as welcome as earlier.

An important difference between the first and second suitcase farming frontiers was the difficulty of obtaining housing in the later wheat boom. Governmental wartime controls were in effect at the beginning and shortages in building materials continued for several years. Some who might otherwise have become residents operated their new farms from their old homes. A further difference between the older and newer suitcase farming country was the addition of new bases from which absentees carried on their part-time wheat growing. Attention will be given to this matter in the next chapter.

Even as the plow-up went on, several instances of local dust storms were reported, which probably reinforced local resistance to additional sodbreaking. The down-to-earth writer of the Haswell News column in a neighboring weekly probably spoke for many as she wrote, "Much discussion ensues with regard to the breaking of good grassland for wheat land. Old timers feel we will have a reversion of the former 'dust bowl' days, only more severe. . . . We only hope that it turns out for the best, for those who are permanently located here."[68] From neighboring Baca County, with relatively less extension of wheat farming by absentees, it was claimed that "the bad part of the present sod breaking is that big blocks of grassland are being broken by non-resident owners who will leave the county when conditions get tough. . . ." Added to the report of the great wheat harvest at Haswell in 1948 was the reservation "the wheat business is tremendous as viewed today, though some people 'in the know' seem to think the land is doomed to desolation under this kind of farming." From the dry, western margin came the generalization "there has been a difference of opinion between the cattlemen and the wheat growers as to the advisability of making this a wheat section, but that difference of

68. *Bent County Democrat,* May 16, 1947; August 8, 1947; July 9, 1948.

opinion is not going to cause any big arguments now for occasionally we hear cattlemen wondering if they have been passing up a good bet these many years."[69] Actually, the boom profits from wheat had just begun and were to be of short duration, but local opposition was weakening. By 1954 resident wheat farmers outnumbered suitcase operators throughout the new wheat country of Colorado, as will be described in the next chapter.

Local opposition to the widespread extension of wheat farming was expressed through several governmental agencies. The action of the gasoline rationing board and the rules of the conservation program in Greeley County, Kansas, have been noted. In Colorado, governmental controls of several types were intended to reduce or prevent the extension of crop farming at the expense of grassland. The Agricultural Commodities Program (ACP), which was a continuation of the AAA, soil conservation programs, sod-breaking ordinances of soil conservation districts, and federal land utilization projects were agencies of varied effectiveness. Since both the sod ordinances and land utilization projects were geographically localized rather than of broad regional distribution, discussion of them will be reserved for the spatial analysis of the new suitcase farming country in the next chapter. However, locally elected AAA committees in nearly all of the new suitcase farming country opposed the new plow-up. Such opposition to new sod breaking was documented for Arapahoe County, immediately to the east of Denver:

> I went to work for [the AAA] in 1949 in Arapahoe County. At that time there was a penalty of $3.00 per acre for breaking sod. But the only way we could collect it was by deducting it from the producers ACP payment in the current year. If the producer did not receive an ACP payment the penalty was not collected. This was County wide in Arapahoe County. As I remember it this stopped about 1951 or 1952. I think that it started about the end of World War II.[70]

Regulations similar to those described for Arapahoe County were in effect in Kiowa County, and apparently in all of southeastern Colorado.[71] With good crops and good prices, farmers became independent of government controls. At best, the regulations only slowed the wheat boom.

The second big expansion of wheat farming led by nonresidents was over by 1954. Probably little land considered suitable lay beyond and

69. *Ordway New Era,* May 28, 1948.
70. Letter from Earl McDonnell, office manager, Lincoln County ASCS Committee, May 13, 1966.
71. Letter from Kathlyn Forster, office manager, Kiowa County ASCS Committee, May 24, 1966.

returning drought resulted in widespread failure of crops. Strictly speaking, there was no longer a suitcase farming frontier. Instead, a new Dust Bowl threatened and stagnation and retreat followed.

CHAPTER EIGHT

The Suitcase Farming Frontier in the Early 1950s

Introduction

The story of the second big advance of nonresident farmers into the semi-arid grasslands of the central Great Plains has been told in the foregoing chapter. With the return of drought, the advance slowed, shortly giving way to retreat. Although 1951 was the peak year for wheat acreage planted in much of the new wheat country, the run of good years was already over. Planted-acre yields averaged three bushels or less for unirrigated wheat in Bent County for four consecutive years, starting with 1950. Bent County was fairly representative of the dry margin of the land invaded by wheat farmers a few years earlier. All too often, the experience was that reported for the Haswell locality, in the neighboring western part of Kiowa County: Mr. and Mrs. Cook of Childers, Texas, found their wheat "all gone"; and for William Kent of Pond Creek, Oklahoma, as for "most out-of-state farmers who return, it was very discouraging to find his wheat all gone." With wry humor, the same reporter wrote, "We do not know whether the out-of-state farmers need to return or not. Maybe their land has just blown to them."[1]

As in the 1930s, there were recriminations against nonresidents for having plowed the grassland. The criticism of the big plow-up in Bent County by a Texan has been noted. Fear was expressed that someone

1. *Bent County Democrat,* February 18, 1955; May 26 and June 2, 1950; March 5, 1954.

would be killed on the road nearby because of dust from the blowing fields.[2] In Cheyenne County, where nonresidents had plowed up large acreages, the county agent, in his annual report for 1954, pointed out that a 1954 survey by extension service workers showed that those questioned considered getting rid of suitcase farmers the most urgent need and the prevention of the breaking of sodland as the second most important. Drought and dust had again polarized local farmers against the nonresidents. But the absentee farmers, no doubt, found crop failure and perhaps land damage more harmful than criticism.

The marked reversal in the results of wheat farming discouraged many nonresidents. A comparison of the names of suitcase farmers operating in the Haswell area of Kiowa County in 1945-50 and in 1953 with the ASCS wheat list of 1954 for the Haswell-Arlington community shows that many had dropped out.[3] Of thirty-one different individuals named specifically who were construed to be carrying on suitcase farming, only seven appeared as operators of farms in the community in 1954. Four continued as suitcase farmers (actually two continued, being joined by two others with the same family names), and three had moved to the locality. In addition, one suitcase farmer from Texas appeared on the 1954 wheat list in the Karval community of Lincoln County. He was listed with a Haswell address, although a local resident identified him as a suitcase farmer. The long-time secretary in the office of the county agent and the ASCS county office manager verified that many of the early suitcase farmers of the Haswell locality mentioned in newspaper stories actually had farmed in the county, but they frequently commented, "He quit," or "He sold out."[4] It appears that a large majority of the early suitcase farmers near Haswell had dropped out before 1954.

An examination of the records for individual farms on the 1954 wheat lists suggests that a number of suitcase farmers were in the process of giving up the struggle against crop failure or had actually already done so, although they were still shown as the farm operators on ASCS records. Bent County community number 2, the large upland community south of

2. Ibid., April 22, 1955.
3. The names of suitcase farmers for 1945-50 and 1953 were gleaned from the Haswell column of *The Bent County Democrat.* The ASCS wheat listing sheets for 1954 were the earliest official lists of wheat farmers found. The listing of addresses of wheat growers permitted classifying farmers as suitcase or local. The Colorado records examined for 1954 and other dates prior to 1959 were stored in the Federal Records Center at Denver.
4. Velda Benner, secretary, office of Kiowa County agricultural extension agent, Eads, interview, June 10, 1966, and Kathlyn Forster, office manager, Kiowa County ASCS Committee, Eads, July 11, 1966.

the Arkansas River, was affected most of the eight communities on the dry margin whose records were checked.[5] In southern Bent County sixteen of the thirty-five suitcase farmers on the 1954 list did not sow wheat in either 1952 or 1953, but went to the trouble and expense of fallowing in 1952. In other words, at that time they were still in the wheat-farming business or hoped to be. However, none of these sixteen suitcase and only three of the twenty local farmers fallowed in 1953. Perhaps the decision to get out of the wheat farming was made when it was decided not to fallow in 1953. Not one of the sixteen suitcase farmers failing to sow in both 1952 and 1953 was on the 1957 wheat list for the community. It is not surprising that farmers, or speculators, from such places as Casper, Wyoming; Wichita, Kansas; Morton, Illinois; Troy, New York; Springfield, Oregon; and Hollister, Oakland, and Long Beach, California, should decide to give up wheat farming.

In Crowley County, with even less precipitation on the average than Bent County, the 1957 ASCS records covering the period 1952-55 show that 1954 and 1955 were the years when farmers, especially suitcase farmers, all but one from eastern Colorado, Kansas, and northern Texas, gave up wheat. Of the fourteen suitcase farmers with historical averages of more than fifteen acres of wheat, nine planted no wheat in either 1954 or 1955. Four of twenty-five local farmers residing in Crowley or adjacent counties made the same decision. Three suitcase farmers and one local farmer with historical averages of more than one thousand acres each kept on planting wheat.

"Laying out," that is, not planting wheat, two years in a row in the early 1950s appears not to have been generally characteristic of suitcase farmers in eastern Colorado, although it was in both Crowley and Bent counties. The ASCS records in four other communities on the forward margin showed that only three absentees of the ninety-three listed for 1954 and one of the eighty-nine on the 1957 list failed to plant wheat two years in a row in the period 1951-55.[6] However, the 1954 record for the Haswell-Arlington community of Kiowa County was put together too late to include most of the suitcase farmers who dropped out.

Although the ASCS wheat lists of 1954 were the earliest generally available, it is doubtful that they showed suitcase farming at its peak. Both a decline in the number of nonresidents and the entry of resident farmers

5. The communities were number 2 in Bent County, the three communities in Crowley County, Haswell-Arlington in Kiowa County, Karval in Lincoln County, and First View and Kit Carson in Cheyenne County.

6. These four dry-margin communities were Haswell-Arlington, Kiowa County; First View and Kit Carson, Cheyenne County; and Karval, Lincoln County.

into wheat had the effect of reducing the percentage of wheat farmers who were absentees. Statistically, except for the great Garvey-Kriss and Garvey plow-ups which revolutionized farming in parts of Kiowa County, it is difficult to show that suitcase farmers dominated wheat farming in the new wheat country.

If summer rather than winter addresses had been recorded on 1954 ASCS wheat lists with any regularity, a number of communities may have had at least 50 percent suitcase farms. As listed, not one was. That only thirty-four out-of-state operators were recorded on the 1954 ASCS wheat lists for Bent County, compared with the forty-three out-of-state claimed for the county's dryland farms by the county soil conservation head,[7] suggests that some suitcase farmers were reported as residents. If, as seems likely, the small number of farmers for whom no addresses were given were actually suitcase operators, their percentage should be increased by a few points in several communities. Figures 17, 18, and 19 are conservative representations of suitcase farming in eastern Colorado.

Geographical Distribution of Suitcase Farming

Figure 17 shows the percentage of wheat farms credited to suitcase farmers in eastern Colorado and western Kansas in 1954, the earliest year for which information was generally available. Although there are gaps in the data for Kansas, the coverage is sufficient to show the general distribution.[8]

As in 1933, the distributional pattern was consistent. The highest incidence of nonresident operation was again at the western margin of

7. *Bent County Democrat,* March 5, 1954.
8. A complete count was made of wheat farms in eastern Colorado as shown on the 1954 wheat listing sheets except for a few illegible entries and a few lacking addresses. In the northeasternmost community of Prowers County, part of the record appeared to be missing. In Kansas all farms were classified in Wallace and Wichita counties, the sample was one-third (one page in three) or more for Grant, Logan, Haskell, Scott, and Morton counties. For outlying counties, smaller samples were taken: one-in-five in Clark, Comanche, Edwards, Gray, Kiowa, Seward, Sheridan, and Trego counties, and one-in-ten for counties on to the east or north. Unfortunately, records for several counties were not found and on some records no addresses were given for farm operators. In the case of the key counties of Greeley and Hamilton, addresses were given for the operators of single tracts but not for the larger number of operators of multiple tracts. In neighboring Wichita County, over-all the percentage of suitcase farmers ran nearly 18 percent, with the single tract farmers representing a much higher 32 percent. Since single-tract farmers were 33 percent nonresident in Greeley and 39 percent in Hamilton, overall estimates of 18 and 20 percent were made for Greeley and Hamilton counties.
Most records for Kansas were examined at the Kansas City Federal Records Center but some were found in county ASCS offices.

important wheat farming, a land which had become important only recently. Kiowa County, Colorado, led at 33 percent and was followed closely by Cheyenne and Crowley counties. If only dryland farmers had been counted, Crowley, Prowers, and Bent would have run substantially higher. Whether the old core area in western Kansas can be included in the core area of 1954 is debatable, because of lower percentages of absentees and uncertainties in the data. However, nonresident wheat farmers in Kansas were relatively most numerous in the same area as they were twenty-one years earlier.

Figure 18, a map showing the percentage of suitcase farmers in eastern Colorado by the communities then recognized by the ASCS, gives more detail. Arapahoe community in the eastern part of Cheyenne County, and Sheridan Lake and Brandon-Chivington in Kiowa County, reached or exceeded 40 percent nonresident operation, roughly equal to the 43 percent shown for out-of-county farmers in Greeley County in 1933. In addition, two other communities in Cheyenne, two others in Kiowa, two in Crowley, and one in Bent reached 30 percent for suitcase farmers and one district in northern Prowers County, despite its spanning the irrigated Arkansas Valley, came close at 27 percent. In the southern portion of Washington County, two communities constituted a secondary high at 17 and 19 percent.

Of course, the ASCS wheat lists contained information only for farms on which wheat was sown. Thus, figures 17 and 18 are representative of farms only to the degree that wheat was included as a crop. A comparison of the ASCS wheat lists with federal census reports shows that wherever the percentage of suitcase farmers ran high, the number of wheat farms equaled or nearly equaled the number of census farms in most counties having little irrigation. ASCS wheat farms exceeded in number all census farms in Kiowa, Kit Carson, and Baca counties and were at least 90 percent as numerous in Washington, Cheyenne, Lincoln, and Elbert, but the percentages ran low to the southwest in Pueblo, El Paso, and Las Animas. Similarly, the ASCS wheat lists recorded more cropland than was found on all census farms in Kiowa, Cheyenne, Washington, Kit Carson, Lincoln, and Elbert counties. Even assuming that the census takers missed some farms operated by absentees, figures 17 and 18 are closely representative of the percentage of all farms operated by nonresidents where the percentages ran high or fairly high in areas with little irrigation. Prowers, Crowley, and Bent counties contained many irrigated farms.

Figure 19, showing the distribution of the farms operated by suitcase farmers on the plains of Colorado, represents another view of the distribution of farming by absentees. In all, 1,007 such farms were counted in eastern Colorado. Kiowa County had a good lead with 200, followed by Prowers, 150; Cheyenne, 135; Washington, 118; Kit Carson, 92; and Baca, 60. Suitcase farms were fairly common in most areas where wheat was important (fig. 20), but their percentage was unusually high where the density of farms in general was high (fig. 18). The average wheat acreage of suitcase farms was larger in this core area than elsewhere in eastern Colorado. The new wheat country, centering on Kiowa and Cheyenne counties, ran especially high in the percentage of farms operated by absentees, the concentration of such farms, and the acreage planted to wheat on them.

Sources of Suitcase Farmers in Eastern Colorado

The apparently almost complete coverage of wheat farms in eastern Colorado by the ASCS wheat lists of 1954, including the names and addresses of the wheat farmers, permitted the first comprehensive analysis of the sources of absentee farmers operating in Colorado. Figures 21, 22b, and 23 are cartographic presentations of the findings. Figure 21 shows the dominance of Kansans among suitcase farmers in most localities in eastern Colorado where absentees were numerous or relatively important. Generally, the divide separating Kansas-based suitcase farmers from those from Colorado lay as far west as the big increase in wheat farming had extended. Understandably, Nebraskans were most numerous among the absentees in the north, but not in the region of the great incursion of the 1940s. There were a few exceptions to the dominance of nonresident farming by Kansans in the main suitcase farming area. Farmers from Oklahoma outnumbered Kansans in two communities and Texans led in one.

Two cases of domination by non-Kansans in the heart of the new suitcase farming country appear to represent the results of successful real estate operation. In the community in north-central Prowers County where absentees were especially numerous, a real estate dealer from Oklahoma is given credit for promoting land sales. The 1954 ASCS list showed Alva, Oklahoma, as the most common out-of-area address for that community, and nearby Cherokee, Oklahoma, the former home of the real estate dealer, ranked third.

The large number of suitcase farmers from Texas in the Haswell-Arlington community probably was largely the result of land promotion by a former Texan whose job was made easy by the spectacular early wheat farming by Garvey. B. O. Stavely was quoted as saying, "I made no money at first when I moved in here three years ago [1945] from Snyder, Texas, and now I have four real estate salesmen and three offices and I can't take care of all my business."[9] Figures 22a and 22b show that many nonresidents came from the Texas panhandle. Although there were a few exceptions, Kansans generally dominated suitcase farming in the new suitcase farming frontier. For all of eastern Colorado, 413 farmers had addresses in Kansas sufficiently distant to qualify as suitcase. There were 204 from Colorado, 75 from Nebraska, 68 from Texas, and 22 from California.

The home bases of suitcase farmers in eastern Colorado in 1954 are shown in figure 23. The old core area of suitcase farmers bounded approximately by Dodge City, Great Bend, Hutchinson, and Wichita is emphasized. Other newer source areas are shown as important, however, among them northern Oklahoma, southwestern Kansas, northwestern Kansas, and a belt along the eastern base of the Rockies in Colorado. Portions of the panhandles of Oklahoma, Texas, and Nebraska were other sources. An area in the shadow of the Rockies was the only important source mainly outside the region of dry-land wheat farming and was primarily urban in character.

The leading sources of nonresidents in order of numbers were as follows: Denver; Alva, Oklahoma; Dodge City, Kansas; Bennett, Colorado; Enid, Oklahoma; Garden City, Kansas; Colorado Springs; Wichita, Kansas; and Cherokee, Oklahoma. The importance of Bennett is probably partly due to the narrowness of Arapahoe County as a separation from wheat farms in Elbert County to the south.

The prominence of Denver, Colorado Springs, and other towns and cities near the Colorado Front Range had been foreshadowed in assessors' reports of suitcase farmers in western Kansas in 1936 (fig. 9). To a considerable degree, the early suitcase farmers from Colorado had formerly been resident farmers in Kansas, as noted earlier (chap. 4, 00-00). Much of the importance of the foothills of the Colorado Rockies as a source for suitcase farmers in Colorado in 1954 is probably a result of the same process that occurred in Kansas—local farmers moving away but retaining operation of their farms. Washington, Weld, and Kit Carson counties—the three having the largest number of suitcase farmers based in cities along the mountains—were old wheat-growing areas. This fact supports the foregoing explanation and tends to minimize the role of Coloradoans as pioneers in the suitcase farming frontier.

An Interpretation of the Spatial Aspects of
the Second Suitcase Farming Frontier

Some of the general conditions under which the suitcase farming advance was resumed in the mid- and late 1940s have been noted in chapter

9. *Denver Post,* August 12, 1948.

7. Here an attempt will be made to interpret the regional distribution of suitcase farming.

The spatial relationships of the first and second suitcase farming frontiers were very similar. A comparison of figures 17 and 19, showing the distribution of absentee wheat farming, with figure 16, the map of the increase in cropland, suggests the importance of suitcase farmers in the plow-up. Again pasture became wheatland. As in Kansas earlier, the new wheat country was adjacent to older, more crowded wheat country. The new wheat country was physically similar to the old, although more droughty and commonly having thinner soils. There was level land in abundance. The deepest penetration of suitcase farming took place where level land extended farthest west, through Kiowa County and into Crowley County, on the high plains north of the Arkansas River. Figure 13 indicates the westward extension of level land there. As mapped by Edwin H. Hammond, land characterized as over 80 percent in slopes of less than 8 percent and with local relief of less than three hundred feet extends farther west there than elsewhere in eastern Colorado.[10] Much of the upland plain in Colorado, as in western Kansas, is mantled with loess.[11]

The map of important wheat districts (fig. 20) identifies the loess areas of Colorado reasonably well. Even the fingers of loess-covered upland extending into eastern Las Animas and southeastern Lincoln counties and outliers of loess in southeastern Elbert County have wheat. Except for the patchy strip of loess just south of the Arkansas River in Otero and Pueblo counties and several small, rather out-of-the-way areas in the southwestern part of the plains, the loesslands of eastern Colorado were usually claimed by the wheat farmer, even to or beyond the twelve-inch average annual rainfall line in eastern Crowley County. Generally speaking, the loesslands of the northern one-half of the plains of Colorado, already in farms, were not available to the new wheat farmers. This was true to a considerable degree of marginally located Kit Carson County, and in Baca County, in the extreme southeast, despite the considerable abandonment of wheat during the drought period.

Absentee ownership of land was essential for the formation of the second suitcase farming frontier as it was for the first. The dependence of farmers from a distance on land owned by nonresidents is shown clearly in

10. Edwin H. Hammond, "Classes of Land-Surface Forms in the Forty-eight States, U.S.A.," Map Supplement Number 4, *Annals, Association of American Geographers* 54, no. 1 (March 1954).

11. *Pleistocene Eolian Deposits of the United States, Alaska, and Parts of Canada* (map), comp. by the National Research Council Committee for the Study of Eolian Deposits, Division of Geology and Geography (Geological Society of America, 1952).

an analysis of ASCS records for 1954 for localities near the outer limit of important suitcase farming. Of seventy-seven suitcase farms for which ownership data were available in four communities, owners operated forty-nine, compared to twenty-eight farmed by tenants.[12] Eighteen owners of these twenty-eight tenant-operated suitcase farms had the same addresses as those of the tenant farmers, eight had other suitcase addresses, and two had local addresses. With only two of the seventy-seven suitcase farms rented from owners living in the locality of the farms, 97 percent of the suitcase farms had absentee owners.

Table 25 gives a breakdown of land ownership in east-central and southeastern Colorado in 1936. In all seven counties, out-of-county residents owned at least 42 percent of the land; in Kiowa and Cheyenne they held over 50 percent. Only in Baca County was resident ownership as great as that of nonresidents.[13] Ownership by absentees in 1954 had probably increased above that for 1936, as suggested for Greeley and Hamilton counties, in Kansas, and Kiowa and Cheyenne counties, in Colorado. However, the buying of land by the United States government for land utilization projects in the late 1930s probably more than offset the acquisitions of outsiders in southern Baca County.

As an owner of an especially large acreage in eastern Colorado, and smaller amounts of land in Kansas, John W. Baughman of Liberal, Kansas, deserves attention. A long-time landowner in southwestern Kansas and Baca County, Colorado, he had been a developer and for a short time an operator of farms. He was probably by far the largest landowner in the new wheat country of Colorado. As early as 1927, Baughman was reported farming in Baca County, and in 1933 he was listed as the owner of at least nine tracts for which AAA wheat applications were made. It appears that he remained a nonresident landowner throughout the Dust Bowl period. In 1942 his operations in Baca County were sufficiently important to require representation by a resident farm manager.[14]

The acreages published by the local paper at the time of his visit to Las Animas, Colorado, at the height of the plow-up may well have been fur-

12. The four communities were Towner and Haswell-Arlington, both in Kiowa County, and First View, and Kit Carson, in Cheyenne County. One of the Kiowa County communities is located in the eastern and one in the western extremity of the county; those in Cheyenne are in the central third of the county. The ownership data were not given for some twenty-five multiple-tract operations. If ownerships had been determined for these usually larger operations, the percentage of tenant operation might have been higher.

13. "Land Use Survey of the Southern Great Plains Region," pp. 73, 74.

14. *Democrat Herald*, July 1, 1927; October 12 and 19, 1933; July 29, 1937; February 17, 1938; and August 31, 1939; *Denver Post*, August 27, 1942.

nished by Baughman; these add up to either 183,975 or 185,975 acres for eastern Colorado, depending upon whether the figure of 2,000 for Bent and Las Animas counties represents the combined total or separate acreages. One-fifth of Baughman's land was said to be in wheat.[15] Figure 24 shows the location of Baughman's land in eastern Colorado.

According to local informants, Baughman bought land during the 1930s, often at tax sales, and continued his acquisition during the wheat boom. The Kiowa County paper reported that he had brought action to quiet title on fifteen different tracts of land there as the plow-up got under way. His 36,375 acres in Kiowa County in early 1948 had reportedly been increased to about 60,000 in 1954.[16] A knowledgeable local informant said Baughman had approximately 100,000 acres of land at the peak of the plow-up in Kit Carson County.

Baughman was prepared for the demand for wheat land. With the exceptions of southern Washington County and the fringe areas of Bent and Crowley counties, his holdings were well distributed throughout the new wheat country. The chief demand at the outset probably came from experienced wheat farmers and speculators from the outside. The ASCS wheat lists showed that by 1954, however, most of Baughman's tenants were residents of the area. It may be assumed that by then many local farmers were experienced in wheat farming and equipped for it.

Cheyenne County, in which suitcase farmers were numerous, provides an example of the relationship of absentee ownership to land use. Figures credited to the community development and public affairs committee of the county cited in the annual report of the county agent for 1953 showed that in each of the six county-school districts the land owned by nonresidents was more completely in cultivation than land owned by residents of the county. Altogether 60.4 percent of the land owned by nonresidents was cultivated but only 29.9 percent of that belonging to residents.[17] Probably nonresidents both bought land suitable to crops and insisted that

15. *Bent County Democrat*, April 16, 1948. Adams, 17,478; Arapahoe, 3,189; Baca, 24,986; Cheyenne, 28,024; Kiowa, 36,375; Kit Carson, 39,499; Lincoln, 27,035; Morgan, 160; Prowers, 5,229; and Bent and Las Animas, 2,000. Most of the 250,000 acres of land credited to Baughman by *Life Magazine* and *Fortune* was in the former Dust Bowl portion of Colorado. ("Southwest Has a New Crop of Super Rich," *Life Magazine,* April 5, 1948, p. 23; "The Land of the Big, Rich, Freewheeling Enterprise in that Capitalistic Oasis, the Southwest, U.S.A.," *Fortune,* April 1948, p. 103.)

According to the home-town *Southwest Daily Times,* January 21, 1970, the Baughman lands have been sold by the heir.

16. *Kiowa County Press,* November 2, 1945, and April 23, 1954.

17. "Annual Report" of county agent, Cheyenne County, 1953.

land belonging to them be cropped. In the early 1950s this meant mainly wheat. Here and elsewhere, many absentee owners were wheat farmers themselves.

It is probably true that local concern over the possibility of the return of Dust Bowl conditions would have delayed or reduced greatly the big plow-up in the Dust Bowl had it not been for absentee landownership, which made it possible for suitcase ·farmers to defy local sentiment as wheat farmers became independent of government payments. Two types of government land-use programs restrained the spread of suitcase farming, however: both the ordinances against breaking sod of some soil conservation districts and the federal land utilization projects appear to have helped restrain nonresident farming in eastern Colorado. These restraints had no parallel in the first suitcase farming frontier.

Nine soil conservation districts having land-use ordinances to limit the plowing up of grassland were in existence in eastern Colorado at the onset of the invasion of suitcase farmers (fig. 25). The approval of the district board of supervisors was required before grassland could be plowed, and in several cases, land not cultivated since 1933 was added to the land subject to control. In Kit Carson County the ordinance was very restrictive in that only Class I land (of which there was virtually none in the two districts) was made subject to the mandatory granting of plowing permits.[18]

Most of the sod-land ordinances were in effect only in the earlier stages of the influx of absentee farmers due to the action of the state legislature in 1945 that set aside all existing land-use ordinances and required that readoption, adoption, or amendment of an ordinance should be by a 75 percent majority of land owners voting in person or by proxy. The organization of absentee landowners against the ordinance in a proxy campaign could defeat the reestablishment of the sod-breaking ordinances in most areas. In two districts in Kit Carson County and one in Cheyenne County efforts to readopt were defeated. In several other cases the ordinances lapsed without a vote. Only three soil conservation districts in eastern Colorado had sod-breaking ordinances in effect in 1952 (fig. 25). They were Horse-Rush Creek and Big Sandy, both mainly in Elbert County, and Timpas, in Otero County.[19] Absentee ownership in these areas was probably lower than farther east, and because these districts were somewhat remote from the main source areas of suitcase farmers in Kansas, the

18. Voelker, *Land-Use Ordinances,* pp. 16, 21, 22. In the two districts in Elbert County, the two in Kit Carson, the one in Otero, and the one in Cheyenne County, land not cultivated since 1933 could not be plowed without permission.
19. Ibid., p. 29.

opposition of local landowners to restrictions on the plowing of grassland may have been small because of limited demand for land by absentees.

The sod ordinances, however, seem to have had little effect on the degree to which the land had been put into wheat by the early 1950s (fig. 20). Nor did they prevent suitcase farming. In the districts near the Kansas border, the control of sodbreaking by the soil conservation districts did not last beyond 1945, which was fairly early in the plow-up. In the three most northerly districts, the supervisors had turned down most requests to break out sod; but between 1945 and 1948 there was considerable plowing in these districts, partly because "non-resident operators moved into the Cheyenne District in large numbers and a few into the Smokey Hill and Plainview Districts" in Kit Carson County.[20]

In Timpas District in Otero County the enforcement of the ordinance—actually the threat of enforcement during the incursion of suitcase farmers—was an effective tool in keeping suitcase farmers out. Here, according to Voelker, "more than 50 potential land buyers—most of them nonresident farmers from Texas, Kansas and Oklahoma—started to buy land in the Timpas District," despite its dryness, "but went elsewhere upon learning of the ordinance."[21] Perhaps the ordinance helped keep suitcase farmers out of the Horse-Rush Creek and Big Sandy districts. At the height of the sodbreaking in eastern Colorado in 1948, the Elbert County agricultural agent reported, "The sod breaking laws in Horse-Rush and Big Sandy districts have been carried out very forcefully as there has been a great influx of suitcase farmers within these districts,"[22] although Voelker reported later that most applications to plow were granted.[23] Figure 19 shows fewer suitcase farms in this part of Elbert County than in some other localities having poor land. The conclusion seems warranted that although the sod ordinances had little effect on the distribution of suitcase farming, the advance was slowed at the west.

The federal land utilization projects were a different matter. These lands were not available for plow-up because the United States government had bought them and maintained control, although there was demand for cropping them as early as 1942.[24] They have been kept in grass and leased for grazing, and now are administered by the Forest Service as national grasslands.

20. Ibid., pp. 49, 47. The county newspaper, the *Cheyenne County News,* gives an account of the activities of opponents and supporters of the land-use ordinance in Cheyenne County and the great surge of sod-breaking that followed the defeat of the ordinance.

21. Voelker, *Land-Use Ordinances,* p. 38.

22. "1948 Annual Report," Elbert County agricultural extension agent.

23. Voelker, *Land-Use Ordinances,* p. 49.

Within the general boundaries of the land utilization projects (shown in fig. 25), privately owned and government land are intimately interspersed. Since the government land is commonly leased for grazing, many adjacent landowners have some inducement to maintain stock-raising operations, combining the use of private and public land. According to Peter Freeman, a long-time resident in what is now the Pawnee National Grassland, located in eastern Weld County adjacent to the Nebraska border, the existence of the federal grazing lands tended to reduce the plow-up of the privately owned land that was intermingled with government land:

> The existence of Gov't. owned tracts used in conjunction with privately owned lands has tended to reduce plow-up following World War II but this discouragement of suitcase wheat farming did not extend to those privately owned lands which had no connection with nearby Federal lands. In other words, if no grazing privilege extended to certain private lands, there was little hesitancy in plowing up unless the operator were a long-term resident established in the livestock business.

In contrast, in eastern Weld County outside the grassland, Freeman wrote, "There has been an increase of plowed land southeast of Briggsdale, south of New Raymer, and in the Grover-Hereford area, all outside of the boundaries [of the land utilization project] except a portion of the Grover area lying North and East of Grover toward Bushnell, Nebr." These areas, adjacent to the national grassland, are shown in figure 17 as areas of greater concentration of wheat than within the general boundaries of the national grassland. As to his personal experience, Freeman reported that following his discharge from the United States Army in 1945, he returned to ranching just outside the land utilization project, using 1,600 acres of his own land, 640 acres of grassland leased from the state, and 960 acres of leased privately owned land. He included feed crops and 100 acres of wheat in his operation. With the relaxation of acreage controls on wheat and the setting of a guaranteed price of $1.80 a bushel at the time of the Korean War in 1950, all 960 acres of privately owned land that he had leased were bought by suitcase farmers.[25] Without the land utilization project, the plow-up in Weld County probably would have been substantially greater.

To the south, the Comanche National Grassland includes about 205,000 acres in Baca, 158,000 in Otero, and a smaller acreage in Las

24. *Denver Post*, August 27, 1942.

25. Letter from Peter Freeman, a manager of the Pawnee National Grasslands, employee of the national grassland since 1955 and long-time stockman, Chicago Ranch, Briggsdale, Colorado, November 1, 1969.

Animas County. The same relationship seems to exist between private and public land here as in the Pawnee National Grassland.

The low incidence of absentee farmers at the southern margin of important suitcase farming can be ascribed partly to the restraints of the land utilization project and those continued in the national grassland. A comparison of figure 25 with figures 17, 18, and 19 supports this conclusion. Probably the considerable amount of sandy land and the persistence of many resident farmers through the Dust Bowl era in Baca County also reduced the opportunities for a big plow-up by outsiders in the 1940s.

A secondary role must be accorded the sod ordinances of surviving soil conservation districts and federal ownership in the land utilization projects in restricting the second advance of suitcase farmers. Probably the distributional pattern of suitcase farming would have been a little different without them.

Decline of Suitcase Farming in Western Kansas

Suitcase farming had declined in the former Suitcase Farming Frontier in western Kansas. A comparison of figures 7 and 21 shows a general reduction in nonresident wheat farmers in western Kansas too large to be accounted for by differences in definition (out-of-county in 1933 and more than one county away in 1954).

A generally applicable interpretation is that resident farmers had joined the absentees in wheat farming, competing with them for land owned by nonresidents. The increasing use of irrigation in parts of western Kansas was also unfavorable to absentee operation because of its greater labor requirements and the substitution of other crops for wheat under irrigation. According to the United States census, the leading counties in irrigated acreage in 1954 were Finney with 54,778 acres, Scott with 39,164, and Grant with 24,165. The increases were most notable in Scott and Grant counties. The decrease in nonresident wheat farming in both of these counties was large, on both an absolute and a relative basis. Data to permit the determining of the number of suitcase farmers in Finney and Stanton counties in 1954 unfortunately were not available.

Some Comparisons of Suitcase and Local Farming

The 1954 wheat listing sheets of the ASCS contained several types of data useful in identifying farming practices, for example, total acres in the farm; acres of cropland; acres of wheat planted in 1951, 1952, and 1953;

and acres fallowed in the same years. The names and addresses of the owners were listed for farms consisting of single tracts. The kinds of information provided permit some comparisons to be made between suitcase and locally operated farms.

The average size of farms in 1954 was calculated for the 221 suitcase and 661 other farms in ten communities in eastern Colorado.[26] The farms of the two groups averaged about the same size despite the inclusion of a few exceptionally large suitcase operations, but otherwise there were clear-cut statistical differences. The farms of the suitcase farmers consisted more completely of cropland, and a substantially higher percentage of the cropland was planted to wheat. As might have been anticipated, the farms operated by local farmers had larger acreages devoted to pasture and crops other than wheat. Well over one-half of all the farm land operated by suitcase farmers was planted to wheat; for the farmers living on the farm or close to it only a little more than one-third was in wheat. Averages and percentages are shown in table 26.

The surprising thing is not that suitcase farmers emphasized wheat, but rather the degree to which the numerous local farmers had become dependent on it. With well over one-half of their cropland in wheat, in addition to land summer-fallowed for wheat, and more than one-third of all their farm land in wheat, the local farmers who sowed wheat had made that crop their chief concern.

The data on fallowed land, recorded for most communities, show that the use of fallowing varied far more between the members of each group than between groups. For well over two-fifths of each group, there were recorded at least as many acres fallowed as in wheat; and more than two-thirds of the suitcase farmers and almost two-thirds of the others had at least one-half as much fallow as wheat sown. A somewhat larger percentage of the suitcase operators than of the locals tried to get by without summer fallowing (table 27).[27]

It is understandable that a considerable number of absentees tried to grow wheat with minimum expense and time spent in the area. The count in Crowley, the driest area included, showed a majority of both suitcase (thirteen of sixteen) and local farmers (twenty-six of thirty-six) as not

26. The communities were community 2 of Bent County; Towner and Haswell-Arlington in Kiowa County; Arapahoe, First View, Kit Carson, and Wild Horse in Cheyenne County; Karval in the southeast of Lincoln County; Anton in Washington County; and Kim in Las Animas County.
27. The communities covered were community 2 in Bent, First View and Kit Carson in Cheyenne County, Haswell-Arlington in Kiowa County, Karval in Lincoln County, and the three communities of Crowley County.

fallowing. It is very unlikely that many suitcase farmers were irrigating their wheat since 320 acres was the smallest amount planted in the peak year on any suitcase farm not practicing fallowing. Almost all of the wheat sown by local farmers without benefit of summer fallow in the county was almost certainly on unirrigated land because only three locally operated farms included were credited with fewer than 120 acres sown in the peak year. The conclusion is reached that dryland wheat farmers made the smallest use of summer fallow in the very driest part of the suitcase farming frontier. The very long odds on harvesting a crop were made even longer by using a practice adapted to much more humid country—that of growing wheat as a continuous crop. Small wonder that, in the words of a local rancher, wheat farmers rarely got their seed back. Seven suitcase and five local farmers gambled on more than 1,000 acres of wheat each in a year. Two suitcase farmers bet on more than 4,900 acres each.

A check of the addresses of the suitcase farmers of 1954 who did not fallow for wheat in Crowley County showed that five came from Hutchinson south into northern Oklahoma, where the average annual rainfall is nearly thirty inches; one farmer from southwest of Amarillo, Texas, which has around twenty inches of rain yearly; one from Greeley, Colorado, in an irrigated area; but three farms were operated by one farmer from semiarid Baca County, Colorado.

In those cases in which farmers were especially heavily committed to wheat through a rotation emphasizing wheat and summer fallow, it is possible to determine many cases of the abandonment of the wheat crop. For example, if in a given year the entire acreage of cropland was seeded to wheat and was also reported to be entirely fallow, the conclusion is that the entire wheat crop was plowed under as a loss. If less than the entire crop acreage was planted to wheat, but wheat and fallow together exceeded the total crop acreage, there had been at least some abandonment of wheat. A summer crop, such as grain sorghum, was an alternative for summer fallow after abandonment of wheat. Since local farmers were more likely to try the summer-crop option, adding up wheat and fallow acreages in order to determine the occurrence of wheat abandonment shows suitcase farmers at a disadvantage. Their failure would more likely be disclosed.

Table 29 gives a comparison of indicated wheat abandonment.[28] The rate of abandonment—fairly high in the record and undoubtedly much higher in actuality—is to be understood in terms of the very dry years

28. Data from wheat listing sheets for 1954, including records for 1951-53, for community 2 of Bent County, First View and Kit Carson in Cheyenne County, and Haswell-Arlington in Kiowa County.

covered and the forward position of the communities on the dry margin of wheat farming. The Haswell-Arlington community, in the western part of Kiowa County, made an especially poor showing: thirty-one indicated cases of abandonment for thirty-two suitcase farms and thirty-nine for sixty-five local farmers in the three years 1951 through 1953.

Not planting wheat in some years, rather than doggedly sowing the same amount regardless of soil moisture and weather conditions, may be taken as a sign of desirable flexibility in farm operations. For the suitcase farmer, not planting would seem to indicate an awareness of prospects, and usually took the form of the hazardous practice of summer fallowing land, probably already in a condition to blow, or letting the land lie idle. The local farmer had the additional practical alternative of waiting until late spring or early summer to plant summer crops. In some cases the absentees doubtless made use of this option.

The record indicates only a moderate amount of flexibility in farming practices as measured by the failure to plant any wheat in at least one year of the three in the period 1951 through 1953. The farmers who consistently planted wheat one year and summer fallowed all their wheatland the next, of course, were not counted as showing this sign of flexibility unless they broke the sequence. Examination of the records for twelve communities showed that 32 of the 277 suitcase farmers and 77 of the 727 local farmers failed to sow wheat in at least one year of the three.[29] The difference between the two groups was very small, with about 12 percent of the suitcase farmers and about 11 percent of the locals not sowing. This measure of flexibility was not found to a great extent in either group.

The fallowing and planting of all their wheatland in alternate years, a measure of regularity, was followed on a surprisingly large number of farms—forty-two suitcase and sixty-four locally operated—in the twelve communities. That more than one-seventh of the absentees farmed in this manner may be taken as an evidence of their effort to hold the amount of time spent in the area to a minimum and also to cut down on the number of times farm machinery would need to be transported back and forth.

In the Kansas suitcase farming country, where the emphasis on wheat was of longer duration than in Colorado, suitcase farmers continued to

---

29. The twelve communities (except for Towner in eastern Kiowa County, Arapahoe in eastern Cheyenne County, and perhaps Anton in southwestern Washington County) were located on the dry western margin of important wheat farming. They were community 2 for Bent County; Haswell-Arlington, Kiowa County; the three communities of Crowley County; First View, Kit Carson, and Wild Horse, Cheyenne County; and Karval in Lincoln County.

stress wheat more than local farmers did, although the differences were less pronounced than in Colorado. Table 29 summarizes the place of wheat in the land use of the 106 suitcase farmers operating in 1954 in the four counties of Wichita, Sherman, Scott, and Grant, as compared with matching local farmers (selected automatically as the next on the wheat lists after the nonresidents).[30] On the average, local farmers had somewhat larger farms; suitcase farmers had somewhat more cropland, planted more wheat, and summer fallowed more land. In percentages, the farms of non-residents were more largely in wheat and in fallow. For both groups, the fallow acreage amounted to more than 80 percent of the wheat acreage, with wheat and fallow together exceeding 100 percent of the acreage in cropland, a circumstance understandable only as a sign of the fallowing of wheatland after early abandonment. It may be assumed that the differences between average suitcase and local farms were actually somewhat greater than shown because not all local farmers grew wheat; these, of course, were not included on the ASCS wheat lists.

Conclusion

An effort has been made to picture suitcase farming on the new suitcase farming frontier shortly after the daring and rapid advance had ground to a halt. In many respects there were important parallels to conditions existing in the older suitcase farming frontier from about 1933 to 1936. Drought was again heavy on the land, and crop failure and dust were again among the legacies of the extension of the wheat country. The Dust Bowl was in trouble again, posing problems for its citizens and its part-time farmers from the outside. As before, national attention was directed to the plight of the central Great Plains and the fundamental problem of its future was raised again.

30. Data from wheat listing sheets of 1954, Kansas City Federal Records Center.

CHAPTER NINE

Aftermath: Suitcase Farming in the 1960s

Introduction

Neither the late 1950s nor the 1960s were times favorable for wheat farming in the suitcase farming country. Hence, they were not good times for suitcase farmers, whose main concern was wheat. Kiowa County, Colorado, in the heart of the newer suitcase farming country, experienced wheat abandonment of 70 percent or more in nine of the fourteen years in the period 1955 through 1968. Only in the five consecutive years from 1958 to 1962 were wheat failures lower.

The acreage reserve option of the Soil Bank program provided farmers a major windfall for not planting crops in 1957. ASCS records show that payments amounting to over $900,000 were made in each of nine counties of eastern Colorado—Kit Carson, Kiowa, Prowers, Baca, Cheyenne, Weld, Adams, Lincoln, and Washington. Kit Carson led, at nearly $4,250,000, followed by Kiowa, with almost $2,750,000. Most of the counties of western Kansas received more than $900,000 each but payments in none equaled those of Kit Carson and Kiowa counties. In 1958 Kiowa County, Colorado, was the only one in the Colorado-Kansas plains to exceed $900,000.[1] It seems safe to assume that the acreage reserve option kept many wheat farmers, both suitcase and local, from going under.

---

1. Figures on acreage reserve payments obtained from the state ASCS offices, Denver and Manhattan.

Further support for harassed farmers was available in the conservation reserve of the Soil Bank, in which cropland was, in effect, leased to the government for periods of three to ten years. In the western margin of the suitcase farming country, where the land retirement program was most popular, the usual lease was for ten years. The program was open for sign-up from 1956 to 1960, beginning in a period of protracted wheat failure. Suitcase farmers, in particular, chose to collect from the government rather than to take their chances on wheat.[2]

Incidence of Suitcase Farmers about 1960

Figure 26 shows the percentage of suitcase operators among farmers on the wheat lists about 1960. The counts were complete in Colorado except that only dryland farms were tallied in several counties; the percentages were based on complete counts in Greeley and Hamilton counties and on extensive samples elsewhere in Kansas. The over-all distributional pattern was reasonably consistent, with the major concentration of absentees occurring toward the west near the Colorado-Kansas border.

The core area marked by both a large number and a high percentage of suitcase farmers centered on Kiowa and Cheyenne counties in Colorado and Greeley County, Kansas. In each well over one-fifth of the wheat farms were operated by absentees; the count, based on ASCS entries, was 262, 146, and 138, respectively but somewhat less if reductions are made for duplications due to some farmers operating more than one farm. The high percentages for dryland farms in Otero, Crowley, and Bent counties (44, 30, and 31) were based on small numbers of suitcase farm entries (4, 17, and 43). In contrast, Kit Carson County, Colorado, next north of the core area, had a count of 118 suitcase farms but a percentage of only 8. Except for the apparent but unreal westward extension based on the use of data for dryland farms only in 1961-62, the distribution of suitcase farmers was much the same in about 1960 as in 1954.

Figure 27, the companion map to figure 26, shows percentages of suitcase farmers in eastern Colorado by communities recognized by the ASCS. Kiowa, most of Cheyenne, and Bent counties are emphasized, as well as Crowley and Otero, which are not differentiated by communities. High percentages of farmers from a distance continued to characterize that part

2. Leslie Hewes, "The Conservation Reserve of the American Soil Bank as an Indicator of Regions of Maladjustment in Agriculture, with Particular Reference to the Great Plains," in *Festschrift, Leopold G. Scheidl Zum 60. Geburtstag,* vol. 2 (Vienna: Ferdinand Berg & Son, 1967), pp. 331-46.

of Colorado in which the greatest plow-up took place in the 1940s. The western margin of the major wheat-growing area continued to be marked by the relative importance of suitcase farmers, except to the north and in southern Baca County.

Figure 28, comparing the situation of about 1960 with that in 1954, shows that suitcase farming had suffered a fairly general decline. The most important exception was Greeley County, Kansas, for which there was uncertainty about the accuracy of the estimate for 1954, as explained earlier. Several counties having moderate to low percentages of nonresident farmers at both times showed little or no change. A few small increases along the margins of the suitcase farming frontier were recorded. The fairly general decline in suitcase farming suggests that with the passage of the period of expansion, the advantages in boldness, know-how, and equipment of suitcase farmers were soon lost and/or that suitcase farmers were more easily discouraged than local farmers.

Persistence and Nonpersistence from 1954

A check of the wheat lists shows that a majority of the suitcase farmers operating wheat farms in 1954 in the then new suitcase farming country of Colorado had dropped out before 1961 or 1962.[3] It seems likely that the less able, less well financed, and less optimistic among them were generally eliminated by the early 1960s although positive proof would be difficult or impossible to find. The ASCS county office managers and other long-term residents provide what must be considered informed—often expert—testimony that many less efficient farmers were eliminated. It seems safe to assume that those lacking in either financial reserves or faith in the future could not or would not choose to continue in the face of heavy crop losses. It can be proved that nonresidents with small farms dropped out before those with larger ones and that tenants left before landowners.

Only in three of twelve communities in the new suitcase farming country of Colorado checked were more than one-half of the suitcase operators of wheat farms in 1954 shown as persisting as absentee farmers. Towner community, the easternmost district of Kiowa County, was the only one in which the number of persisters was at all large—eighteen of thirty-five absentees; an additional four suitcase farmers of 1954 had moved into the locality by 1960. The communities studied showing the

3. The ASCS wheat-listing sheets for 1954 were examined at the Denver Federal Records center. Equivalent records, consisting of a series of individual record cards on microfilm for 1961 and 1962 were made available for study at the Colorado state ASCS office, Denver.

lowest rates of persistence were Wild Horse, the westernmost community of Cheyenne County, with no suitcase persisters and one farmer becoming local among seven absentees; Karval, in southern Lincoln County, with three of fourteen continuing; "A" community in Crowley County, with three of twelve persisting; community 2 in Bent County, with ten of thirty-three continuing; Anton, in southwestern Washington County, with eleven of thirty-one remaining; and Haswell-Arlington, the westernmost community of Kiowa County, with eleven of thirty persisting and two others becoming local.[4]

On the average, suitcase farmers who persisted from 1954 were markedly different from those who did not and both groups of nonresidents were different from local farmers. Table 30 summarizes the differences. Persisting suitcase farmers had the largest farms, the largest acreages of cropland, the highest percentage (85) of farm land in crops, the largest amount and percentage (64) of cropland in wheat, and the next to the lowest percentage (27) of farms having 320 acres or less of cropland. Nonpersisting suitcase farmers had the smallest farms and were a poor third in amount of cropland per farm, second in percentage (76) of their farms in cropland, third in amount of wheat acreage, second in percentage (61) of cropland sown to wheat, and a good second in percentage (44) of farms containing 320 acres or less of cropland.[5]

Large farms, large amounts and high percentages of cropland, large amounts and high percentages of cropland in wheat were especially characteristic of suitcase farmers who persisted, although several very large farms operated by suitcase farmers tended to raise the averages for persisting suitcase farmers. The records examined did not show whether the wheat farmers of the ten communities farmed elsewhere as well.

An analysis of the 1954 records of five communities in the heart of the suitcase farming country showed that 33 of 58 farms (57%) of the suitcase persisters were owner-operated. Thirty-four of 81, or 42 percent, of nonpersisting suitcase farmers were owner-operators. Of the local farmers who

4. The communities checked in detail were as follows: number 2 in Bent; Arapahoe, First View, Kit Carson, and Wild Horse in Cheyenne County; "A" in Crowley County; Towner and Haswell-Arlington in Kiowa County; Flagler in Kit Carson County; "B" in Las Animas County; Karval in Lincoln County; and Anton in Washington County. In Flagler, Kit Carson County, the 1955 record was used because that for 1954 was not available.

5. The communities whose persisting and nonpersisting suitcase and local farmers were subjects of this analysis were: community 2 of Bent County; Arapahoe, First View, Kit Carson, and Wild Horse in Cheyenne County; Towner and Haswell-Arlington in Kiowa County; "B" or Kim in Las Animas County; Karval in Lincoln County; and Anton in Washington County.

persisted, 40 of 186, or 21 percent, owned their land; 15 of 113, or 13 percent, local farmers were owner-operators.[6] Ownership, indicative of a greater capital investment, appears to have been a factor of some importance in the persistence of suitcase and other farmers.

Irrigation as a Factor in Decline

The reduction in the percentage of suitcase farmers was pronounced in several areas of expanding irrigation. By 1959, according to the United States census, seven counties in the old suitcase farming country of western Kansas—Finney, Haskell, Wichita, Scott, Stanton, Grant, and Kearny— each had more than 35,000 acres of irrigated land. The increase from 1954 was substantial in all seven but especially great in Haskell (from 11,825 to 61,694 acres) and Finney (from 54,778 to 100,749 acres). Decreases in the percentage of suitcase farmers were recorded for the four counties of the seven with percentages shown for 1954 and 1960. In two, Haskell and Grant, the reductions ran over 50 percent. In Finney, Kearny, and Stanton (without records for 1954) the percentage of suitcase farmers for 1960 were 3, 8, and 11, far below the out-of-county figures of 1933. Irrigation was an increasingly important factor in persistence—one highly unfavorable to suitcase farming.

Absentee Ownership

The collection of considerable data on out-of-county ownership of land for 1969,[7] less than a decade after the year for which figure 26 represents the distribution of suitcase farmers, permits a reappraisal of absentee ownership as a factor in suitcase farming. The significant correspondence of the distribution of nonresident farmers (fig. 26) and nonresident ownership (fig. 29) continued. A correlation coefficient (Pearson moment product) of +.6295 was determined for the twenty-three counties for which both types of data were available.

---

6. The locations of farms in Colorado analyzed are Arapahoe, First View, and Kit Carson in Cheyenne County and Towner and Haswell-Arlington, Kiowa County. Farms consisting of multiple tracts, with ownership not given, were not counted.

7. The estimates (in a number of cases they were precise acreages) by county ASCS office managers were provided in response to requests for estimates of the amount of farm land owned out-of-county. In a number of cases it was specified that the percentages were for cropland; in other cases the figures were for farm land, and in some instances for percentage of owners.

The Conservation Reserve as a New Factor

An important factor in part of the suitcase farming country in the 1960s was a new government land-retirement program, the conservation reserve of the Soil Bank, which served to maintain absentees on the ASCS wheat lists, at least in the more hazardous western portion of the suitcase farming country. Many were only nominally wheat farmers, having retired all of their cropland for a ten-year period; others after, in effect, leasing part of their cropland to the government, continued wheat farming on the remainder. Some absentee landlords are reported to have become nominal operators in order to collect both the tenant's and the landowners' share of the "lease" money. Similarly, nonresidents became nominal suitcase farmers by buying land—ordinarily cheap land—for the purpose of collecting conservation reserve payments until safeguards against this practice were written into the program for the last year of the sign-up period. In addition, some long-term resident farmers, apparently hard pressed to show a profit from farming, went into partial retirement or took jobs in towns at a distance while maintaining their status as actual or nominal operators of farms. In the several ways noted, the conservation reserve program tended to maintain or even increase the number of suitcase farmers, especially toward the west.

The degree to which suitcase farmers were wheat farmers in name only is shown for the communities of eastern Colorado in figure 30.[8] Along the dry, western margin of important wheat farming and beyond, well north of the center of the state in eastern Colorado, a majority of those residing far enough away to qualify as suitcase farmers had substantially all of their cropland in the Conservation Reserve. In the case of the few suitcase farmers of Otero County, the sign-up was 100 percent. The restriction that no landowner or operator might receive more than five thousand dollars per year in conservation reserve payments, as well as perhaps the quotas imposed by ASCS administrators, prevented even greater participation in the program in some localities. In only three communities in the heart of the suitcase farming country of Colorado—two in eastern Kiowa County and one in eastern Cheyenne—did over 75 percent of the suitcase farmers decide to continue growing wheat rather than retire the land for 10 years. Evidence has been presented elsewhere that the high failure of crops,

8. The microfilmed record cards of 1961 and 1962 for wheat farmers included acreages of cropland that had been placed in the conservation reserve. Thus farm-by-farm, community-by-community, and county-by-county data on the degree to which farms had been retired for a period of years from crop farming were available. The farm record cards are identified as "156" cards and were examined in the Colorado State ASCS office.

especially wheat, in the early and mid-1950s was a major reason for farmers entering the program in the southern portion of the plains of Colorado.[9] That wheat failure was less common during the latter portion of the sign-up period appears not to have offset the effects of the earlier losses. Away from major suitcase farming areas, the high percentages of nonpersisting wheat farmers shown for parts of Yuma County, adjacent to the Kansas-Nebraska border, were based on a small number of absentee farmers, presumably operating at least partly on sandy or rough land. Incidentally, absentee farmers went into the conservation reserve program to a greater extent than local farmers.

The official records support the charge that nonresidents became nominal wheat farmers in order to collect Conservation Reserve payments; they also show that, in fact, local farmers had become suitcase farmers—both actual and nominal—by moving away. Unfortunately, the wheat lists for 1957, before the land retirement effort was well under way, generally failed to list the owners, thus preventing the determination of the degree to which absentee owners displaced their tenants.

The wheat lists for thirteen communities in Colorado[10] showed 111 suitcase farmers listed as operators in 1961 or 1962 who had not been listed in either 1954 or 1957. Of these 111 new nonresidents, 57 had substantially all of their cropland (at least 95 percent or all but four acres) in the conservation reserve in 1961 or 1962, 13 had part in, and 41 had none in. In six key communities on the dry southwestern margin, the count among the 56 new suitcase farmers ran as follows: 42 farmers were almost entirely in the Conservation Reserve; 4 were partly in; and 10 were not in at all.[11] Circumstantial evidence that absentees acquired land or eliminated renters for the purpose of receiving the major part or all of the conservation reserve payments is strongest for the area in which wheat farming had proved especially risky. In the remaining seven communities checked, either new suitcase farmers were few or a majority had no land in the conservation reserve.

An examination of the wheat lists for 1962 for the other communities in eastern Colorado showed that a considerable number of operators changed their addresses. Forty-six former local farmers had become suit-

9. Hewes, "Conservation Reserve," pp. 338-40.

10. Community 2 in Bent County; Arapahoe, First View, Kit Carson, and Wild Horse in Cheyenne County; all three in Crowley County; "A" in Elbert; Towner and Haswell-Arlington, Kiowa County; Flagler in Kit Carson County; and Karval in Lincoln County.

11. Number 2 in Bent County, the three in Crowley County, Haswell-Arlington in Kiowa County, and Karval in Lincoln County.

case farmers by moving; of these, twenty had placed substantially all their cropland in the conservation reserve, nine had part of it in the program, and seventeen had no land in it. It seems safe to assume that the guaranteed government payments helped induce former local farmers to move away. In several instances, ASCS county office managers considered the moving away of former residents as the most important factor contributing to the continuation of suitcase farming. In one case, the explanation given for the percentage of suitcase farmers being higher than in other communities in the county was that the land was poorer—less able to support full-time farmers.

Source Areas about 1960

Nonresidents from Kansas continued to dominate suitcase farming in both the first and second suitcase farming frontiers, but absentees from other parts of Colorado had succeeded Kansans in several marginal areas in Colorado and had replaced Oklahomans in one community, while Kansans had replaced Oklahomans in one community and Texans in another (fig. 21). The shift to Colorado bases resulted in part from the flight of former local farmers to cities to their west. The changes in addresses of farmers shown on the Colorado wheat lists of 1962 and those determined by a comparison of the addresses of 1954 and 1961 or 1962 for a dozen communities showed that forty-six of the ninety-one local farmers who had become suitcase operators had gone to live elsewhere in Colorado. Thirty-one had moved to the piedmont belt, with eight to Denver, six to Colorado Springs, and four to Loveland, the leading cities. Twenty went to Kansas, eight to Texas, seven to Oklahoma, and ten to other states, some as distant as Florida, Arizona, Oregon, and Washington.

Figure 31, showing the bases from which suitcase farmers operated in eastern Colorado and western Kansas, represents the continued dominance by Kansans. The early main source area in south-central Kansas, extended somewhat to the west, was most important. The newer important bases included the strip along the Colorado Front Range, western Kansas, northern Oklahoma, the Texas pandhandle, and part of Nebraska bordering Colorado.

As viewed closer up, the continuity of sources of absentee farmers was marked, as in Greeley and Hamilton counties in Kansas and the Haswell-Arlington community in Kiowa County, Colorado. Figure 15b, Greeley County, is much like 15a; figure 6b, Hamilton County, is similar to 6a, and figure 32a, Haswell-Arlington, resembles figures 22a and 22b, although Texans no longer led.

By this time, metropolitan Denver had become the most common address of suitcase farmers in the central Great Plains. Its only close rival was Dodge City, Kansas. Other addresses credited to operators of more than thirty farms were Colorado Springs, Wichita, Garden City, Great Bend, Hutchinson, Larned, and Pratt. There is no indication whether these absentee farmers lived in town except when street or hotel addresses were given.

A check of the addresses of 958 listed suitcase operators of wheat farms in eastern Colorado listed for 1961 and 1962 (roughly 85 percent of the total) resulted in 264 positive identifications of urban dwellers, 157 of them from Colorado, 89 from Kansas, 33 from Texas, 23 from Oklahoma, and 54 from other states. The leading urban bases were Denver with 60 operator addresses, Dodge City with 25, and Colorado Springs with 24. Other cities with 8 or more suitcase addresses given were Cañon City, Colorado; Garden City, Great Bend, Hutchinson, and Wichita, Kansas; Enid, Oklahoma; and Amarillo, Texas.

East from the suitcase farming core, the percentage of suitcase farmers having listed street addresses increased if the following examples are representative. According to the official ASCS wheat referendum lists of 1963,[12] 37 of 104 suitcase operators in Greeley County, Kansas, had street addresses; in Haskell County, Kansas, the count was 11 of 24; and the listing of suitcase farmers in the *Official Grant Farm Plats* book, 1963 edition, showed that 9 of 18 suitcase farmers in Grant County, Kansas, had street addresses. For the three counties combined, Dodge City, with 8, had the largest number of suitcase street addresses; others with 4 or 5 each were Garden City, Wichita, Colorado Springs, and Pretty Prairie, Kansas. Phoenix, Arizona, and Joliet, Illinois, were the most distant such addresses.

Spatial Relationships of Suitcase Farming about 1968

Because of the long duration of the study reported here, an updating of information was undertaken in the summer and fall of 1968. Data for that year, the latest then available, were collected in the Colorado state ASCS office in Denver and in the county offices in three Kansas counties bordering Colorado. Further information was obtained in the Kansas state office, but in this case the last year of record was 1967.[13] Emphasis was placed on

---

12. Examined in the Kansas state ASCS office, Manhattan.

13. Farm record cards in agricultural programs, identified as "156" cards. The 1968 original cards examined in the county ASCS offices in Greeley, Hamilton, and Stanton counties, Kansas. The 1968 records in the Colorado state ASCS office are on microfilm. The cards at the Kansas state office examined were for 1967.

the former core area of suitcase farming, with scattered marginal areas included. The coverage is thought to be representative.

Figure 33 shows the percentage of wheat farmers qualifying as suitcase farmers in the twelve counties and three communities in which complete counts were made and in four counties in which extensive systematic sampling was done. Briefly, the findings were: (1) the old core area along the Kansas-Colorado border continued as the chief suitcase farming area; (2) the percentage of suitcase farmers, especially in the core area, had declined; and (3) there had been little change on the core-area margins.

Figure 34 details the distribution of suitcase farmers by communities in the parts of Colorado covered. Haswell-Arlington, with 37 percent, was highest in percentage of its wheat farmers classed as suitcase. There seems to be ample evidence that the factors recognized earlier were continuing to influence suitcase farming; however, no extension or replacement of the conservation reserve cropland-leasing program, which was ending, was assured. In Stanton County, Kansas, a major increase in irrigation is credited locally with nearly completely eliminating the suitcase farmer.

The reduction in the percentage of suitcase farmers from 1961 (or 1962) to 1968 obviously meant that more nonresidents gave up farming than took it up. Something of the nature of the changes in the operators of wheat farms is apparent in the substitution of some new addresses and the names of some new operators on the 1968 records of wheat farms (called "156" cards). In the Haswell-Arlington and Towner communities, sixteen suitcase farmers were replaced by locals, fourteen suitcase farmers were replaced by other suitcase farmers, one suitcase farmer became local, seven local farmers were replaced by suitcase farmers, and three locals became suitcase farmers. Thus, the most common change was that of local farmers replacing absentees; the net change was a loss of seven suitcase farmers.

Figure 35 illustrates the changes in the percentage of suitcase operations among wheat farms from 1954 to about 1968. The decline in the core area is notable.

Evidence was obtained that the core area of suitcase farming as identified in this study was indeed the focus of suitcase farming in the central Great Plains. A complete count of suitcase farmers of 1965 in the specialized wheat-farming counties of Nebraska, adjacent to the Colorado border, showed a range from nineteen in Kimball County to one in Banner County, with percentages from 4.3 in Kimball to 0.4 in Banner.[14] At the

14. Donald B. Deal, "Sidewalk Farming in the Specialized Wheat Region of Nebraska" (Master's thesis, University of Nebraska, 1967), p. 72. The counties in order of percentages were Kimball, Perkins, Deuel, Cheyenne, Keith, and Banner.

northwestern edge of the hard winter-wheat country, the ASCS county office manager of Platte County, Wyoming, reported in 1964 that there was only one suitcase farmer operating a wheat farm in the county and three whose entire cropland acreage had been placed in the conservation reserve.[15] To the south, the percentage of wheat farmers who were suitcase operators in 1970 varied from 5 percent (Moore and Ochiltree, Texas) to 4 percent (Cimarron, Oklahoma) to only one suitcase farmer in the whole county (Lipscomb, Texas).[16] A student of nonresident farming over scattered parts of the central and northern Great Plains certified that no other county checked equaled Morton County, Kansas, in the percentage of suitcase farmers in about 1954. Still farther north, the highest incidence of nonresident farmers (sidewalk and out-of-area combined) in 1966 was 29.8 percent in a district in Saskatchewan, the Canadian province having the largest number of nonresidents.[17]

There is some evidence that the Dust Bowl of Kansas and Colorado stood out earlier for its suitcase farming. In Perkins County, Nebraska, which was considered representative of a block of counties, there were almost no out-of-county operators of farms in 1936, and in 1958 it was said of a five-county sample in the Texas Panhandle that "a few farmers live outside the area."[18]

No changes of importance in the source areas from which suitcase farmers came were evident. In that portion of Colorado shown in figure 33, non-Kansans were in a plurality only in the marginal areas of Kim community in Las Animas County, and in El Paso, Arapahoe, and Sedgwick counties. Nonresidents from Colorado led in all but the last of these, where Nebraskans had a small plurality. Kansans continued to predom-

15. Letter from Oscar B. Gudahl, ASCS county office manager, Platte County, Wyoming, January 20, 1964.

16. Eight county office managers responded to a request for the percentage of suitcase farmers among the wheat growers in 1970; the counties to the south in order of percentage of suitcase farmers were Moore, Ochiltree, Cimarron, Roberts, Sherman, Hemphill, Beaver, and Lipscomb. Cimarron and Beaver are in the Oklahoma Panhandle; the others are in the northern portion of the panhandle of Texas. In the case of Ochiltree, Texas, it was explained that the increase of irrigation had resulted in a reduction of suitcase farming.

17. Letter from Walter M. Kollmorgen, Department of Geography, University of Kansas, January 24, 1964, for the central and northern Plains; and M. L. Szabo, "Characteristics of Non-resident Farm Operators on the Canadian Prairies," *Geographical Bulletin* 8 (1966): 279-303.

18. P. M. Pevehouse, "Conditions in the Southwestern Wheat Area Which Affect the Rehabilitation Program (as Typified by Perkins Co., Nebraska)," Resettlement Admin. Research Bul. K-3, mimeographed (May 1936), p. 12; for Texas, *Conservation Reserve Program* of the Soil Bank, USDA Inform. Bul. 185. (Washington, D.C.: GPO, March 1958), p. 26.

inate in the heart of the suitcase farming. Kansans constituted a majority of the suitcase farmers in both Kiowa and Cheyenne counties, and equalled all others combined in Anton community of Washington County. A comparison of figure 32b with figures 32a and 22 shows a substantial continuity in the important Haswell-Arlington community. In Kansas, suitcase farmers from Kansas had substantial majorities everywhere except in marginally located Sherman County.

Some Aspects of Suitcase Farming in the 1960s

Table 31 presents pertinent data for a large number of persisting, new suitcase and local farmers in eastern Colorado for 1961-62.[19] Suitcase and local farmers persisting from 1954 differed little in average size of farm or amount of cropland. The percentages of farm land in crops were 58 and 56, respectively, for the two groups. The farms of new operators were smaller on the average, with a larger percentage of cropland (78 percent for new suitcase and 62 for new local farmers). A comparison of these figures with those in table 26 shows that suitcase operators continued to have a larger percentage of cropland than local farmers but that the gap had narrowed since the early 1950s. Perhaps government programs had been an equalizer; the conservation reserve had removed from any type of production more land on suitcase than on local farms. New suitcase farmers had 40 percent of their cropland in the conservation reserve; persisting suitcase farmers, 31 percent; new local farmers, 31 percent; and persisting locals, 21 percent. Productivity indexes[20] varied little between groups except for local persisters, who were credited by the local ASCS committees either with having better cropland or with being better farmers than the other three groups.

The relative commonness of farms having 320 acres of cropland or less varied substantially between groups; their percentages ran as follows: new

19. The Colorado communities covered were number 2 of Bent County; Arapahoe, First View, Kit Carson, and Wild Horse in Cheyenne County; Towner and Haswell-Arlington in Kiowa; Flagler in Kit Carson County; and Karval in Lincoln County. The "156" cards of 1961 and 1962 (ASCS Colorado state office) and wheat-listing sheets for 1954 (Denver Federal Records Center) furnished the data.

20. Overall within a county, the productivity index for cropland averages out at about 100, but in some counties with substantial amounts of irrigated cropland, wheat farms, which are mainly dryland, were rated well below 100—at 50 or 60 in some cases. Accordingly, not even the farms of persisting local farmers averaged 100 in productivity. Productivity indexes were used as the basis of payments for land in the conservation reserve but were recorded for cropland whether it was so retired or not. The "156" cards included information on productivity.

locals, 42; new suitcase operators, 34; persisting suitcase farmers, 28; persisting locals, 19.[21] Offhand, one might assume that most farmers having no more than 320 acres of cropland would have taken refuge in the conservation reserve; however, the degree of participation by small farmers was largely in line with that of other farmers in the community. The Towner and Haswell-Arlington communities of Kiowa County provide good examples. Figure 30 shows that a far lower percentage of all suitcase farms were in the conservation reserve in Towner than in Haswell-Arlington. There was a similar contrast for local farmers. In Towner community, at the eastern end of Kiowa County, none of seven persisting small suitcase farmers, two of five new small suitcase operators, one of seven persisting small local farmers, and none of four new small local operators were entirely in the conservation reserve. However, at the opposite end of the county, the figures for the respective groups were two of two, thirteen of seventeen, seven of nine, and eight of ten. In a community in another county (which will not be identified here), the corresponding counts were one of two, six of seven, four of twelve, and one of five. In this case, it is apparent that most of the small new suitcase farms—probably uneconomic, all owner-operated, and none farmed by the same suitcase operators as in 1957— either were purchased for the purpose of collecting government payments or were taken over from tenants so that the absentee landlords could collect the entire payments.

The detailed land-use records for farmers not participating in the conservation reserve and for those only partly in the program were compiled for seven communities in the heart of the suitcase farming country of Colorado.[22] Tables 32 and 33 show the results. Table 32 indicates that suitcase farmers who elected to stay out of the conservation reserve had more cropland on their farms than local operators who did not go into the program. In addition, suitcase farmers had somewhat more of their cropland in wheat than did resident farmers. Thus, on the average, suitcase operations were more heavily devoted to wheat than were local operations. In other words, suitcase farmers continued to act like suitcase farmers.

Table 33, showing comparisons for farmers partly into the conservation reserve, contains some unanticipated findings, most notably the very large average size of farms operated by nonresidents and their rather small percentage of the farm acreage classed as cropland. As expected, wheat acre-

21. Anton community, Washington County, was added to the nine communities providing data for table 31.
22. The communities were number 2 of Bent County; Arapahoe, First View, and Kit Carson of Cheyenne County; Towner and Haswell-Arlington in Kiowa County; and Flagler in Kit Carson County.

ages and the portion of cropland in wheat were larger on the farms of suitcase farmers than on those of local farmers. However, the percentages of total farm acreage in wheat were identical for the two groups. Surprisingly, of the operators who participated only partly in the land-retirement program, local farmers did so to a greater extent, with 33.9 percent of their cropland, than nonresidents, with 24.0 percent. The observation seems warranted that, because of the large amount of cropland he farmed, the average farmer, suitcase or local, who was partly in the conservation reserve could both take advantage of the guaranteed income of the government program and take his chances on raising wheat. These operators continued as wheat farmers; for many the reduction in crops came in those other than wheat.

Overall, suitcase farmers on the more droughty margins of the wheat country who continued as farmers in the early 1960s were still emphasizing wheat to a greater degree than local farmers, although the differences in land use were less marked than earlier.

Apart from wheat, the chief crops grown in the suitcase farming country are feed grains and hay. The average acreages in the feed grains for 1959 and 1960 were matters of record on the ASCS wheat listings of 1961 for individual farms not having land in the conservation reserve. For farms having land in that program, the feed-grain record was for the last two years prior to the year the conservation reserve leases took effect. Although the acreages planted to grain sorghum, barley, and corn for all the farmers in a number of communities in eastern Colorado were compiled with the purpose of comparing the farming of residents with that of nonresidents, it was decided not to use them. One reason was that the two years of record actually spanned a period of six years since the conservation reserve was open for sign-up from 1956 to 1960. A second was that, as the county office managers explained, the feed-grain acreages ran higher than was usually the case, and therefore the 1961 records were not representative and would tend to confuse a comparison of suitcase and local farming.

Suitcase farmers more commonly than local farmers owned the land that they farmed. This was the situation in western Kansas in 1933 and in eastern Colorado in 1954. The percentage of ownership remained higher among the nonresidents in the 1960s. In 1961-62, in ten communities in the heart of the Colorado suitcase farming area,[23] 172 of 285 farms (60 percent) of the suitcase farms were owner-operated, as compared to 268 of

23. Community 2 in Bent County; Arapahoe, First View, Kit Carson, and Wildhorse in Cheyenne County; Haswell-Arlington and Towner in Kiowa County; Flagler in Kit Carson County; Karval in Lincoln County; and Anton in Washington County.

775 (34+ percent) of the farms of local farmers. A nearly complete count in eastern Colorado showed that 64+ percent, 741 of 1,151, of the farms of suitcase farmers were operated by their owners.[24] Similarly, in western Kansas a higher percentage of absentees than local farmers were owners. The 1963 wheat referendum list for Greeley County identified 45 of the 94 suitcase farmers as owners and 99 of the 282 local farmers. In 1968 in community "A" of Hamilton County, bordering immediately on Greeley County, 22 of the 44 farms operated by suitcase farmers were owned by the farmers themselves or others with the same family name, but the figures were only 35 out of 223 for locally operated farms.

Many nonresidents operate elsewhere as well as in the suitcase farming country, often at home and perhaps in another distant locality. In the spring of 1969 the Kiowa County, Colorado, ASCS office manager made a name-by-name check of long-time suitcase and local farmers and new farmers having both kinds of addresses for the easternmost and westernmost communities of the county to determine whether the farming of these operators was limited to the county. The results were as follows: of the suitcase farmers continuing from 1954, four farmed only in the county and fifteen farmed elsewhere as well; of the suitcase farmers new since 1961, four farmed in the county only and seven farmed elsewhere as well; of the local farmers persisting from 1954, eighteen farmed only in the county and two farmed elsewhere as well; of the new local farmers, five farmed only in the county and two farmed elsewhere as well.[25] Plainly, both persisting and new suitcase farmers more often than local farmers divided their farming efforts between distant farms.

As noted, there were many nominal suitcase farmers, who did little or no absentee farming, carried on the wheat lists in the 1960s. For other suitcase farmers, there were several options in the degree to which they did their own farming, and the efficiency of their operation varied widely. In 1961 the Kit Carson County ASCS office manager estimated that 25 percent visited their farms so infrequently as not to know "what is going on"; and about 20 percent had a man on the farm or were represented by a custom farmer; the rest were able to perform timely farming operations by keeping in touch with residents by telephone, which suggests the variation in operations and results.[26]

24. ASCS "156" cards for 1961-62 for eastern Colorado, excluding Crowley and most of Washington counties.

25. Letter from Mrs. Kathlyn Forster, ASCS county office manager of Kiowa County, Colorado, April 14, 1969.

26. Interview with H. H. Simpson, Jr., ASCS county office manager of Kit Carson County, Colorado, Burlington, August 24, 1961.

Local opinion holds that in many cases suitcase farming is not as careful as that done by local on-the-land farmers. Reconnaissance field work also suggests that weedy and crusted fallow and weedy freshly sown wheat fields are more common in the heart of the suitcase farming country than elsewhere. Of course, one example cannot be the basis of a generalization, but one of the few absentee farmers who responded to a letter inquiring about his farming methods admitted that since he had moved back to Kansas, away from his Kiowa County farm, his farming had fallen below standards he had maintained as a resident farmer. The time lost, particularly in moving equipment into and out of the area, may make the wheat-farming operations of absentees less timely than those of most local farmers.

Generally, the majority of nonresidents either are at the job of suitcase farming for a period of several months or return several times per season in an effort to carry on a profitable operation. In fact, some ASCS county office managers report little difference between the farming of residents and that of absentees. It may be assumed that out-of-area residents who spend the summer away from home carrying on suitcase farming should ordinarily obtain results equal to those of local farmers. One absentee farmer who, in answer to an inquiry, responded on stationery showing addresses and telephone numbers both in Kiowa County and Kansas, was identified as farming only in Kiowa County.

The following detailed classifications may be representative of suitcase farming. As of 1969, the Kiowa County ASCS office manager identified only four of fifteen suitcase farmers of Towner community, located by the Kansas border, as depending on custom farmers. The remaining eleven did most or all of their own farming, two were reported as hiring some seeding done, and four hired some or all of their fallowing.[27] In 1968 the long-time resident superintendent of the local experiment farm classified the farming of the suitcase operators on the 1963 wheat referendum list for Harrison Township, Greeley County, Kansas, as follows: seven did their own farming; two had become local farmers by moving to the community, three depended on resident members of the family, one depended on custom operation, and the arrangements of several were unknown. According to the same source, by leaving their fallowing equipment in the locality, some suitcase farmers were better able to carry on timely operations than those who transported most of their farm machinery back and forth.[28] It appears that most suitcase farmers did much or all of their nonresident farming themselves rather than hiring it done.

27. Letter from Kathlyn Forster, October 23, 1969.
28. Interview with T. Bruce Stinson, Tribune, November 16, 1968.

The most readily available quantitative measures of the results of suit-case and local wheat farming are the productivity indexes compiled for all the farms in a given area in connection with the conservation reserve program and the estimated average wheat yields used in recent government wheat programs. There is some evidence that productivity rates used for the conservation reserve program were converted rather directly into estimated wheat yields. For example, in one community the following conversions were common: productivity 80 = 16.5 bushels; 95 = 19.6; 105 = 21.6; 110 = 21.6 or 22.7.[29]

The estimated yields for wheat farms determined by county ASCS committees are probably meaningful measures of performance. Estimated yields are important since they help to determine payments to farmers for compliance with the government wheat program. Any dissatisfied farmer is entitled to an upward revision in his estimated yields if he produces evidence that higher yields were obtained. In fact, a comparison of the estimated yields of 1964 with those of 1968 for individual farmers showed instances of upward revisions for both local and suitcase farmers.

The dryland wheat farms of local farmers carried somewhat higher estimated wheat yields than those of suitcase farmers, although both groups usually showed a fairly wide range within a single community. For example, in the westernmost community of Kiowa County, Colorado, the estimated yields for 1964 (made in advance and based on previous performance) ranged from sixteen to more than twenty-two bushels for each group, but twenty-eight local farms were credited with more than twenty-two bushels, while only six suitcase farms produced that amount. Sixty-eight local and fifty suitcase farms had yields of sixteen or seventeen bushels. In 1968, after the estimates had been lowered, the unweighted average estimated yields were 16.55 bushels for local farmers and 15.29 for suitcase farmers, a difference of a little over 8 percent in favor of local farmers. In one community in eastern Colorado, the highest yield recorded constituted the mode of estimates for local farmers, but no suitcase farm was credited with that estimate.

Average estimated yields for 1968 for local and suitcase farmers were calculated for a number of localities. In those cases where the coverage was complete the results were as follows: community number 2, Bent County, Colorado, local 15.10 bushels and suitcase 12.66 bushels; Kit Carson, Cheyenne County, Colorado, 18.00 and 16.87; Haswell-Arlington, Kiowa County, Colorado, 16.55 and 15.29; "A" community, Hamilton County, Kansas, 22.46 and 21.79; and Stanton County, Kansas, 26.78 and 21.54.

29. The productivity figures were entered on the ASCS wheat lists for 1962. The estimated yields for 1964 were shown on the "156" cards.

Elsewhere, a complete coverage for suitcase farmers, with estimated yields recorded for the same number of matching local farmers for 1967 showed the following averages for local and for suitcase farmers: Lane County, Kansas, local 27.30 and suitcase 25.15; Logan County, Kansas, 27.05 and 27.73; and Sherman County, Kansas, 30.45 and 27.81.[30] With one exception the results are consistent. In all areas but one, Logan County, Kansas, local farmers were credited with higher estimated average yields than nonresidents. In a few instances, the advantage held by local farmers seems to have been due partly to the irrigation of some wheat, but the local ASCS committees were convinced that local farmers obtained somewhat better results from dryland farming than did suitcase farmers. However, the differences were small in most areas.

Although, as noted, the law provides a safeguard against the arbitrary fixing of wheat yields, giving some assurance that estimated yields approximate actual yields, these records fail to show how good or poor the wheat crop of any particular farmer was in a given year. Such records are not available from the ASCS. Performance records of acreages in wheat and the various feed grains planted and left for harvest kept for a number of years in the 1960s by county ASCS offices in eastern Colorado constitute the closest approach to this type of information.[31]

The performance records permit a comparison of both the acreages of major crops planted by local and suitcase farmers and the acreages intended for harvest up to a short time before the actual harvest. Of course, a sudden late catastrophe, such as a hailstorm, might reduce the actual number of harvested acres below the figures reported, but since wheat and feed grains are not ordinarily abandoned unless the expected yield is too low to pay the costs of harvesting and hauling, a rough measure of crop failure and financial loss is provided. Individual judgments of whether a given field is worth harvesting may vary, depending on whether the farmer owns his combines and, if so, whether they must be transported some distance. Since both the wheat and feed-grain programs of the federal government have the equivalent of built-in free crop insurance, crop yields not worth harvesting may not indicate quite as large a financial loss to the participating farmers as one might think.

A test was made of the performance records of a large number of farmers in and near the core area of suitcase farming in eastern Colorado. The aim was to compare all qualifying suitcase farms with an equal num-

30. Estimated yields from "156" cards for 1967 and 1968.
31. Performance records, cards for individual farms, identified as "578" cards. Those for Colorado, 1964-67, were examined in county ASCS offices.

ber of local farms within a given community. The procedure for each community studied was to record the acreages planted and left for harvest in wheat and each of the feed grains for all the suitcase farms which contained no conservation reserve land, and for an equal number of matching locally operated farms also without conservation reserve land. The method guards against subjective bias in the gathering of data for non-suitcase farms without necessitating complete coverage of that group. The coverage was greatest for 1964 and 1965, which were years of major drought and of high wheat abandonment. These years were of special concern because of interest in learning how the results of local and suitcase farmers compared during the years of high stress. The use of data from 1964 to 1967 for three of the five communities of Cheyenne County and the adjacent Karval community of Lincoln County, a somewhat interrupted east-to-west cross section, permitted meaningful year-by-year comparisons as well as the determination of four-year averages.

The communities for which the 1964 records were canvassed were the northeastern and north-central of Baca County, the most easterly of Kiowa, the most eastern and two middle communities of Cheyenne County, the most southeastern of Lincoln County, and the first, second, fifth, and seventh of the seven communities of Kit Carson County arranged from east to west. In all, the essential records of 119 suitcase and 120 local farms were noted. Table 34a summarizes the results. The most striking findings are that both groups of farmers emphasized wheat to a high degree over feed grains and that a low percentage of wheat was left for harvest. The suitcase farms averaged higher than locally owned farms in acreages sown and acreages left for harvest, and somewhat higher in percentage of the wheat acreage left for harvest. The local farms were credited with somewhat more barley and grain sorghum and higher percentages of crops left for harvest. The small acreages of both barley and grain sorghum planted reflect that few farmers of either group planted these feed grains and that only a few individuals sowed large acreages. Grain sorghum was less often abandoned than wheat or barley.

For 1965 the inquiry was shifted to the remaining four communities of Kiowa County from the communities in Baca and Kit Carson counties. Table 34b shows that local farmers kept somewhat higher percentages of their wheat and grain sorghums for harvest than did absentee farmers. Failure of wheat was very high for both groups, while that of grain sorghum was low. No barley was left for harvest.[32]

---

32. Differences in the disposition of wheat acreage planted in excess of allotments by the two groups does not seem to have been a significant variable. In one of

The 1966 and 1967 records are for the three communities in Cheyenne County and one in Lincoln County. Abandonment in 1966 was very low, with the apparent abandonment of wheat by suitcase and local farmers being nearly equal. In 1967 local farmers had a clear-cut advantage in the percentage of the wheat acreage left for harvest. Tables 34c and 34d summarize the results for 1966 and 1967.

Averages for the four years 1964-67 for these four communities are shown in table 34e. The local farmers had a small edge over the suitcase farmers in the percentage of wheat left for harvest, a greater advantage in grain sorghums, and a still greater advantage in barley, although the acre- age was very small.

As might have been anticipated, the figures show little abandonment by either group in a year of low abandonment, as in the combined Cheyenne County-Karval community area in 1966. Somewhat surprisingly, however, suitcase farmers did not fare markedly worse than local farmers in the worst years 1964 and 1965. The percentage of their wheat abandoned early in 1964, in fact, was smaller than for local farmers.

The overall results, combining all the data, as presented in table 35f, show an advantage of about 5 percentage points to the local farmers in the wheat left for harvest, a smaller advantage in grain sorghum, and a larger advantage for the small amount of barley sown. But 43.2 percent is 111+ percent of 38.3 percent. Thus, local farmers left over 11 percent more of their wheat for harvest than suitcase farmers. Eleven percent approaches the preferential 15 percent on estimated yields said by one ASCS county office manager to have been given the average local farmer. The advantages enjoyed by the average local farmer in productivity and estimated yields, as pointed out earlier, were generally less than 11 percent.

Conclusion

This examination of suitcase farming in eastern Colorado and western Kansas in the 1960s has shown a notable persistence of spatial patterns of suitcase farming. The turnover in suitcase farmers was large, the number of suitcase farmers had shrunk, and areas of concentration had been reduced.

---

the communities, a count shows that allotments were exceeded on 25 of the 121 local farms and on 2 of the 33 suitcase farms. However, excess acres were left for harvest on 16 of the local and the 2 suitcase farms. The excess was destroyed by the farmer in only six cases and by natural causes on the other 3 farms. No wheat was left for harvest on 17 local and 9 suitcase farms. Some grain sorghum was sown on 11 of the 17 local and 6 of the 9 suitcase farms.

South-central Kansas and other established bases continued to be the primary sources of nonresidents.

Judging from official records, the differences between the farms and farming of suitcase and of local farmers were generally moderate or small but may have been significant. Except for their greater use of the conservation reserve, the nonresidents continued more than residents to emphasize wheat.

CHAPTER TEN

Blowland and the Absentee

Introduction

Indictments of absentee land owners and suitcase farmers for creating or aggravating Dust Bowl conditions are numerous and often emphatic.[1] Since in many cases the nonresident operator was also the owner, it is not surprising that both the nonresident owner and operator should be blamed, but the suitcase farmer was the prime target. Some lines of doggerel by Sagebrush Slim probably expressed the prevailing mood in Baca County, Colorado, and elsewhere in the Dust Bowl in the late 1930s:

. . . .

> And the timid suitcase farmer
> Left by car and train and truck;

1. Anderson, "Soil Murder," p. 88; Bell, *Culture of a Contemporary Rural Society,* p. 35; L. C. Gray, "Federal Purchase and Administration of Submarginal Land in the Great Plains," *Journal of Farm Economics* 21 (February 1939), 130; "The Report of the Eleventh Conference of the Regional Advisory Committee on Land Use Practices in the Southern Great Plains Area," April 19-20, 1937, mimeographed, p. 6. Reports of County Agents, Colorado: Bent, 1950, 1953; Cheyenne, 1954; Kiowa, 1935, 1949; Kit Carson, 1935, 1936, 1937. Reports of County Agents, Kansas: Gray, 1932; Greeley, 1935, 1936, 1937, 1953; Haskell, 1934. E. D. G. Roberts, "Land Utilization Program in the Southern Great Plains," *Science,* n.s. 88, no. 2283 (September 30, 1938): 292; Carl C. Taylor, "The Wheat Area," in *Rural Life in the United States,* ed. Carl C. Taylor (New York: A. A. Knopf, 1949), p. 395; Thornthwaite, *The Great Plains,* p. 249.

> But the loyal hearted native
> Damned the wind and dust—and stuck.
>
>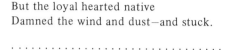
>
> When the man that wrecked the country
> With the wheat he raised so well,
> Has his innings with the devil
> In the lowest pits of hell—
>
> May the little imps of Satan
> Make a burning wind arise
> That will smother him with ashes
> And blow cinders in his eyes.[2]

However, it is apparent that farmers other than nonresidents failed to control dust blowing from their fields. A farmer who held out against dust, crop failure, and depression through much of the Dust Bowl era, admitted, apparently referring to the spring of 1933, "There were only five of us in Meade County who listed [worked the land with a lister] our land. . . . The remaining few who still had funds that might have been applied to the work, simply did not feel like making the effort to check their land from blowing. They felt that losing a crop was tough enough, without battling the wind."[3] The official report for 1935 for the Akron station, on the northwestern margin of the Dust Bowl, contained the statement that "there was ample time from February 21 to March 15 for correcting some of the worst blow spots developed by the first general storm of February 21. However, no field work was attempted" in the surrounding countryside.[4] From Baca County, Colorado, in the heart of the Dust Bowl, the county newspaper acknowledged in late winter of 1936 that 75 percent of the cultivated land was blowing.[5]

There seems to be a dearth of objective, quantitative, comparative studies that might be used to confirm or refute the charge of poor stewardship of the land leveled at nonresidents.[6] Apparently, the Kansas Agricultural Extension Service was concerned with nonresident farming as a cause

2. *Democrat Herald*, May 25, 1939.
3. Lawrence Svobida, *An Empire of Dust* (Caldwell, Idaho: Caxton Printers, 1940), p. 43.
4. Akron (Colorado) 1935, "Dryland Field Report," 1935.
5. *Democrat Herald*, February 20, 1936.
6. An exception is Morris Evans, "Nonresident Ownership—Evil or Scapegoat?" *Land Policy Review* 1, no. 2 (July-August 1938): 15-20. Evans was identified as being in charge of land-economics investigations for the Bureau of Agricultural Economics in the southern Great Plains. His concluding sentence is that "to the more

of blowing dust. The Wichita County agent noted in his annual report for 1935 that a survey of land blowing on resident and nonresident farms had been sent to Manhattan on March 30 of that year. There was no statement of the conclusions of the survey, and neither the county agent nor Kansas State University officials could produce the report. The county agent testified later, however, that local farmers were much more effective than nonresidents in controlling wind erosion, largely because they were at the scene.[7]

In a 1948 report, the superintendent of the Greeley County, Kansas, experiment station identified the southwestern portion of the county as the chief source of dust:

> On November 5, 1948, there was an extremely high wind that started much soil to blowing in the southwest part of the county. Most of this was on fairly new land that had been continuously cropped from two to five years. Of course, when it started to blow it caused the summer fallow with good wheat at that time to blow also.[8]

Although the report contained no specific references to nonresident ownership or operation, it may be taken as an indictment of absentee owners and suitcase farmers. This was the area that had an inadequate water supply, few resident farmers, and very little resident ownership just before the big plow-up, led by absentees (described in chapter 7); and suitcase farming must have been especially concentrated there in the late 1940s. A report produced in 1941 by the County Agricultural Program committee described a so-called area of nearly 132-square miles in the southwestern part of the county in which only eight families lived. Residents were

---

than the casual observer there is frequently little to choose between resident and nonresident ownership." However, he held nonresident farmers more largely to blame for soil damage in a survey made in two counties in southwestern Kansas: "On 275 farms in Haskell and Seward Counties, Kansas, erosion conditions indicate that the nonresident operator was more careless of his land than the resident operator—whether owner or tenant" (p. 17). He also cited a survey made in the Dust Bowl by the Resettlement Administration that showed the following percentages of the land operated as being substantially damaged: rented land of nonresident part owners, 58 percent; nonresident owner-operators 56 percent; resident owner-operators, 53 percent; rented land of resident part owners, 52 percent; land owned by nonresident part owners, 47 percent; and land owned by resident part owners, 37 percent. In each category, the land of the nonresident operator had the worst of it by 3 to 10 percentage points (p. 18).

7. Letter from Roy E. Gwin, Leoti, Kansas, August 24, 1965.

8. "Annual Report," 1948, Tribune Branch of Kansas State Agricultural Experiment Station, Manhattan.

credited with the ownership of only 5,200 of the 84,480 acres. The committee concluded that "this area is not suitable for the permanent establishment of homes due to the fact [that], in general, water cannot be obtained."[9] The area consisted largely of those communities of Greeley County having the highest percentage of out-of-county wheat farmers in 1933.

Measures of Wind Erosion on Absentee- and Locally Owned Lands

Land Use and Wind Erosion, 1936

The detailed maps of land use and erosion condition in the Joel Report, of 1936,[10] provide the means for comparing abandonment and wind-erosion damage on some of the farms in southwestern Kansas, assuming that the status of operators and owners had not changed between 1933 and 1936. Since nonresident operation remained at a high level through 1936 and the rate of absentee ownership was high at both times, a considerable measure of stability in ownership and tenure can be assumed. In fact, ownership records in the Hamilton County courthouse showed that 18.5 of the 24 tracts of 640 acres included in wheat farms in 1933 were still owned in 1936 by the same individuals or within the same families as in 1933, suggesting a fairly stable ownership. Unfortunately, the lists of AAA applications of 1933 published in the local newspapers did not give locations within sections (square-mile units) within the southwestern portion of Kansas mapped in the Joel Report. Thus, the only farm tracts whose locations could be determined readily were those occupying entire sections. In all, the records of abandonment and wind erosion of 70 tracts of 640 acres each were examined. Twenty-four tracts each were located in Hamilton and Stevens counties and twenty-two in Grant County.

The results obtained do not support the claim that a large percentage of cropland was abandoned early by absentee operators. Instead, the local farmers abandoned or let a larger percentage of their cropland lie idle, especially on land they were renting from absentee owners. The following percentages of idle or abandoned land, out of total farm land, were determined for twenty-four sections in Hamilton County: out-of-county owner-

9. United Agricultural Program Progress Report, Greeley County (prepared by J. E. Taylor, chairman, Greeley County Planning Committee, after meeting, March 1941), MS, Greeley County agent's office, Tribune, Kansas.

10. Joel, *Soil Conservation Reconnaissance Survey,* maps 3 (Baca County, Colorado), 4 (Hamilton County), 5 (Stanton County), 6 (Grant County), and 9 (Stevens County).

ship and operation, 12 percent; in-county ownership and operation, 7 percent; out-of-county ownership with in-county operation, 22 percent; overall, out-of-county operation, 12 percent; in-county operation, 18 percent. The breakdown for Stevens County showed the following: out-of-county ownership and operation, 7 percent; in-county ownership and operation, 9 percent; out-of-county ownership with in-county operation, 14 percent; overall, out-of-county operation, 6 percent; in-county operation, 13 percent. In Grant County, the percentages of idle or abandoned land for both out-of-county and in-county operators ran only 4 percent.

An index of wind-erosion damage based on the classification used in the Joel Report was devised.[11] The weighting of categories of damage was as follows: slight removal by wind (less than 25 percent of topsoil lost) = 0; moderate removal by wind (25-75 percent of topsoil lost) = 1; severe removal by wind (more than 75 percent of topsoil or part of upper subsoil lost) = 2; very severe removal by wind (wind erosion into the lower subsoil) = 3. All categories of wind damage, from none to severe, were shown on the idle land and cropland, but no land was found to have been very severely damaged in the localities in Kansas. The procedure was to multiply the number of acres by 0, 1, or 2, then divide the result by the total number of acres. If none of the land had been damaged, or if it had suffered only slight damage, the index number was zero; one-half of the land at slight removal and one-half at severe removal resulted in an average index number of 1, the same as if all the land had experienced moderate removal.

Wind-erosion index numbers for the sections in Hamilton and Stevens counties combined were as follows: out-of-county owners and operators, idle land 1.0, cultivated land .73; in-county owners and operators, idle land .5, cultivated land .39; out-of-county owners and in-county operators, idle land 1.23, cultivated land .68; overall, out-of-county operators, idle land 1.0, cultivated land .76; and, overall, in-county operators, idle land 1.16, cultivated land .52. The worst showing was made by in-county farmers operating land owned by out-of-county owners. The best record was made by in-county farmers operating locally owned land. The overall differences can hardly be called large. Strangely, the idle land on farms operated by residents in Stevens County but owned out-of-county had by far the worst record for wind removal (1.51), but cultivated land (at .48) fared quite well. Most of the accumulated dust reported was on the idle

11. Robert Eikelberry, Lincoln, Nebraska, soil correlator, Mid-West Region, Soil Conservation Service, who had served on field parties responsible for the mapping for the Joel Report, approved the index, advising that the lower categories of damage should be ignored. His advice was followed.

land owned out-of-county but operated locally in Stevens County. Accumulated dust on idle land was, of course, a prime target for future blowing. In neighboring, only slightly damaged Grant County, the calculations showed a standoff in wind-erosion indexes: out-of-county operators, idle land, 1.0, cultivated land, .12; in-county operators, idle land, 1.0, cultivated land, .12.

The net result of testing for the degree of abandonment and wind damage as shown on the detailed maps of the Joel Report is to indicate that absentee-owned land farmed by local farmers (by acres, the chief category) fared worst on both scores, although locally owned and operated land showed somewhat less damage than other land. To this point, it appears that absentees were more victims than villains—that the worst damage had occurred on their land where farmed by local farmers.

A map of fields worked by the county in 1936 in an effort to reduce dust blowing for Stanton County, Kansas,[12] provides identification of what were assumed to be the worst sources of uncontrolled blowing. The owners of blow lands were determined in three townships which contained considerable concentrations of land that was worked by the county, and their names were checked against the lists of inhabitants returned by the assessor in 1936. The three townships included one (T27S, R24W) in the less level northwestern portion of the county, one (T30S, R41W) in a south-central location, and one (T30S, R39W) in the southeast, both southern portions being on the extensive, nearly level plain. The owners of early 1936 were identified as from out of the county, county residents, those having the same family names as residents, and the county itself (which owned land shortly to be sold at tax sale). In this case, no attempt was made to determine the residence of operators.

On the detailed map of the Joel Report, measurement of land-use units of the land indicated as worked by the county showed 2,340 acres of idle or abandoned land, 10,655 cultivated acres, and 1,085 acres of grass. It is assumed that the grassland was mapped inadvertently. Thus, somewhat more than one-sixth of the total land area of the three townships had been treated by the county. Of that land, absentees owned 1,940 idle and 6,904 cultivated acres, while others owned 400 idle and 2,716 cultivated acres. Absentee ownership was thus indicated for 83 percent of the idle and 72 percent of the cultivated land worked by the county. These figures are considerably higher than the 57.9 percent which represents the portion of

12. The map was included in the 1936 annual report of the agricultural county agent for Stanton County. It was the only such map found among the reports of county agents at Kansas State University, Manhattan.

land in the county owned by nonresidents.[13] The nonresidents' share of the land worked by the county may actually have run even higher, since the remainder, except 640 acres of cultivated land, belonged either to the county or to individuals having the same family names as residents. Thus, it is possible that all but 640 acres of the land worked by the county belonged or had recently belonged to out-of-county owners. Nonresidents thus were judged guilty of owning most of the sources of dust that the county commissioners tried to control. Since the percentage of the land farmed by out-of-county operators (about 20 percent of the wheat acreage, as shown in table 15) was less than one-half as great as the percentage of land owned by nonresidents, operators who did not combat blowing dust must have included resident as well as suitcase farmers.

The wind-removal indexes for land worked by the county were as follows: absentee-owned land, idle, 1.09, and cultivated, .58; other ownerships, idle, .94, cultivated, .31. In addition to the greater degree of removal of soil on the absentee-owned land, more than one-half of the idle land owned by absentees had accumulations of dust over six inches thick.

For comparison, the land not worked by the county in the three townships, nearly five-sixths of the total area, included 7,304 acres of idle land, 39,880 acres of cultivated land, and 7,141 acres of grass.[14] A smaller portion of cropland in this category had been idled and the wind-removal index of the idle land, 0.89, was somewhat lower than for the land, whether owned by absentees or others worked by the county. However, the wind-removal index of .78 for cultivated land was higher than for either ownership class of land worked by the county, and more than one-half of the idle land not worked by the county was mapped as having dust accumulations more than six inches deep. For idle and cultivated land combined owned by absentees and worked by the county the wind-erosion index was .70 and for the land not worked by the county the index was .74. One can conclude that, as of 1936, although much land owned by non-residents was blowing without receiving attention from the owners, presumably impartial, scientific observers failed to find that it had been damaged more than other land in the same area. Of course, 1936 was fairly early in the Dust Bowl period and later surveys in Dust Bowl localities showed greater damage than is shown in the Joel Report.[15]

By 1936, as pointed out in chapter 5, especially hard-hit Baca County,

13. "Land Use Survey of the Southern Great Plains Region," p. 74.
14. The overall error in measurement is slightly more than 1 percent, combining all acreages in the three townships.
15. John J. Underwood, *Physical Land Conditions in the Western and South-*

in the center of the Dust Bowl, had experienced widespread abandonment of land and emigration of farmers. Nonresidents constituted less than 10 percent of the farmers. A comparison of land use and of wind damage on land owned by absentees and others in the county was made possible by the mapping of landownership, land use, and soil erosion in 1936.[16]

Northeastern Baca County, the best wheat country in the county, presents a good area in which to test the significance of absentee ownership of land as a factor in wind erosion. Two thirty-six-square-mile areas were selected for the test in the predominantly hard (nonsandy) level land of the northeastern quarter of the county. One square (six miles to the side) was chosen to include mainly absentee-owned land; the other was selected so as to include mainly land owned by residents. The legal description of the first area, of which 66 percent was owned by absentees, was the west half of T28S, R43W, and the east half of T28S, R44W; the second, only 26 percent absentee-owned, consisted of the west half of T30S, R43W, and the east half of T30S, R44W.

In the area of heavy nonresident ownership, 25 percent of the land owned by absentees was idle, 28 percent was cultivated, and 47 percent was in grass. Of the remaining land, 13 percent was idle, 41 percent cultivated, and 46 percent in grass. For absentee-owned land, the wind-removal indexes averaged 1.58 on idle land, 1.26 on cultivated land, and .75 on grassland. The figures for the other land were 1.21 for idle land, 1.72 for cultivated land, and .35 for grassland. In addition, dust had accumulated to a depth of more than six inches on nearly all of the idle land, both that owned by nonresidents and that owned by others.

In the second study area, land use for the two classes of ownership was as follows: 21 percent of the land owned by nonresidents was idle, 24 percent was cultivated and 55 percent was in grass; for other land, 19 percent was idle, 25 percent was cultivated, and 56 percent was in grass.

Wind-erosion indexes in this area were as follows: absentee, idle, 1.29; cultivated, 1.26; grassland, .64; other, idle, 1.07; cultivated, 1.02; grassland, .35. Here absentee-owned land fared consistently worse than other land, but the differences might be described as moderate except for those

eastern Baca County Soil Conservation Districts, Colorado, Physical Land Survey, no. 30, USDA Soil Conservation Service (Washington, D.C.: GPO, 1944); *Physical Land Conditions in Kit Carson County, Colorado,* Physical Land Survey, no. 43, USDA Soil Conservation Service (Washington, D.C.: GPO, 1949). The former was surveyed in 1937-39, the latter in 1939-40.

16. "Land Use in Baca County, Colorado," p. 12, maps landownership. The types of landownership recognized were resident, nonresident, state, corporation, county tax sale, and federal. Only resident and nonresident ownerships exceeded 5 percent.

in the grassland category. Dust accumulations in excess of six inches were mapped only on the idle lands—on about one-third of that owned by absentees and on a somewhat larger part of other idle land. Combining the results for the seventy-two-square miles in northeastern Baca County, land-use figures were as follows: absentee-owned land, idle, 23.4 percent, cultivated, 26.6 percent, and grassland, 50.0 percent; land owned by others, idle, 17.5 percent, cultivated, 30.2 percent, and grassland, 52.3 percent. The following wind-erosion indexes were determined: absentee-owned land, idle, 1.50, cultivated, 1.27, and grassland, .45, idle and cultivated combined, 1.38, all uses combined, .91; land owned by others, idle, 1.12, cultivated, 1.41, grassland, .37, idle and cultivated combined, 1.30, and all uses combined, .82.

Apparently a large amount of land was left idle as a consequence of drought and related crop failure. Wind erosion and dust accumulation were probably both largely results and partly causes of the abandonment. In this case, the charge is sustained that land owned by absentees was abandoned in large amounts and became a major source of dust. Absentee-owned land, whether abandoned or used for crops or pasture, suffered more wind removal than land owned locally, except for cultivated land in the first area studied. It may be surmised in that case that local farmers worked too hard and unwisely under most discouraging conditions. Although the charge that absentee-owned land was a major contributor to Dust Bowl conditions is given limited support, land damage and blowing dust would still have been severe, assuming the ways in which the land was being used, if it had all been owned locally.[17] Of course, suitcase farmers who operated almost entirely on absentee-owned land and who were in considerable measure responsible for the plow-up, are in part—a part apparently impossible to determine—to blame for Dust Bowl conditions. The judgment in this case must be that absentee landlords and probably suitcase farmers were guilty of contributing to dust bowl conditions, but not to the degree charged. The fact that northeastern Baca County is still, or again, largely in crops should refute the conclusion of *Deserts on the March* and *The Plow That Broke the Plains* that a desert was being formed.[18]

17. Evans, "Nonresident Ownership," p. 18, gives some supporting data in his statement of 1938 "that analyses of abandoned land on purchase projects reveal a higher percentage for nonresident than resident owners," citing figures of nonresident ownership of 52 percent of the pasture and 63 percent of the abandoned cropland in Baca County. It is assumed that he was referring to land acquired by the government in the southern and western part of the county.

18. Paul B. Sears, *Deserts on the March* (Norman: University of Oklahoma Press, 1935); *The Plow That Broke the Plain,* Resettlement Admin. documentary film, 1936.

Blowland Violations

Other sources of information were used in an effort to determine the degree to which absentee ownership and suitcase farming were responsible for the blowing dust that has plagued the suitcase farming country repeatedly. These sources included the minutes, or journals, of meetings of county commissioners, as well as records of county clerks, among them files of complaints against land owners and operators, records of hearings, and assessments of costs to the county for working blowing land. In some cases, addresses were given for the individuals named; in others, the county clerk, assessor, register of deeds, or ASCS county office could provide addresses. For the early years, the names of those accused of having sources of dust and those who were assessed for having their land worked in Kansas counties were checked for residence against the assessors' lists of inhabitants. In cases in which only legal descriptions were given, it was necessary to check for names among the records of the register of deeds. In all, a large list of landowners and a smaller list of farm operators were compiled. Here, then, was a considerable body of evidence, assuming the evenhandedness of county officials and complaining citizens.

The commissioners' journal, Stanton County, Kansas, volume 3, covering the latter half of the Dust Bowl period, provides abundant data on soil drifting.[19] Under the date of April 15, 1936, an entry was made for a voucher of $4,037.20 for the soil drifting fund, apparently for the working of blow land—perhaps as mapped by the county agent in 1936—during the previous month (commonly at the rate of fifty or sixty cents per acre). For the years 1937, 1939, and 1940, an analysis of eighty-five specific charges of violations and a few records of the payment of charges levied resulted in the following breakdown of the place of residence of landowners; five were local, thirteen had local family names, five had specific suitcase addresses, and sixty others came from out of the county. At the maximum eighteen, at the minimum only five, of the eighty-five accused offenders were residents of the county. The percentage of absentees was thus much greater than the 57.9 percent of landowners who were nonresidents in 1936. The evidence strongly supports the responsibility of absentee owners for soil drifting, and is consistent with the results of the analysis of the map showing land worked by the county in 1936.

The complaints of soil drifting on file with the county clerk of Stanton County for the period 1955-68 frequently named the operators as well as the landowners, thus permitting the identification of operators as well as

19. "Commissioners' Journal," Stanton County, Kansas, vol. 3, 1927-53.

owners in most cases.[20] The number of complaints for the various groups was as follows: local owner-local operators, twenty-eight; suitcase owners-local operators, twenty-one; suitcase owners-suitcase operators, nine; owners unknown address-local operators, seven; suitcase owners-operators of unknown address, three. Complaints were charged to suitcase owners thirty-three times, local owners twenty-eight times; suitcase operators nine times, and local operators fifty-six times. Thus, suitcase owners were named only a little more often than local owners; local operators were charged more than six times as often as suitcase farmers. In view of the recent estimate of 50 percent out-of-county ownership and a 1960 figure of 11 percent suitcase operation in the county, it would appear that the record of absentee owners and operators had improved to the point that their control of soil drifting was nearly equal to that of residents.

The journal of the county commissioners of Greeley County, Kansas, volume 5, includes records for 1954, a year of major soil blowing.[21] Seven suitcase and three local owners appeared at hearings that year and thirteen assessments for the working of blowing land were made against the land of suitcase owners. The number of complaints by ownership and operation categories was: suitcase owner-local operator, five; suitcase owner-suitcase operator, three; suitcase owners other than those listed above, seventy-five; address of owner unknown, one; address of owner unknown-suitcase operator, one, local owner, five; and owner in next county, three. Summarizing, there were eighty-three suitcase ownerships, five in-county ownerships, three next county ownerships, four suitcase operators, and five in-county operators. The proportion of out-of-county ownerships involved was somewhat greater than the percentage of land owned out-of-county in 1936 (73.8 percent) or that estimated for 1970 (75 percent). Apparently, absentee owners, possibly absentee operators, were guilty of neglecting their land as charged by residents.

The Greeley County files of complaints about dust blowing for the years 1961-68 typically listed both owners and operators.[22] The breakdown of these records shows thirty-four suitcase owners-operators not identified or as having uncertain addresses, twenty-nine suitcase owners-resident operators, seventeen suitcase owners-suitcase operators, nine local owners-operators not identified, eight suitcase owners-next-county oper-

20. File of soil drifting complaints, 1955-68, county clerk, Stanton County courthouse, Johnson, Kansas.

21. "Commissioners' Journal," Greeley County, Kansas, vol. 5, 1943-1955, courthouse, Tribune.

22. File of Soil Blowing Complaints, 1961-68, county clerk's office, Tribune, Kansas.

ators, six next-county owners-no operators shown, three in-county owners-in-county operators, two next-county owners-next-county operators, two owners not identified-local operators, one local owner-suitcase operator, and one owner not identified-operator not identified. In all, eighty-eight suitcase, thirty-four in county, and ten next-county owners were identified. The percentage of out-of-county owners named thus was 74, almost the same as their share of the land. The percentage of accused suitcase operators ran somewhat higher at 29 percent than the percentage they constituted of operators in the county in 1960 (23 percent) and in 1968 (12 percent). Neither absentee ownership nor absentee operation stood out as a major hazard.

Kiowa County, Colorado, as the center of suitcase farming in the dry and dusty mid-1950s and during the varied weather since, provides another test of the degree to which suitcase owners and operators were charged with leaving blowing fields unworked. A summation of the results of an analysis of the records of the county commissioners for several years follows.[23] In 1953 warning notes were sent by the county commissioners to fifty-five suitcase and sixteen local owners. Two and a half cases of suitcase and sixteen and a half of local operation (there was one case of joint operation) were identified. The record shows that assessments were made in 1954 against twenty-one suitcase and two local owners. In 1955, assessments were reported against eleven suitcase owners, one local owner, and eight whose addresses could not be determined. Notices, including some assessments, were sent to twenty-two suitcase and five local owners in 1956. The only operators identified were four local tenants on farms of suitcase owners. Warning notices were sent in 1957 to thirteen local owners and twenty-four suitcase owners, of whom one was identified as the operator.

The complaints alleging drifting soil in Kiowa County were examined for recent years.[24] The 1958 file showed thirteen suitcase owners, of whom four were owner-operators, and two local owners. The last year (through the summer of 1968) in which more than ten complaints were filed was 1959, with nineteen against suitcase and five against local owners. The following number of complaints, by ownership and operation categories, was filed for the period 1961-November, 1968: suitcase owner, nineteen; suitcase owner-local tenant, fifteen; suitcase owner-suitcase operator, four; suitcase operator, one; local owner, two; and local oper-

23. "Commissioners' Records," Kiowa County, Colorado, vol. 7 (1953-55); vol. 8 (1956-57), courthouse, Eads.
24. File of Soil Blowing Complaints, 1957-68, county clerk's office, Eads, Colorado.

ator, one. These categories were mutually exclusive. There were thirty-nine suitcase owners, five suitcase operators, two local owners, and sixteen local operators.

To place the counts of ownership and operators in context, it should be recalled that out-of-county owners had title to 55.3 percent of the land of Kiowa County in 1936 and 62.3 percent of the cropland in 1969, and that suitcase farmers constituted 33 percent of the operators of wheat farms in 1954, 28 percent in 1961, and 26 percent in 1968. Identified suitcase landowners consistently accounted for more than 62 percent of the accused offenders. The case against suitcase operators is less clear because operators were not identified as frequently. The largest number of operators was identified in 1953, when local operators outnumbered suitcase operators sixteen and a half to two and a half, and in the period 1961-68, when local operators outnumbered suitcase operators sixteen to five. Since suitcase owners farmed substantial amounts of the land they owned, it is unlikely that they were adequately represented in the records. However, the number of complaints, by ownership and operation categories, in two years in which both owners and operators were identified was as follows: 1964, suitcase owner-suitcase operator, two; suitcase owner-local operator, two; local owner (almost certainly local operator), two; 1965, suitcase owner-local operator, eight.

Conclusions

Absentee ownership quite clearly increased the hazard of dust blowing and land damage in the Dust Bowl era, but appears to have been no more hazardous than local ownership in recent years in two of the three counties whose records were examined. There is little solid support for the charge that absentee farm operators were responsible for most of the dust storms and land damage. It appears that neither local nor suitcase farmers had a good record of stewardship of the land during the 1930s. In fact, the close-up studies in southwestern Kansas suggest that the damage was greatest on land owned by absentees but worked by local tenants.

The comparative responsibility of suitcase and local farm operators for more recent blowing of dust is difficult to assess because of the frequent failure of the records of complaints of dust blowing to identify operators. Although more local than suitcase operators were the subjects of complaints, it may be true as charged that in proportion to their numbers suitcase farmers more often failed to protect their fields from blowing. In Stanton County, where the identification of operators was fairly complete, the control of soil drifting by suitcase farmers was nearly equal that of local farmers, but it is uncertain whether Stanton County is representative of the general area.

In the three counties—Stanton, Greeley, and Kiowa—for which recent complaints of soil drifting were studied, it is said by several ASCS county office managers that most of the poorer suitcase farmers have been eliminated and that with increased mobility and improved communications, operators from a distance are now better able to protect their fields from blowing than earlier and realize the need to do so. Doubtless, the record of the absentee farmer has improved. However, the authoritative statement by an ASCS county office manager that the Baughman Land Company of Liberal, Kansas, which had been using some outside operators, went over almost completely to local tenants for its many farms in Kiowa and adjoining counties after the severe dust storms of 1954 is a strong circumstantial argument that the stewardship of local farmers was better.

CHAPTER ELEVEN

Summary, Interpretation, and Prospect

Summary

Spatial Relationships

Figure 36 summarizes some of the basic spatial aspects of suitcase farming in the central Great Plains. The map suggests the essential dynamics of absentee farming, most importantly the movement of seasonal farmers from the main source area—the long-established specialized wheat country in central Kansas—first to an early, then to a later suitcase farming frontier. Additional sources of absentee farmers are shown, especially for the second advance. The spatial patterns represented in figure 35 have proved remarkably persistent. The first and second suitcase farming frontiers together constitute a large area in which nonresidents continue to raise much wheat. The incidence of absentee operation has declined, especially at the east, but the greatest concentration remains near the western margin where it has been at least since 1954. The main source areas continue to be important and suitcase farmers still move back and forth between their home bases and the wheat country.

Decline—The General Trend

Although the spatial patterns have remained, suitcase farming has suffered a widespread decline. Although the core area of the first suitcase farming frontier is the same as in 1933 and that of the enlarged suitcase farming country is where it was in 1954, the percentage of absentees has been reduced. The point that has been made earlier about the greater persistence of local farmers under trying conditions could be supported by more available evidence. Such local factors as irrigation have brought a notable reduction in the number of nonresidents, but the general decline in the share of absentees in wheat farming suggests that they have lost their original advantages of equipment, experience, commitment to wheat, and perhaps boldness. The emphasis has shifted to staying power.

A series of graphs (figs. 37 and 38) represents trends in both the older and the newer suitcase farming country. Four counties in western Kansas and one county and two outlying communities in eastern Colorado are included. Greeley, Stanton, Wichita, and Haskell counties, in western Kansas, are similar in that all show a decline, although percentages prior to 1940 are for out-of-county rather than suitcase farmers. However, considerable evidence has been given that at that time comparatively few out-of-county farmers were from adjacent counties. Only in Greeley County is it certain that there was an early major decline in the number of suitcase farmers, followed by a later substantial increase. As noted, nonresidents in Greeley County were subjected to both a very high rate of wheat failure and unusually stringent local control programs at the time of especially rapid reduction in suitcase farming. As pointed out earlier, the figure for 1954 is an estimate based on incomplete records. In Stanton County, there seems to be no way of determining whether the decline in the late 1930s reported in the county newspaper was large, or even if it took place. The long-term decline shown is based on only three dates. In Wichita County, adjoining Greeley County on the east, very little reduction took place from 1933 to 1940, perhaps none at all, considering that the earlier figure was for out-of-county farmers and the later was for suitcase farmers. In Haskell County, the big decline took place after irrigation became important. The increase in irrigation also contributed to the decline in suitcase farming in Stanton and Wichita counties. Greeley County had and still has little irrigation. The trend away from nonresident agriculture must be due to factors of a more general character than the increase in irrigation.

Kiowa County, Colorado, having the largest number of suitcase farmers in the whole region (at least since 1954), has experienced a persistent slow decline in the number of nonresidents (fig. 38). The decrease apparently began shortly before 1954 and may have been sharper at that time than since, but there does not seem to be any way to measure suitcase farming before 1954. In the case of Anton community, in the southwestern part of Washington County, the reduction in the number of nonresidents was interrupted by a peak in 1962, probably largely as a result of the attractions of the conservation reserve of the Soil Bank, both for absentee owners and for former local residents who moved away but continued to be at least nominal operators of farms. Community 2 of Bent County, a dryland area in the southern portion of that county, also showed a peak in suitcase farming during the period of maximum participation in the Conservation Reserve. No position for 1957 is graphed because the number of suitcase farmers in this community in 1957, as shown in the ASCS records, was so much smaller than in 1954 and in 1961 as to raise questions about the completeness of the list. If the list was complete, both the downturn from 1954 to 1957 and the upturn from 1957 to 1961 were sharper than in Anton, in Washington County. Subsequently, the decline in the number and percentage of suitcase farmers in southern Bent County has been pronounced, probably due to the combination of very poor crops and the expiration of conservation reserve contracts.

The Character of Suitcase Farmers and Farming

It is difficult to generalize about suitcase farmers and their farming. The chief way in which suitcase farmers differ from other farmers is in living at a distance from their farms. Even in this respect, the distinction may be blurred by absentees becoming local and residents becoming suitcase farmers by moving away. At the outset, suitcase farmers were commonly innovators. Having the advantages of equipment and experience, they introduced large-scale wheat farming and appear to have obtained higher yields than local farmers. Later the residents caught up in equipment and experience and for some time have obtained equal or better yields, while often doing a somewhat better job of controlling soil drifting. The differences in both respects appear to be small, however. On the average, absentees continue to emphasize wheat but only slightly more than residents. In the 1960s, nonresidents made more use of the conservation reserve, in effect leasing their cropland to the government, especially on the dry, western margin of the suitcase farming area. Although they more often owned the land they worked, suitcase farmers have been far less persistent than residents. For part-time farmers from a distance, dropping out does not mean giving up their homes and long-term associations.

It is likely that the costs of wheat farming are a little less for suitcase farmers than for others. Somewhat fewer operations in summer fallowing, some economy in the use of equipment in several localities, and capital costs and taxes that are somewhat lower because of the lack of farm buildings are examples of presumed economies in suitcase farming. On the other side of the ledger are the somewhat lower returns credited to the absentees. Insofar as income depends on the guaranteed payments for compliance with government programs, a small difference has been verified. Probably no one is in position to say with authority how the economic returns to the two groups compare.

It is certain that a few good years can offset several poor ones, although claims made by suitcase farmers that they can keep going on one good crop in three—or even in four—may raise questions about their method of cost accounting. It is necessary to assume that most of the successful nonresidents who have been farming for thirty years or longer took the long view and had the necessary reserves of capital or credit to continue despite several consecutive years of loss and that their cost accounting has been realistic.

Interpretation

The thesis has been developed that technological advances in mechanization and mobility permitted two great but somewhat speculative advances of wheat farming from nearby areas of earlier development. The nonresidents have shown less staying power than local farmers, who joined and have been replacing them. Nevertheless, there has been a remarkable persistence of suitcase farming where it was established as much as half a century ago. Suitcase farming has become a regional characteristic.

That suitcase farming in the central Great Plains developed and continues in a region characterized by drought, Dust Bowl conditions, wheat failure, cycles of boom and bust, absentee ownership of land, and recency of settlement raises basic questions about the nature of the associations involved. In effect, the question is, What is the ecology of suitcase farming? If answers can be determined, some understanding of the fundamental character of the region should result. Here the major concern will be to try to determine how suitcase farming fits into the picture.

The following hypothesis of cause and effect relationships is advanced. Drought and other natural hazards have caused heavy crop losses, periodically albeit irregularly discouraging crop farming. Low land prices have resulted. At such times or as recovery from poor years began, outsiders who were less hard-hit than residents have bought land in the hope of speculative gains. Beginning in the early 1920s, many of the absentee owners went into wheat farming or rented land to other nonresident farmers when rainy years, high prices, or technological advances were viewed as opportunities to plow up the grassland. With the plow-up, the stage was set for another retreat. The cycle was complete—bust to boom to bust.[1]

Variations in yearly and seasonal precipitation are common in the Great Plains. In the western Plains, the upward and downward departures from the critically low averages result in the climate from year to year ranging from subhumid through semiarid to desert.[2] The comparatively humid years are usually good ones for the crop farmer and stockman. The dry periods, especially if continued several years, often damage pasture, reduce water supplies, destroy crops, and bring on dust storms.

The good and the poor years of the wheat farmers, and presumably of stockmen and other farmers, in the suitcase farming country are commonly bunched. The abandonment of wheat, elsewhere shown to be an important index of risk,[3] will serve to show how frequently good and poor wheat years come in series in the heart of the Dust Bowl. An abandonment rate of 50 percent or more of the wheat acreage sown may be considered high and less than 30 percent low in this region of high risk. Each of the four western Kansas counties of Greeley, Hamilton, Stanton, and Morton experienced wheat abandonment of 50 percent or more in either six or seven of the nine years from 1932 to 1940. But in seven, eight, or nine

1. Several essential aspects of the ecology of suitcase farming as presented here seem to have been anticipated by a senior agricultural economist of the Bureau of Agricultural Economics in the Dust Bowl period (Charles R. Loomis, "The Human Ecology of the Great Plains Area," *Proceedings of the Oklahoma Academy of Science* 17 [1937]: 14-28). Although he took only incidental notice of suitcase farmers, the following passage calls attention to variable precipitation, uncertain returns, speculation, and suitcase farming in the Dust Bowl: "Reports have shown that in the most drought-stricken, dust-blown counties a few rains have been sufficient to bring back many migrants ready to try for another crop. Their very life has been one of gambling against nature and the market and the odds have been extreme. Since the advent of tractors, combines, disk plows and power drills, the whole work on a large tract—both harvesting and planting—can be accomplished in six weeks. Under these conditions suitcase farming flourishes. There is no longer any necessity for living on the land. This generation of Great Plains farmers probably never had its parallel in previous history. Increase in the number of establishments retailing these farm machines in some of this area and in bordering areas of distress is sufficient evidence to prove that the drought has only temporarily arrested the extension and perpetuation of the 'dust bowl' " (p. 25). He also refers to overexpansion following a series of rainy years and high grain prices. Although increases in tenancy were recognized, no emphasis was given to absentee ownership.

2. C. W. Thornthwaite, *Atlas of Climatic Types in the United States, 1900-1939,* USDA Soil Conser. Service, Misc. Publ., no. 421 (Washington, D.C.: GPO, 1941).

3. Leslie Hewes and Arthur C. Schmieding, "Risk in the Central Great Plains: Geographical Patterns of Wheat Failure in Nebraska, 1931-1952," *Geographical Review* 42 (1956): 375-87; Leslie Hewes, "Causes of Wheat Failure in the Dry Farming Region, Central Great Plains, 1939-1957," *Economic Geography* 41 (1965): 313-30.

years of the ten-year period from 1941 to 1950, these counties had failures of less than 30 percent. Together they had ten cases of failures of 50 percent or more in a possible twenty from 1954-57. No county had abandonment as great as 30 percent in the five-year period 1958 to 1962. Fifteen cases of abandonment of 50 percent or more in a possible twenty-four occurred from 1963-68. The record of abandonment in the three Colorado counties of Baca, Kiowa, and Cheyenne showed even greater bunching of high and low rates of abandonment. (Prowers County, located between Baca and Kiowa, was omitted as unrepresentative because of its considerable amount of irrigation.) In nine years, from 1932 to 1940, there were either seven or eight years of abandonment of 50 percent or more in each of the three counties. In the ten years from 1941 to 1950, each county had either seven or eight years of abandonment of less than 30 percent. All three counties had wheat abandonment of 50 percent or more in all four years from 1954 to 1957; but from 1958 to 1962, only one county experienced abandonment as great as 30 percent in any year. Twelve cases of abandonment of 50 percent or more of a possible eighteen in the years 1963 through 1968 followed.

Ninety-seven cases of high abandonment—50 percent or more—of a total of 110 in the thirty-seven years of 1932 to 1968 occurred in the seven counties in the three periods of high abandonment. There were 104 cases of an abandonment rate of 30 percent or less for winter wheat. Ninety-two of the 104 cases of low failure were bunched in the two periods indicated. At the extremes, there were 26 instances of abandonment of 90 to 100 percent and 60 of 10 percent or less. Abandonment in the middle range of 30 to 50 percent took place less than one-sixth of the time—42 out of a possible 259 times. The average weighted abandonment rate for Baca County was 50.8 percent; the other six counties had averages ranging from 31.8 to 49.0 percent. The average was seldom realized; instead it was compounded mainly from considerably higher and lower rates.[4]

---

4. Abandonment of wheat acreages was determined by subtracting harvested acres from planted acres. The data in most cases were those given by the state agricultural statisticians. Data for Kansas are in the *Biennial Reports of the Kansas State Board of Agriculture,* vols. 28-38 (Topeka: Kansas Printing Plant, 1932-53), and *Farm Facts,* Kansas Crop and Livestock Information, Report of the Kansas State Board of Agriculture, vols. 39-51 (Topeka, 1956-68). Data for Colorado are from *Colorado Agricultural Statistics* Colorado Dept. of Agr., with the USDA (Denver, 1932-68); Reed, "Winter Wheat, Total Acres Planted"; and the USDA Field Crops Statistics Branch, Agr. Estimates, Agr. Marketing Service, Washington, D.C. unpublished planted acreages of wheat for Colorado, 1931-38. For Colorado, the acreages given by Reed have been used where statistics do not agree.

As would be expected from the great variation in the acreage of wheat abandoned from year to year, highly variable yields have been the rule in the Kansas and Colorado portion of the Dust Bowl. The coefficients of variation in wheat yields in terms of seeded acres in the region for the years 1926-48 were the highest in the United States. The count by states of counties in the nation showing variability as great as 80 percent was Kansas, thirteen; Colorado, six; Texas, two; South Dakota, two; and Oklahoma, one, giving a Great Plains and national total of twenty-four. The 19 counties in Kansas and Colorado formed a single block, which was continuous with the county in the Oklahoma Panhandle and two in the Texas Panhandle, as shown in figure 38.[5] Variability has been especially great along the Colorado-Kansas border. Suitcase farming has been concentrated in the area of extreme fluctuation in wheat yields.

It appears that the closest attempt to determine the profitability of wheat farming over a large part of the Dust Bowl portion of the central Great Plains is a study of the counties of eastern Colorado lying between the Arkansas and South Platte rivers for the years 1929-56. Assuming a fixed price for wheat, the study showed that operating (cash) costs of raising wheat were covered least often where the variability in yields was greatest. During the twenty-eight years covered, for the ten counties included in the study it was calculated that operating expenses were not met in as many as twelve years for some counties. In numbers of years that they did not meet expenses, the counties are in descending order: Cheyenne, twelve; Kiowa, twelve; Kit Carson, eleven; Lincoln, eleven; Washington, seven; Elbert, seven; Phillips, five; Yuma, four; El Paso, three; and Douglas, none.[6] The percentage of variability in wheat yields for these counties, in the same order, was 92, 89, 86, 84, 82, 57, 69, 72, 43, and 39. As noted, the percentage of suitcase farmers has been high in Kiowa and Cheyenne counties, moderate in Kit Carson, Lincoln, and Washington, and low in the others.

5. E. Lloyd Barber, "Variability of Wheat Yields by Counties in the United States," mimeographed, USDA Bur. of Agr. Econ., September, 1951. The percentages by county were Greeley, 93 percent; Wallace, 93; Baca, 92; and Cheyenne, Colorado, 92; Kiowa, Colorado, 89; Hamilton, 89; Stanton, 87; and Morton, 87.

6. Harry G. Sitler, *Economic Possibilities of Seeding Wheatland to Grass in Eastern Colorado,* ARS 43-64, USDA Agr. Res. Serv. (Washington, D.C., February 1958), p. 24. A study by E. Lloyd Barber, *Meeting Weather Risks in Kansas Wheat Farming,* Agr. Econ. Report, no. 44 (Kansas Exper. Sta., September 1950), pp. 8-12, including the averages of five Kansas counties on the northern and eastern margins of the Dust Bowl, serves mainly to show that risk and variability in yields and income decreased rapidly away from the Dust Bowl and that long-term profits increased as the Dust Bowl was left behind.

Calculations of the gross value of wheat harvested per seeded acre for the period 1929-55 have been published for two Dust Bowl counties of Colorado. Since actual state average prices were used, the figures should be especially meaningful. In Kiowa County, the value of wheat during the six-year period 1932-37 ran from 9¢ to 80¢ per acre per year, and in Baca in the six-year period 1933-38, from 2¢ to 64¢ per acre. By contrast, in Kiowa County during the eight years between 1942 and 1949, the average values ranged from $12.41 to $44.60; the figures for Baca County during the same period ran between $14.32 and $48.17.[7] The earlier period was one of heavy losses, the later one of large profits—perhaps large enough to pay for the land in one year.

The alternation of good and poor crops, particularly the occurrence of several good crops together after a series of poor crop years, would seem to be made to order for a speculative view both of land and of wheat farming. Also, the sequence had the effect of encouraging periodic expansions and contractions of crop farming on the frontier.

Since "land acquires its value from a series of anticipated net returns that will become available over a period of years,"[8] it follows that the big periodic variations in the returns from wheat farming should lead to big variations in land values. The major distress of the thirties and the great recovery of the forties resulted in a large decline, quickly followed by a rapid advance in land values in the Dust Bowl area of the central Great Plains. According to the United States census, the national decline of farm real estate values per acre between 1930 and 1940 was about 35 percent (from $48.52 to $31.71) and the increase from 1940 to 1950 was about 105 percent (from $31.17 to $64.96), but the changes in much of western Kansas and eastern Colorado were much greater.

Figure 40 emphasizes the counties in western Kansas and eastern Colorado in which the decline in land value in the 1930s and the increase in the 1940s were especially great. In large part these counties were then or shortly became a part of the suitcase farming country. Variations farther east in Kansas were smaller than shown in figure 40. Only four counties to the east lost as much in land value as 50 percent from 1930 to 1940; and

7. Charles W. Nanheim, Warren R. Bailey, and Della E. Merrick, *Wheat Production: Trends, Problems, Programs, Opportunities for Adjustment,* USDA Agr. Res. Serv., Infor. Bul., no. 179 (Washington, D.C.: GPO, March 1958), p. 82. McPherson County, in east-central Kansas, had only two years of less than five dollars and only eight below ten dollars in the twenty-six years.
8. John E. Reynolds and John F. Timmons, "Factors Affecting Farmland Values in the United States," *Research Bulletin, no. 566,* Agriculture and Home Economics Experiment Station (Ames: Iowa State University, February 1969), p. 333.

no county in Kansas east of those shown had an increase even as great as threefold from 1940 to 1950.

The low cost of land in the Kansas-Colorado portion of the Dust Bowl as the Depression ended presented an opportunity to acquire land as an investment or for speculation and permitted the government to add to its holdings. It may be taken for granted that relatively few buyers were residents of the drought-stricken area. The federal government was one of the large purchasers: 240,000 acres were under option on December 15, 1939, for the land utilization project in Baca and Las Animas counties (mainly in Baca) at an average purchase price for land and improvements of $3.25 per acre.[9] This was not an exceptionally low price, average valuations of less than $4.00 per acre in 1940 being reported for Kiowa, Cheyenne, and Lincoln counties. There had been similar buying opportunities earlier.

Much of the subsequent increase in land value in the newer part of the suitcase farming country resulted from the conversion of grassland to wheat under favorable conditions of moisture and price. Suitcase farmers led the way—on absentee-owned land. Absentee ownership was a speculative reaction to wide fluctuations in land values; it was also a condition favoring sharp upturns in value.

The hypothesis stated consists of the following sequence of conditions: climatic variability → variations in crop yields → changes in land values→ absentee ownership of land → suitcase farming. If the hypothesis is essentially correct, the geographical distribution of these phenomena should be similar. Such is the case. The northern one-half of the Dust Bowl (fig. 1) provides the setting of unstable semiarid climate. Within this area, wheat yields are the most variable to be found in the United States (fig. 39). Here land values have fluctuated widely (fig. 40), with absentee landownership (figs. 14 and 29) having much the same pattern. The incidence of suitcase farming has been and is presently high (figs. 7, 17, 26, and 33) in the same area, within the two suitcase farming frontiers (fig. 35). Several of the maps are so similar that they could be interchanged with only the discriminating student being aware of the substitution.

The several maps of related phenomena, although generally similar, contain several important discrepancies. The fact that suitcase farming is no longer important in much of the earlier suitcase farming frontier, as noted, may be understood as resulting from the nonresident farmers' loss of their initial advantages and the spread of irrigation into some areas. The

9. M. G. Fuller, "The Land Purchase and Development Program in Baca Co., Colorado," *Soil Conservation* 5 (1940): 215.

three counties that stand out as having much lower percentages of suitcase farmers than the violent fluctuations in wheat yields and land values would forecast are Morton, the most southwestern county of Kansas, Baca in the extreme southeastern corner of Colorado (both in the heart of the Dust Bowl), and Kit Carson, Colorado (located at the northern margin of the Dust Bowl). All three of these counties have peripheral positions relative to suitcase farming. Baca and Morton counties, at least in part, and Kit Carson County, to some degree, were included in the first great surge of nonresident farming. In all three a considerable corps of experienced wheat farmers weathered the great Depression and drought. They were in a position to compete with the newcomers when wheat farming became profitable again in the 1940s. In addition, much of Morton County and part of Baca County are so sandy as to have little attraction for wheat farmers. By the 1940s, government rescue operations, the land utilization projects, protected much of Morton and Baca counties against plow-up and the conversion of these projects to the Cimarron and Comanche National Grasslands continue to prevent a plow-up. Recently, irrigation has become important in parts of Baca and Kit Carson counties.

A realistic appraisal of the mechanism hypothesized is that it has worked, but somewhat unevenly because of other important circumstances.

In respect to a question posed in the preface, suitcase farming does seem to be more a result of high risk than a cause of wheat failure, although absentees have contributed to soil drifting and abandonment. The contribution of these part-time nonresident wheat farmers to the disintegration of rural communities and their towns deserves study. This type of damage will exceed that done to land and crops.

The suitcase farming in an area of especially high risk may provide a partial answer to the basic problem posed by Isaiah Bowman when he wrote, "How far one can go in reaping the bounty of the land and yet escape the penalties of recurrent drought is the perennial question of the dry-farming and farming-ranching country of the West." It appears that the suitcase farmer has gone too far but is unusually well qualified to move in rapidly to garner the rewards of a series of good years and to cut back or pull out when times get bad. Of course, continued climatic fluctuations are to be expected.[10]

10. John R. Borchert, in "The Dust Bowl in the 1970's," *Annals of the Association of American Geographers* 61, no. 1 (March 1971): 1-22, anticipates a return of drought to the Great Plains. He points to a number of drought-related problems of a social-economic character that would have to be met.

The Future of Suitcase Farming

The rate of high turnover of absentees and the considerable reduction in their number show unmistakably that the poor results of wheat farming have discouraged many suitcase farmers. The conservation reserve agreements that many accepted rather than trying to raise crops permitted former wheat farmers, especially those from a distance, to remain as nominal farmers for a decade. Participation in this land-retirement program signified that farmers and owners either had exhausted their financial resources or considered their crop prospects unpromising. Many nonresidents have elected to get out of wheat farming altogether.

Kiowa County, Colorado, the leading suitcase farming county, illustrates the plight of many absentee owner-operators who were only nominal farmers for a decade, collecting conservation reserve payments. Now they do not have those payments and many have no income from crop farming. As of September 1, 1970, about 100,000 acres of 188,000 planted to grass under the conservation reserve program were still in grass. Most of the acreage was in the dry, western half of the county, much of it on former wheat farms that were owned and operated by nonresidents.[11] Since many nonresident former wheat farmers are loath to plow up the grass, it must be concluded that they do not wish to go back into wheat farming. Apparently many hope that further government land-retirement programs will allow them to get out of wheat farming without the necessity of taking heavy losses.

A further reduction in the wheat farming by absentees may be expected, assuming that corporations, presently of little importance in the farming of wheat in the region,[12] will not take over the enterprise. Even so, several conditions favor the continuation of suitcase farming, including, for example, the large amount of land owned by absentees and the tradition of wheat farming by nonresidents, as well as the moving away of local farmers prepared to continue as absentee wheat farmers.

There is still the possibility that short-term speculative gains due to high grain prices or a series of good crop years might be a lure for the reoccupation of ground lost by nonresident wheat farmers. But the general lack of level loess-covered land beyond the limits reached in the second great surge of absentee farmers in 1954 seems to rule out a third great advance of suitcase farming. The dependence of wheat farmers on government pro-

11. Letter from Kathlyn Forster, February 23, 1971.
12. George W. Coffman, "Corporations with Farming Operations," Agr. Econ. Report, no. 209, USDA Economic Research Service (June 1971), pp. 5, 40.

grams is another factor that would have a retarding effect. It is true, however, that the second suitcase farming frontier came as a surprise, after even greater dependence on government assistance than now.

Appendix A: Figures

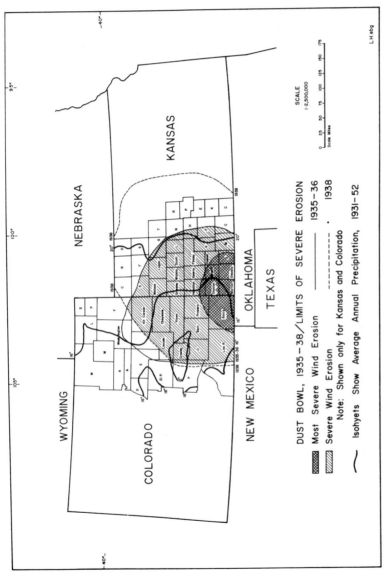

Fig. 1. Setting of suitcase farming frontier. The shaded area, consisting of land which suffered severe wind erosion in both 1935-36 and 1938, is here defined as the northern part of the Dust Bowl. The first suitcase farming frontier was formed mainly between the 20- and 16-inch rainfall lines. The second was mainly from the 16-inch line to the 12-inch isohyet. In both cases, most suitcase farming activity occurred in the Dust Bowl area. Map based on information from *Report of Soil Conservation Service: Problems of the Southern Great Plains* (April 1954), Appendix, p. ii, and United States Weather Bureau.

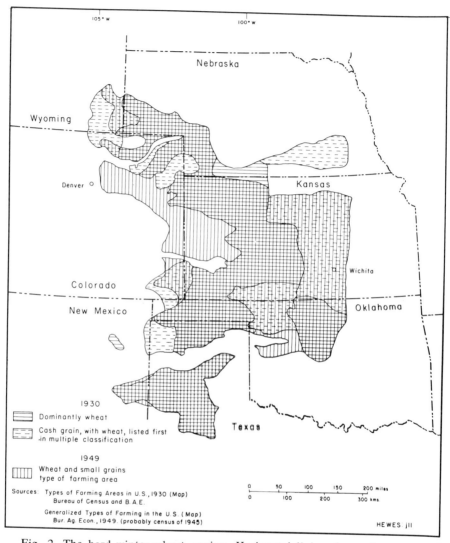

Fig. 2. The hard winter wheat region. Horizontal lining shows the extent of region in 1930. Vertical lining by itself represents the addition between 1930 and 1945. Probably the area mapped for 1930 extends too far west along the Colorado-Wyoming border and not far enough west farther south, from near Denver due east into Kansas. Hence, the extension of wheat farming between 1930 and 1945 is exaggerated somewhat.

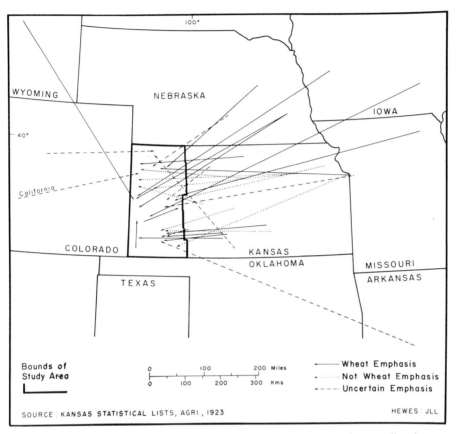

Fig. 3. Suitcase farmers in western Kansas, 1923. Although not all suitcase farmers were covered, the pattern shown was probably fairly representative and indicative of things to come.

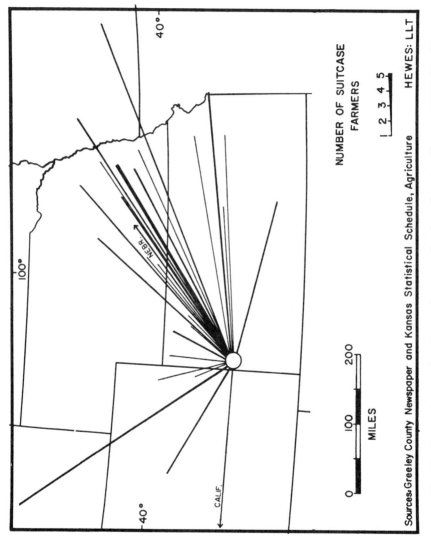

NUMBER OF SUITCASE
FARMERS

1 2 3 4 5

HEWES: LLT

Sources: Greeley County Newspaper and Kansas Statistical Schedule, Agriculture

Fig. 4. Home bases of suitcase farmers, Greeley County, Kansas, 1920-32. The dependence on southeastern Nebraska as a source of nonresidents was both unusual and fairly temporary.

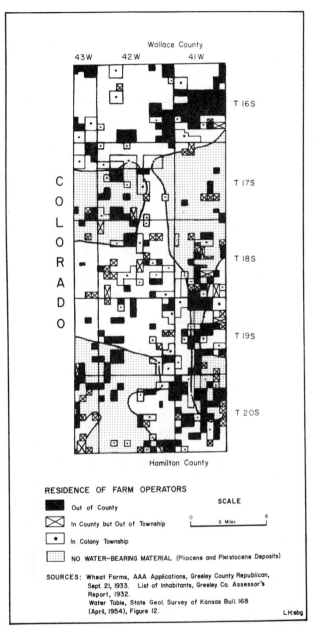

Fig. 5. Wheat farms in Colony Township, Greeley
County, Kansas, 1933. The prominence of out-of-county
farmers is evident, especially in parts of the township
without a water table. Colony Township was essentially at
the western limit of important wheat farming.

193

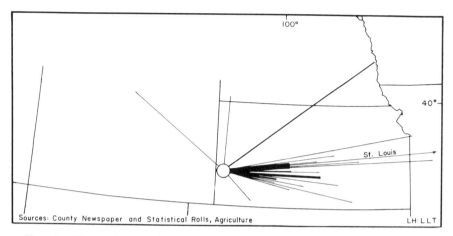

Fig. 6a. Home bases of suitcase farmers, Hamilton County, 1924-32. The dependence on older wheat country to the east was marked.

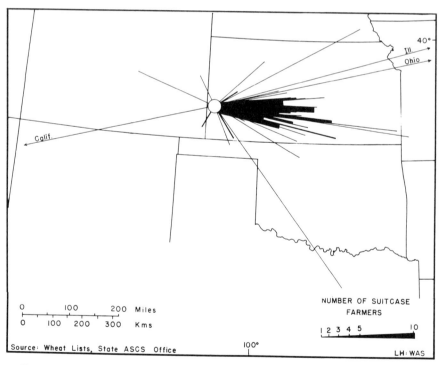

Fig. 6b. Home bases of suitcase farmers, Hamilton County, 1960. The modern pattern is much like that in the early years.

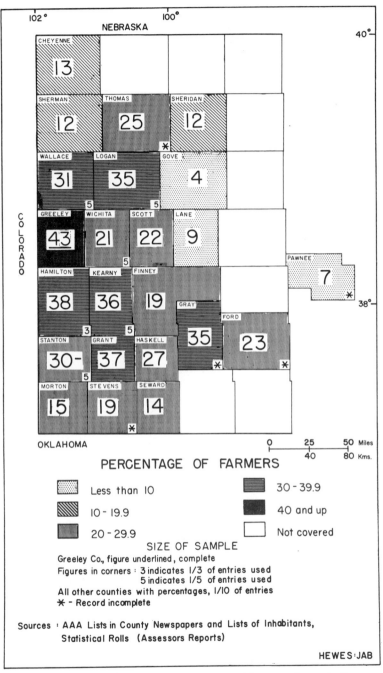

Fig. 7. Percentage of wheat farms operated by out-of-county farmers in western Kansas, 1933.

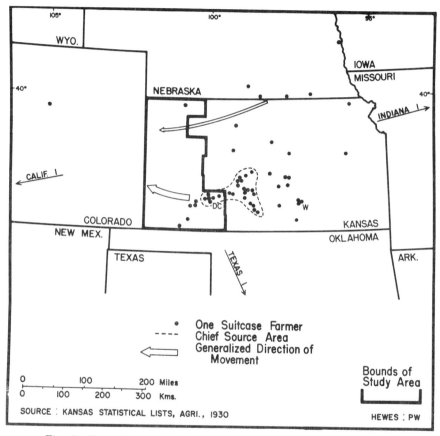

Fig. 8. Home bases of suitcase farmers in western Kansas, 1930. Although the listing in the assessors' reports was very incomplete, it appears to have been representative.

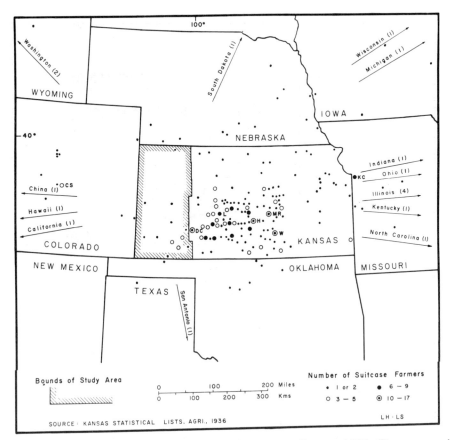

Fig. 9. Post offices of suitcase farmers in western Kansas, 1936. The assessors' reports included an exceptionally large number of nonresident farmers. The major source area from Dodge City to Wichita and Moundridge is shown plainly.

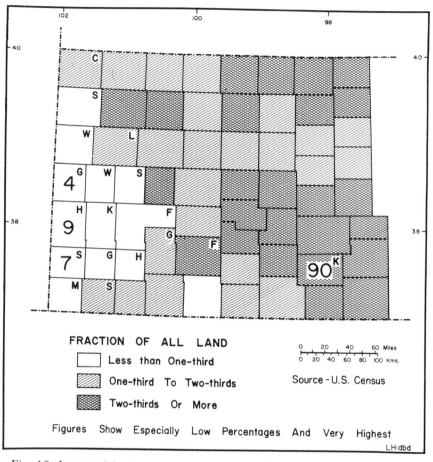

Fig. 10. Improved land in central and western Kansas, 1920. The openness of most of the counties soon to be included in the suitcase farming frontier is apparent. In the case of Logan County, marked by the letter "L," the amount of improved land may have been exaggerated.

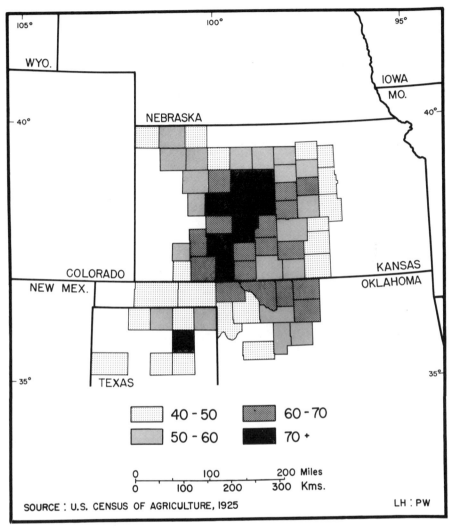

Fig. 11. Large percentages of cropland in wheat, 1924. The area a short distance to the east of the developing suitcase farming frontier was the chief region in or near the central Great Plains in which the emphasis was on wheat. Nowhere else in the general area was the wheat gradient so steep.

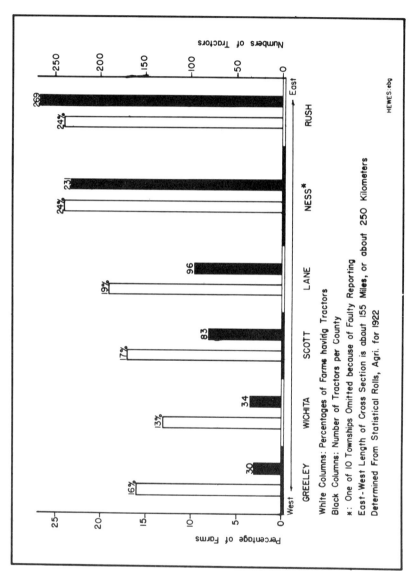

Fig. 12. Tractors in western Kansas, 1922. Tractors were of greater absolute and relative importance immediately to the east than in the suitcase farming frontier in the first year for which the assessors' reports provide coverage.

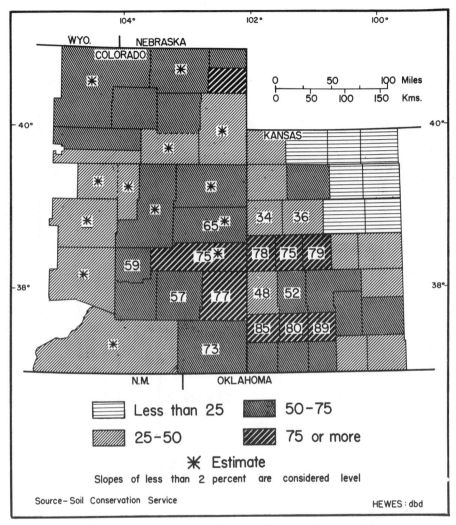

Fig. 13. Percentage of level land. Most of the land was level in the country into which suitcase farmers went in numbers to create both the first and second suitcase farming frontiers, especially on the interfluves to both the north and south of the Arkansas River. Hamilton County, cut by the valley, and Logan and Wallace counties, all important in early absentee farming, were the least level.

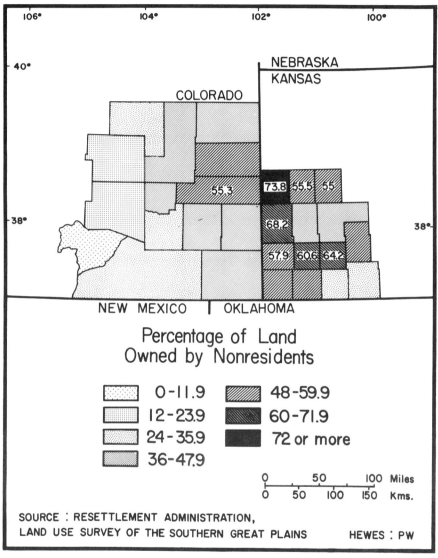

Fig. 14. Land owned by nonresidents, 1936. The correspondence with the percentage of out-of-county farmers in 1933 in western Kansas, as shown in fig. 7, is close. A large amount of land owned by absentees westward in Colorado aided the later expansion of suitcase farming there. Percentages are given for the counties in which as much as 55 percent of the land was owned by nonresidents. No information was available for the parts of Kansas and Colorado not designated.

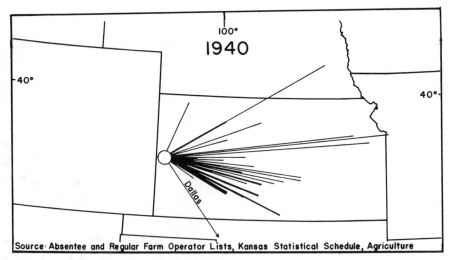

Fig. 15a. Home bases of suitcase farmers, Greeley County, Kansas, 1940. The assessors' list is judged to have been complete or nearly so. Most suitcase farmers from southeastern Nebraska had dropped out.

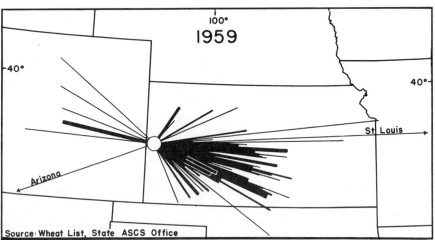

Fig. 15b. Home bases of suitcase farmers, Greeley County, Kansas, 1959. Except for a big increase in numbers, probably occurring largely in the 1940s, and the greater importance of bases in front of the Rockies, 1959 was much like 1940.

203

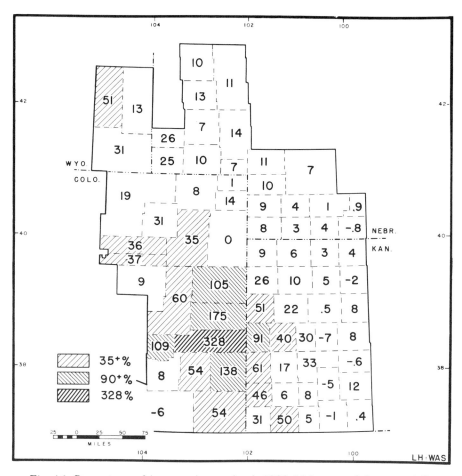

Fig. 16. Percentage of increase in cropland, 1939-54 in part of the central Great Plains. Generally, the large increases in suitcase farming were in the counties that experienced the greatest expansion in cropland.

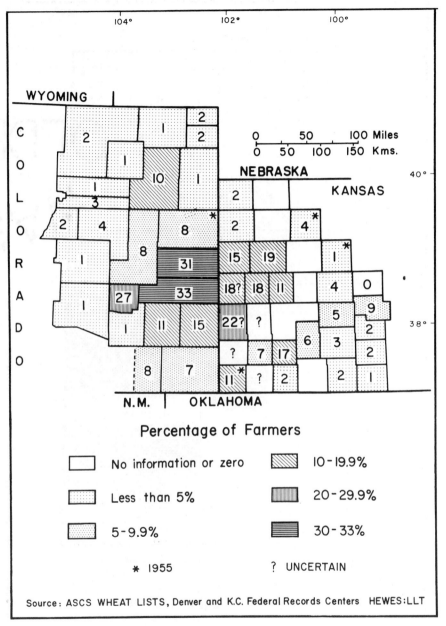

Fig. 17. Suitcase farmers in western Kansas and eastern Colorado, 1954.

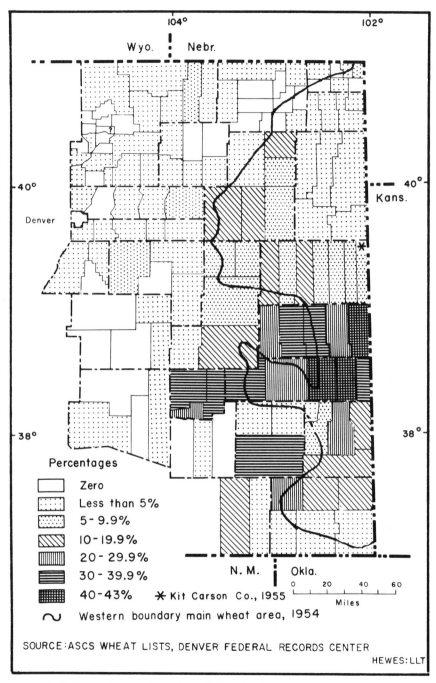

Fig. 18. Suitcase farmers in eastern Colorado, by communities, 1954. This map emphasizes, in detail, the pattern shown on fig. 17. The heavy line, based on fig. 20, emphasizes the border, or marginal, location of suitcase farmers.

206

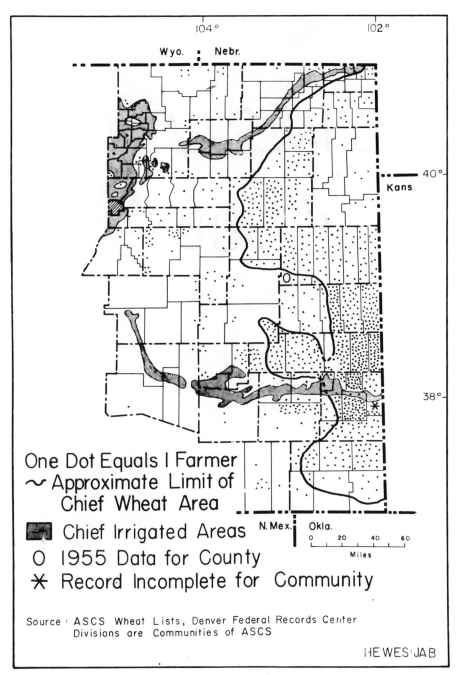

One Dot Equals I Farmer
~ Approximate Limit of
   Chief Wheat Area

▨ Chief Irrigated Areas

O 1955 Data for County

✳ Record Incomplete for Community

Source : ASCS Wheat Lists, Denver Federal Records Center
    Divisions are Communities of ASCS

HEWES:JAB

Fig. 19. Suitcase farmers in eastern Colorado, 1954. Most suitcase farms were located within the chief wheat area.

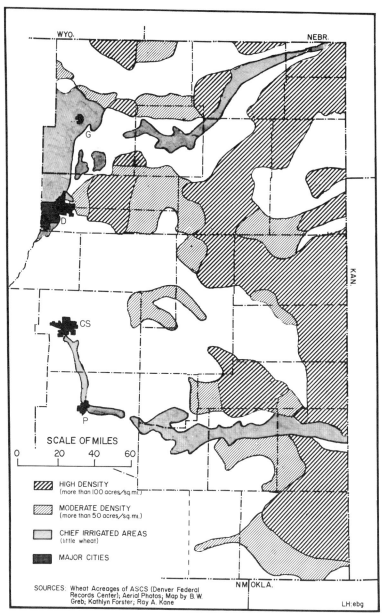

Fig. 20. Chief wheat areas of eastern Colorado, about 1954. Generally, the loess-covered plains were important for wheat. Rougher land, heavy clay, and loose sand were commonly avoided. In Weld County, in the northwest, the wheat areas, with one exception, lay outside the general limits of the national grassland.

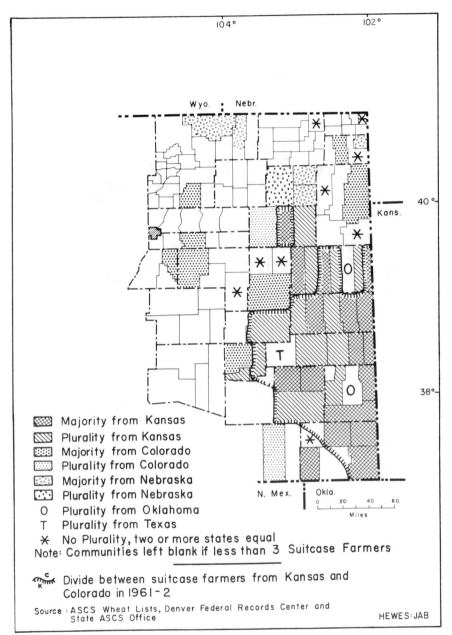

Fig. 21. Sources of suitcase farmers in eastern Colorado, by communities, 1954. A line has been added to show the divide between Kansas and Colorado suitcase farmers in 1961-62.

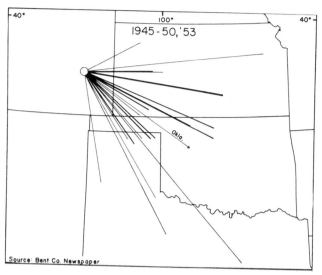

Fig. 22a. Home bases of suitcase farmers, Haswell area, Kiowa County, 1945-50, 1953. Most of the early suitcase farmers came from older wheat country to the southeast and east.

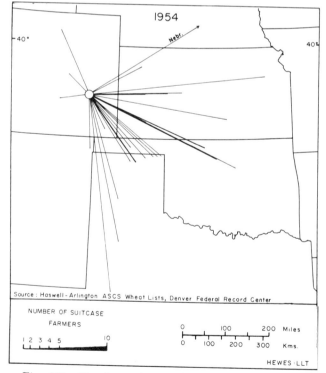

Fig. 22b. The home bases of suitcase farmers in the Haswell-Arlington community in 1954 were similar to those at the beginning of suitcase farming.

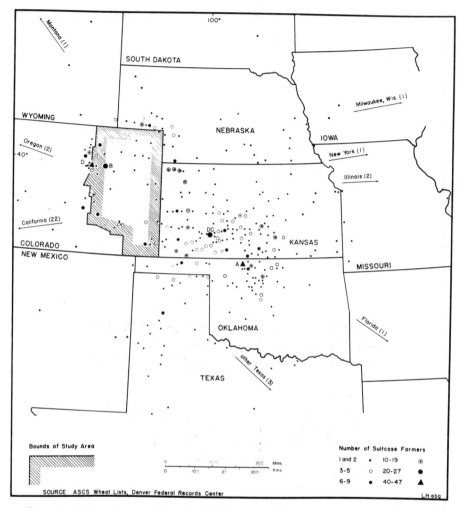

Fig. 23. Home bases of suitcase farmers in eastern Colorado, 1954. Although Denver and Alva, Oklahoma, were the two most common addresses, the old source area of suitcase farmers in south-central Kansas still provided the largest numbers of suitcase farmers in the second suitcase farming frontier. Altogether, approximately one thousand absentees operating in eastern Colorado are represented.

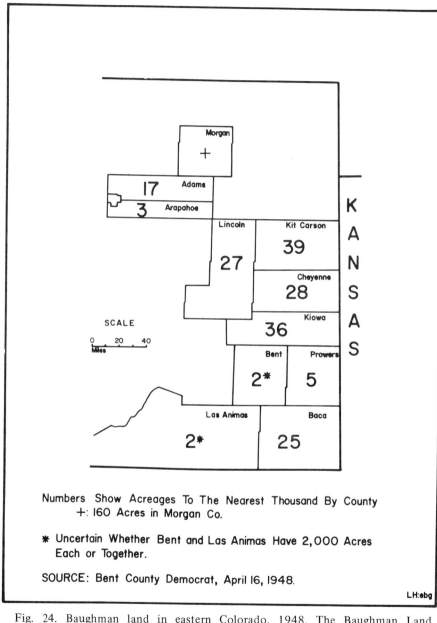

Numbers Show Acreages To The Nearest Thousand By County
+: 160 Acres in Morgan Co.

* Uncertain Whether Bent and Las Animas Have 2,000 Acres
Each or Together.

SOURCE: Bent County Democrat, April 16, 1948.

LH:ebg

Fig. 24. Baughman land in eastern Colorado, 1948. The Baughman Land Company of Liberal, Kansas, was probably the biggest landlord of wheat farmers on the new suitcase farming frontier.

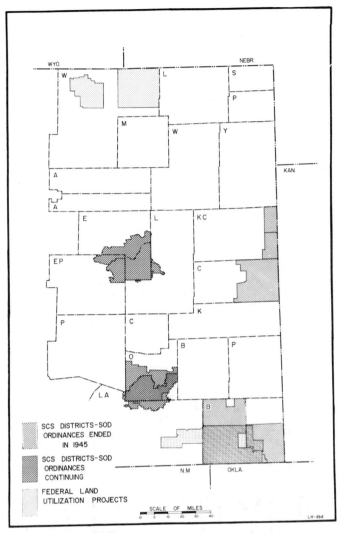

Fig. 25. Soil conservation districts having sod ordinances and land utilization projects in eastern Colorado. Only the districts with sod-breaking ordinances lasting after 1945 and the land utilization projects, now national grasslands, were important barriers to the spread of suitcase farming. Their deterrent effects are not clear; perhaps the distance from major sources of nonresidents and poor land and dryness were more important drawbacks of such areas.

Sources: Voelker, *Land Use Ordinances*; Underwood, *Physical Land Conditions*; SCS, *Progress in Soil Conservation Work Completed in Soil Conservation Districts* (map) (December 21, 1951); SCS, "Horse-Rush Creek Soil Conservation District" (manuscript map); Forest Service, *Commanche National Grassland, San Isobel National Forest, Colorado* (Washington, D.C.: GPO, n.d.); *Colorful Colorado* (map) (State Department of Highways, Colorado, 1966).

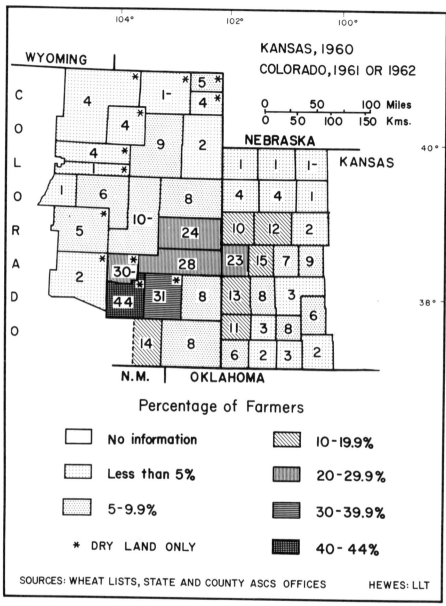

Fig. 26. Suitcase farmers in western Kansas and eastern Colorado, about 1960. While Kiowa and Cheyenne counties in Colorado and Greeley County in Kansas led in numbers of nonresident farmers; counting dryland farmers only, the three adjacent counties of Otero, Bent, and Crowley, beyond the limit of important wheat farming, had higher percentages. Some large declines had occurred in Kansas. The counts were complete in eastern Colorado except for the restriction to dryland farms in several counties. In Kansas, the count was complete in Greeley and Hamilton counties; the other percentages are based on extensive samples.

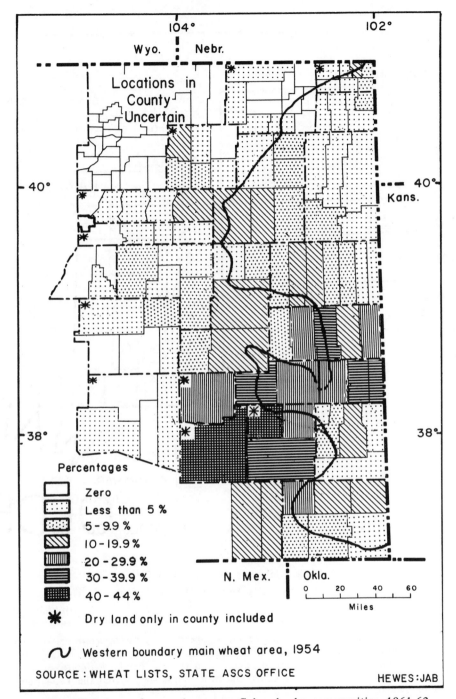

Fig. 27. Suitcase farmers in eastern Colorado, by communities, 1961-62. Kiowa County ran highest except to the southwest, where there were few dryland wheat farmers.

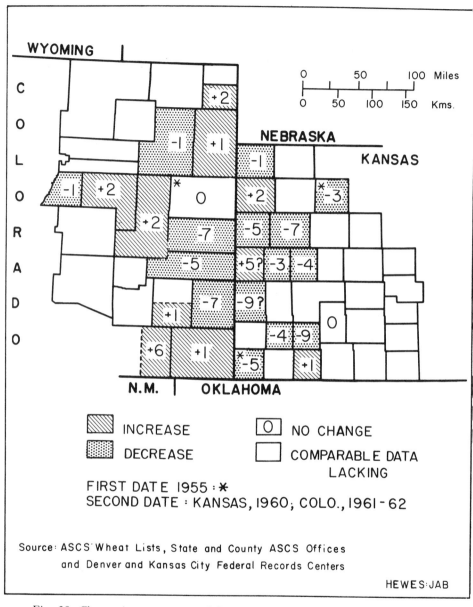

Fig. 28. Change in percentage of farms operated by suitcase farmers, 1954 to about 1960. Decline was general in the heart of the suitcase farming country, where only Greeley County, Kansas, showed an increase over the estimate of 1954. Several marginal areas showed gains. Question marks signify that the 1954 figures were estimates.

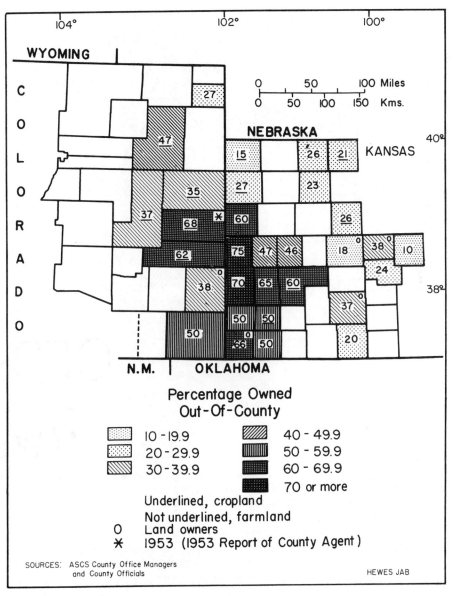

Fig. 29. Land ownership by nonresidents, 1969. Absentee ownership was high in the suitcase farming country, although local farmers rather than suitcase farmers were using most of the absentee-owned land, especially in the older suitcase farming frontier.

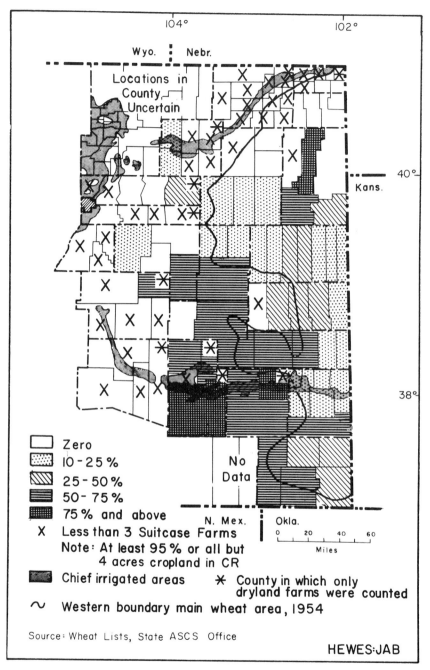

Fig. 30. Percentage of suitcase farms in conservation reserve in eastern Colorado, 1961-62. The concentration at or beyond the margin of important wheat farming in the southern half of the map is evident. The high percentages in two communities near the Kansas-Nebraska boundary are based on small numbers of farms.

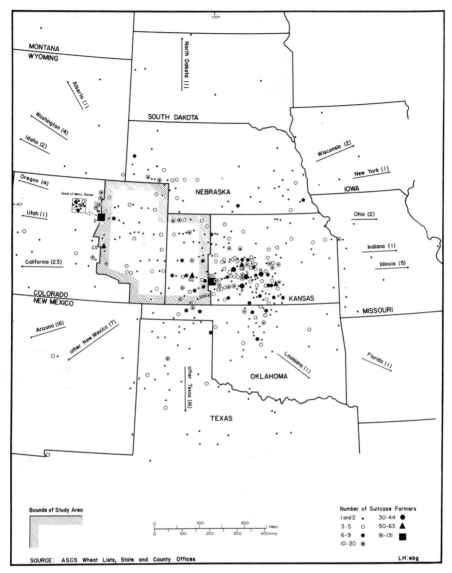

Fig. 31. Home bases of operators of suitcase farms in eastern Colorado and western Kansas, about 1960. South-central Kansas continued as the leading source. The great majority of suitcase farmers were from wheat-farming country; a largely urban belt along the Colorado Front Range was the chief exception. Note the inset of metropolitan Denver area. The figure 93 refers to Denver proper.

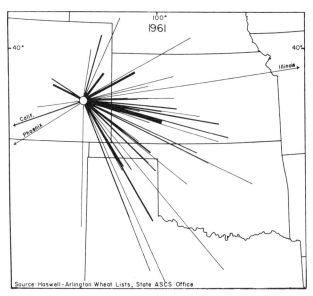

Fig. 32a. Home bases of suitcase farmers, Haswell-Arlington community, 1961. Most suitcase farmers were based within 300 miles of the land they farmed to the southeast, east, and northeast.

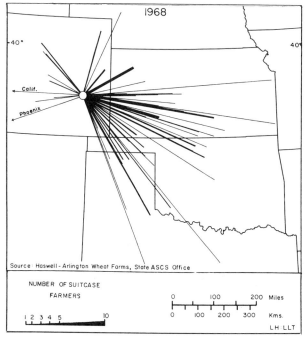

Fig. 32b. Home bases of suitcase farmers, Haswell-Arlington community, 1968.

220

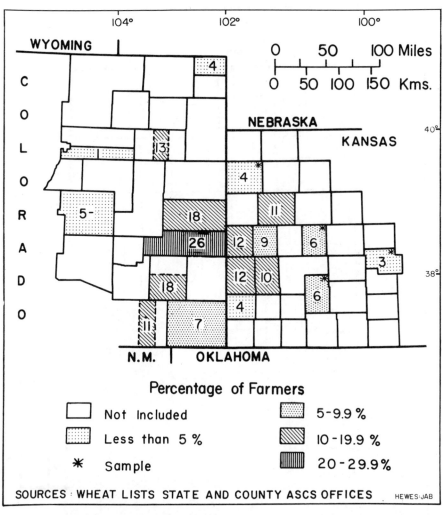

Fig. 33. Suitcase farmers in western Kansas and eastern Colorado, 1967-68. The percentages for Colorado and Greeley and Himilton counties, Kansas (both 12 percent) are for 1968. Percentages in the other counties of Kansas are for 1967. Coverage is sufficient to show the general distribution of the persistence of suitcase farmers. The core area showed further decline.

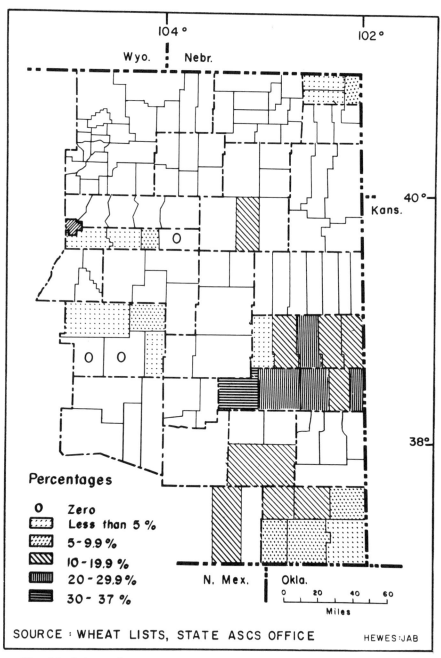

Percentages

O	Zero
	Less than 5 %
	5 - 9.9 %
	10 - 19.9 %
	20 - 29.9 %
	30 - 37 %

SOURCE : WHEAT LISTS, STATE ASCS OFFICE

HEWES:JAB

Fig. 34. Suitcase farmers in eastern Colorado, by communities, 1968.

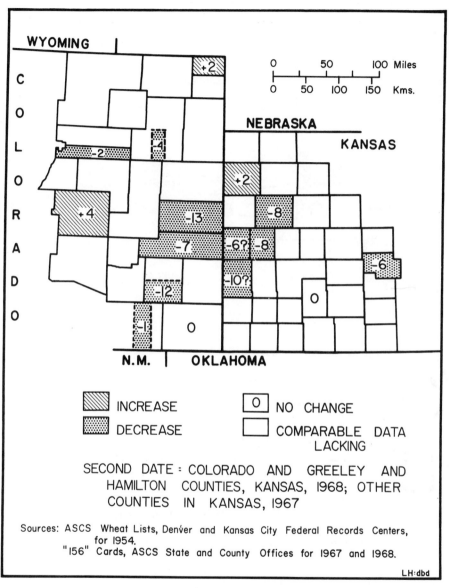

Fig. 35. Change in percentage of suitcase farmers, 1954 to about 1968. The decline was general except in some marginal locations. Changes are in percentage points; hence, percentage of change is greater.

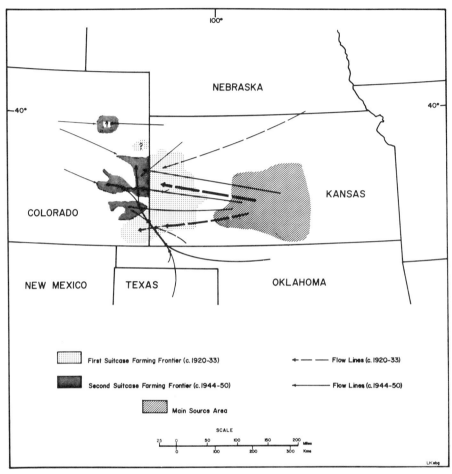

Fig. 36. Suitcase farming frontiers in the central Great Plains. The map shows the portions of Kansas and Colorado in which farmers from a distance are judged to have played leading parts in expanding wheat farming in two great advances, and generalizes the places from which they came to the new wheat farms. Information gathered about the two areas in Colorado marked by question marks was not sufficient for positive identification. Actually, the second suitcase farming frontier overlapped the first, at least in Greeley and Hamilton counties in western Kansas.

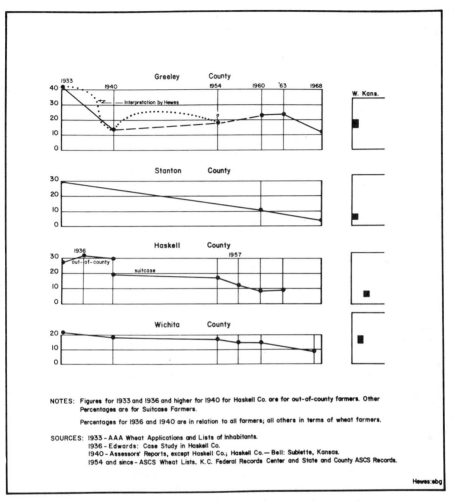

Fig. 37. Trends in the percentage of suitcase farmers in Kansas. The four counties are presented as representative of the important suitcase farming country of Kansas. In all, decline has been marked, although interrupted in the case of Greeley County. The dotted line is preferred for Greeley County.

225

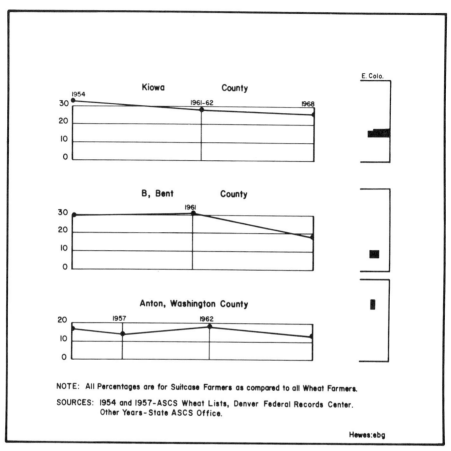

Fig. 38. Trends in the percentage of suitcase farmers in Colorado. The areas selected are considered representative of the important suitcase farming country of Colorado. Kiowa County represents the heart of the area; the other areas are in peripheral portions at the south and north and contained fewer suitcase farmers. Decline characterizes all three areas, although there was less than in Kansas. The time period covered in Colorado is shorter, possibly an important consideration in the smaller decline there. The gains of 1961-62 are interpreted as effects of the conservation reserve program.

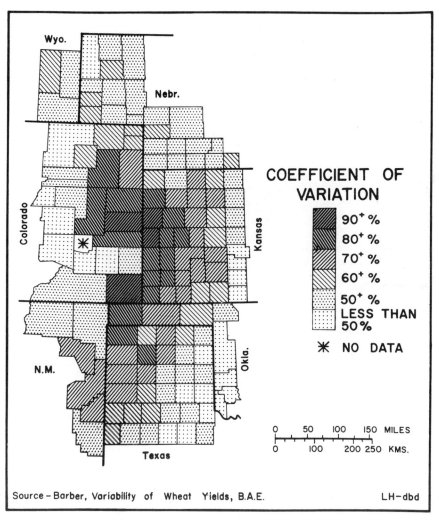

Fig. 39. Variability of wheat yields, 1926-48.

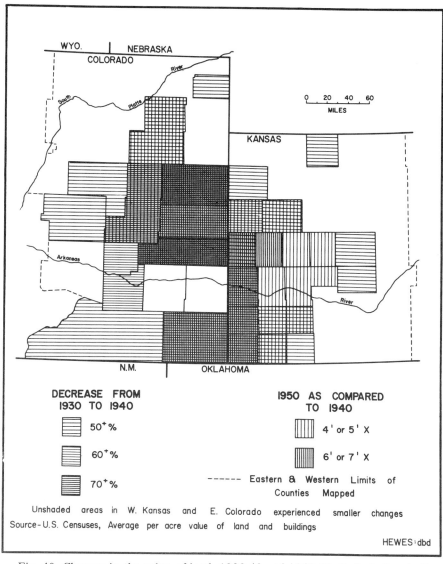

Fig. 40. Changes in the value of land, 1930-40 and 1940-50. Both decline in the earlier period and increase in the later period were great. This combination is favorable to the absentee ownership.

Appendix B: Tables

TABLE 1
GREELEY COUNTY, KANSAS, WHEAT, 1912–27

Year	Acréage Seeded	Acreage Harvested	Percent Abandoned	Average Yield per Harvested Acre	Experiment Farm Yields
1912	690	179	75	4	
1913	231	24	90	6	
1914	....	905	....	11	
1915	283	283	0	15	
1916	417	313	25	7	
1917	1,231	37	97	5	
1918	263	103	61	4	
1919	....	825	....	9	
1920	864	734	15	12	
1921	19,616	18,635	5	10	
1922	9,334	7,187	23	10	
1923	20,368	7,536	63	7	
1924	15,632	14,382	8	15	21.1
1925	16,656	10,993	34	7	8.2
1926	30,442	27,398	10	8	15.2
1927	57,676	22,494	61	2	2.3

SOURCE: T. B. Stinson and H. H. Laude, *A Report of the Tribune Branch Agricultural Experiment Station*, Agri. Exper. Sta., Bul. no. 250, Kansas State Agricultural College (Manhattan, March 1930), pp. 12, and 13.

TABLE 2
LARGE WHEAT FARMS, GREELEY COUNTY, KANSAS, 1920–25

	Farmers from Greeley and Adjacent Counties	Suitcase Farmers
A. Acres of wheat, 1920–25		
100–500	94	23
500–1,000	12	6
1,000 and up	4	6
Total	110	35
B. Bushels of Wheat, 1920–25 (if no acreage given)		
500–1,000	7	2
1,000–2,000	3	4
2,000–4,000	1	2
4,000–8,000	2	0
8,000 and up	0	1
Total	13	9

SOURCE: Assessors' reports, Statistical Lists, Agriculture, Greeley County.
NOTE: A and B are mutually exclusive but counts are cumulative; that is, one farmer could be counted six times if there were records for six years.

TABLE 3
Wheat Yields in Greeley County, Kansas, 1920–25

Bushels per Acre	Local Farmers (Greeley and Adjacent Counties)	Suitcase Farmers
Less than 1	2	0
1–5	14	1
5–10	7	3
10 and over	8	3

SOURCE: Assessors' Reports, Statistical Lists, Agriculture.

NOTE: Figures are for farms for which acreage was given one year and production in the next year.

TABLE 4
Residence of Greeley County, Kansas, Wheat Farmers, 1933

District	Rural In-County		Local Towns		Out-of-Co.		
	Farmers Resident	Family Names	Farmers Resident	Family Names	Farmers	Per-centage	Total
N. Tribune	21	9	3	6	24	38.1	63
S. Tribune	30	12	8	5	17	23.6	72
N. Harrison	35	14	8	4	41	40.2	102
S. Harrison	14	6	4	0	35	59.3	59
W.N. Colony	16	5	7	2	22	42.3	52
E.N. Colony	7	3	4	2	9	36.0	25
W.S. Colony	15	4	5	3	28	50.9	55
E.S. Colony	13	2	5	1	21	50.0	42
County	151	55	44	23	197	40.2	470
	206		67				
Totals*	175		45		164	42.7	384

SOURCES: AAA lists, *Greeley County Republican*, September 21, 1933, and lists of inhabitants, Statistical Rolls, Greeley County, 1933 and 1932.

NOTE: If a family name was encountered in both a farm location and a town, the farm location was given precedence.

* Avoiding duplication between townships.

TABLE 5
Farms of Out-of-County Wheat Farmers, Greeley County, Kansas, 1933

District	Farm Land Acres	1930 Wheat Acres	1930 Wheat Bu.	1931 Wheat Acres	1931 Wheat Bu.	1932 Wheat Acres	1932 Wheat Bu.	3-Yr. Av. Acres	Acres Sown for 1933
N. Tribune	12,520	5,160	72,484	8,635	151,420	10,825	34,558	8,207	9,625
S. Tribune	7,520	5,110	67,530	5,710	68,948	6,570	10,150	5,797	6,410
N. Harrison	17,700	12,310	165,386	15,720	204,141	15,215	28,227	14,415	15,308
S. Harrison	19,298	7,480	100,044	18,906	312,787	18,146	14,120	14,844	17,028
W.N. Colony	17,268*	1,850	27,520	7,548	143,885	12,638	81,583	7,345	9,318
E.N. Colony	3,040*	520	4,240	2,025	29,660	2,120	4,549	1,555	1,410
W.S. Colony	10,020	2,960	29,605	7,980	90,977	8,657	20,050	6,533	8,425
E.S. Colony	8,480	4,450	53,860	7,445	75,522	6,825	12,668	6,240	7,232
County Totals	95,846	39,840	520,669	73,969	1,077,340	80,996	206,405	64,935	74,756
County Totals for All Farmers	222,419	104,257	1,268,670	164,122	2,295,190	175,167	377,390	147,845	169,140
Out-of-County Percentages of County Totals	43.09	38.21	41.04	45.07	46.94	46.24	54.69	43.92	44.20

SOURCES: AAA lists, *Greeley County Republican*, September 21, 1933, and lists of inhabitants, Statistical Rolls, Agriculture, 1933 and 1932.

* An addition of about 5,700 acres should be made to E.N. Colony and the same amount deducted from W.N. Colony due to crediting an entire large farming operation to W.N. Colony because its headquarters was located there. A similar shifting of acres and bushels of wheat is needed.

TABLE 6

Farms of Resident Rural Wheat Farmers, Greeley County, Kansas, 1933

District	Farm Land Acres	1930 Wheat		1931 Wheat		1932 Wheat		3-Yr. Av. Acres	Acres Sown for 1933
		Acres	Bu.	Acres	Bu.	Acres	Bu.		
N. Tribune	15,512	7,965	97,310	10,342	154,620	10,557	40,035	9,621	10,530
S. Tribune	16,240	8,099	95,097	10,874	135,955	11,199	8,975	10,057	9,830
N. Harrison	26,722	18,160	246,517	19,525	262,365	20,485	22,013	19,390	20,821
S. Harrison	7,520	2,430	28,183	5,440	98,744	6,260	25,199	4,710	6,070
W.N. Colony	10,863	3,030	28,855	6,530	79,199	7,755	20,400	5,772	7,830
E.N. Colony	2,884	1,140	3,400	1,484	17,440	1,334	980	1,319	1,684
W.S. Colony	8,760	3,420	40,770	6,640	104,030	5,970	16,080	5,343	7,040
E.S. Colony	6,560	4,350	32,980	5,210	53,745	5,290	6,096	4,950	5,925
County Totals Overall	95,061	48,594	573,112	66,045	906,098	68,850	139,778	61,162	69,730
Resident Rural Farmers'	222,419	104,257	1,268,670	164,122	2,295,190	175,165	377,390	147,845	169,140
Percentages of County Totals	42.74	46.61	45.17	40.32	39.48	39.31	37.04	41.09	41.23

SOURCE: Data from AAA applications of 1933 and lists of inhabitants, 1933 and 1932.

TABLE 7

FARMS OF GREELEY COUNTY TOWN FARMERS (HORACE AND TRIBUNE), 1933

District	Farm Land Acres	1930 Wheat Acres	1930 Wheat Bu.	1931 Wheat Acres	1931 Wheat Bu.	1932 Wheat Acres	1932 Wheat Bu.	3-Yr. Av. Acres	Acres Sown for 1933
N. Tribune	7,380	1,930	21,100	4,300	73,467	4,580	5,350	3,603	4,650
S. Tribune	7,754	3,723	36,800	4,878	64,175	5,819	6,770	4,807	5,604
N. Harrison	7,200	6,300	80,233	6,700	80,147	6,720	1,360	6,573	6,880
S. Harrison	720	560	4,896	720	7,075	720	690	667	720
W.N. Colony	2,880	890	6,300	1,650	25,400	2,140	6,400	1,560	1,460
E.N. Colony	1,800	800	8,180	1,800	23,580	1,800	2,340	1,466	1,800
W.S. Colony	2,498	820	5,440	3,100	24,306	2,260	7,520	2,056	2,260
E.S. Colony	1,280	800	12,440	960	12,600	1,280	780	1,013	1,280
County Totals	31,512	15,823	174,889	24,108	312,750	25,319	31,210	21,745	24,654
Overall	222,419	104,257	1,268,670	164,122	2,295,190	175,165	377,390	147,845	169,140
Town Farmers' Percentages of County Totals	14.17	15.18	13.79	14.69	13.63	14.46	8.27	14.71	14.58

SOURCE: Data from AAA applications of 1933 and lists of inhabitants, 1933 and 1932.

TABLE 8

PERCENTAGE OF FARM LAND SOWN TO WHEAT, GREELEY COUNTY, KANSAS, 1930–33

Group	1930	1931	1932	1933
Local Rural Farmers	51	61	72	73
Local Town Farmers	50	73	80	78
Out-of-County Farmers	42	77	84	78

SOURCE: Data from AAA applications, 1933, and lists of inhabitants, 1933 and 1932.

TABLE 9

AVERAGE WHEAT YIELDS PER ACRE, GREELEY COUNTY, KANSAS, 1930–32

Group	1930 Bushels	1931 Bushels	1932 Bushels	3-Yr. Av. Bushels
Local Rural Farmers	11.79	13.71	2.03	8.82
Local Town Farmers	11.05	13.53	1.24	8.10
Out-of-County Farmers	13.22	14.56	2.56	9.26

SOURCE: Data from AAA applications, 1933, and lists of inhabitants, 1933 and 1932.
NOTE: Planted-acre basis.

TABLE 10

HIGH AND LOW YIELDS OF WHEAT, GREELEY COUNTY, KANSAS, 1930–32

Group	Number of Tracts	Not Harvested 1930–32 (Any Year)	1 Bu. or Less 1930–32 (Any Year)	1+ but Less Than 5 Bu. 1930, 1931	20 Bu. or More, 1930, 1931	5 Bu. or More, 1932
Rural In-County Farmers	240	187	18	22	52	35
Local Town Farmers	79	63	2	4	10	8
Out-of-County Farmers	240	184	11	8	79	62
Total	559	333	31	34	141	115

SOURCE: Derived from applications for wheat allotments, *Greeley County Republican*, September 21, 1933, and lists of inhabitants, Statistical Lists, Agriculture, 1933 and 1932.

NOTE: Operations of family name farmers were omitted. Yields in middle range omitted. Each tract reported separately. Except for number of tracts, counts are cumulative. Yields are bushels per planted acre.

TABLE 11

OWNER AND TENANT OPERATIONS, COLONY TOWNSHIP, GREELEY COUNTY, KANSAS, 1933

Group	Owner-Operation*	Tenant-Operation
Local Rural Farmers	29	86
Local Town Farmers	13	40
Out-of-County Farmers	45	80

SOURCE: Based on 1933 AAA wheat applications and lists of inhabitants, 1933 and 1932.
NOTE: Each tract reported separately; not a count of farms.
* Including ownership by those of same family name.

TABLE 12

OWNERSHIP OF RENTED WHEAT FARMS, COLONY TOWNSHIP, GREELEY COUNTY, KANSAS, 1933

Tenants	Locally Owned Tracts	Tracts Owned Out-of-County
Local Rural	9	77
Local Town	6	34
Out-of-County	15*	65

SOURCE: Based on AAA applications; residence on assessors' reports (lists of inhabitants) 1933 and 1932.
* Counting as local three tracts owned by Kansas Agriculture Development Company.

TABLE 13
HAMILTON COUNTY, KANSAS, WHEAT FARMS, 1933

Group	Farm Land Acres	1930 Wheat Acres	1930 Wheat Bu.	1931 Wheat Acres	1931 Wheat Bu.	1932 Wheat Acres	1932 Wheat Bu.	3-Year Average Acres	3-Year Average Bu.	Acres Sown for 1933
Local Rural	31,409	14,074	161,176	23,821	457,231	23,087	166,259	20,324	261,555	21,271
Sidewalk (Local Town)	6,437	1,780	25,945	4,580	55,912	4,828	22,611	3,729	34,823	4,667
Out-of-County	24,946	7,870	103,800	23,203	445,345	21,048	156,265	17,373	235,137	17,391
County Totals	62,782	23,724	290,921	51,604	958,488	48,963	345,135	41,426	531,515	43,329
Percentage for Out-of-County Farmers (37.6% of farmers)	39.8	33.2	35.7	45.2	46.5	43.0	45.3	41.9	44.2	40.1

SOURCE: Based on sample of every third farm listed in AAA applications in the *Syracuse Journal*, September 15, 1933. Thus, all county totals given are only about one-third of actual totals, and the same is true of the three groups of farmers. Residence was checked in the list of inhabitants in the assessor's report of 1933.

TABLE 14

AVERAGE WHEAT YIELDS IN HAMILTON COUNTY, KANSAS, 1930–32

Group	1930	1931	1932	3-Yr. Av.
Local Rural	11.38	19.19	7.20	12.38
Local Town	14.57	12.20	4.68	9.34
Out-of-Co.	13.19	19.19	7.42	13.53
County Averages	12.26	18.57	7.04	12.83

SOURCE: One-third sample, AAA listing, *Syracuse Journal,* September 15, 1933. Residence based on lists of inhabitants in assessor's report for 1933. Yields are on a bushels per planted-acre basis.

TABLE 15
STANTON COUNTY, KANSAS, WHEAT FARMS, 1933

Groups	Farm Land Acres	1930 Wheat Acres	1930 Wheat Bu.	1931 Wheat Acres	1931 Wheat Bu.	1932 Wheat Acres	1932 Wheat Bu.	3-Yr. Av. Acres	3-Yr. Av. Bu.	1933 Acres Wheat
Local Rural Farmers	36,580	19,257	191,591	22,968	398,442	22,943	218,081	21,723	269,371	24,541
Sidewalk Farmers	2,960	1,777	16,566	2,097	38,587	2,220	17,704	2,031	24,286	2,710
Out-of-Co. Farmers	8,010	5,207	47,930	6,897	127,715	6,382	52,584	6,162	76,076	6,584
Total	47,550	26,241	256,087	31,992	564,744	31,545	278,369	29,916	369,733	33,835
Percentage Out-of-Co.	16.8	19.8	18.7	21.2	22.6	20.2	18.2	20.6	20.5	19.5

SOURCE: Data from AAA applications, *Johnson City Pioneer*, September 28, 1933. Classification of farmers based on the list of inhabitants, Statistical Rolls, Stanton County, 1933.

NOTE: Based on one-fifth sample, but entries in one of the nine communities and part of two others were not visible because they were covered by the newspaper binding. Thus, all totals probably should be more than five times as large as shown.

TABLE 16
LAND USE, SAMPLE AREA, HASKELL COUNTY, KANSAS

	Resident-Operated Farms		Local Nonresident-Operated Farms		Farms Operated Out-of-County	
	Acres Cropland	Acres Pasture	Acres Cropland	Acres Pasture	Acres Cropland	Acres Pasture
1936						
Locally Owned Farms	5,695	1,505	0	0	0	0
Farms Owned Out-of-Co.	10,625	495	640	0	4,080	0
Total	16,320	2,000	640	0	4,080	0
1925*						
Locally Owned Farms	3,345	3,855	0	0	0	0
Farms Owned Out-of-Co.	2,715	8,405	160	480	2,320	1,760
Total	6,060	12,260	160	480	2,320	1,760

SOURCE: Computed from maps in A. D. Edwards, *Influence of Drought and Depression on a Rural Community: A Case Study in Haskell County, Kansas*, pp. 35, 41. The thirty-six square miles constitute the western one-half of T28S, R33W, and the eastern one-half of T28S, R34W.
* Assuming owner-operation status of 1936.

TABLE 17

WHEAT GROWING BY OLD AND NEW FARMERS, KANSAS, 1920 AND 1927

| | 1920 | | 1927 | | |
	Wheat	Not Growing Wheat	Wheat	Wheat, 300 Acres or More	Not Growing Wheat	% of Acreage in Wheat
Colony Tp., Greeley Co.						
Farmers, 1920	14	63	17	4	13	32.9
New Farmers	....	....	23	9	24	67.1
Harrison Tp., Greeley Co.*						
Farmers, 1921	7	21	7	1	5	6.7
New Farmers	....	....	32	19	5	93.3
Tribune Tp., Greeley Co.†						
Farmers, 1920	5	40	20	6	11	14.3
New Farmers	....	....	51	20	21	85.7
Lamont Tp., Hamilton Co.						
Farmers, 1920	24	30	11	0	17	18.2
New Farmers	....	....	13	2	13	81.8
Stanton Tp., Stanton Co.						
Farmers, 1920	3	37	8	1	7	26.3
New Farmers	....	....	10	4	22	73.7
Augustine Tp., Logan Co.						
Farmers, 1920	2	17	6	0	7	29.3
New Farmers	....	....	5	2	3	71.7
Hartland Tp., Kearny Co.						
Farmers, 1920	3	25	3	1	12	21.2
New Farmers	....	....	20	2	12	78.8
Lincoln Tp., Grant Co.						
Farmers, 1920	14	41	15	4	3	21.0
New Farmers	....	....	39	20	6	79.0
Overall, 8 Townships						
Farmers, 1920	72	274	87	17	75	17.8
New Farmers	....	....	193	78	106	82.2

SOURCE: Based on Assessors' reports, Statistical Rolls, Agriculture.

* 1921 data for Harrison Township includes Fishman, then a suitcase farmer; Fishman was not reported in the township in 1927.

† Fishman shown as a new farmer in Tribune Township in 1927. If Fishman is considered a persister, the percentage of wheat for that group was nearly 50 percent in 1927.

TABLE 18

IN-COUNTY KANSAS FARMERS GROWING WHEAT, 1933

County	In-Co. Applicants for AAA	In-Co. Farmers (Assessors' Reports)
Grant	302	324
Greeley	272	339
Hamilton	209	391
Kearny	298	319
Logan	184	534
Stanton	385	352
Wallace	88	464
Wichita	356	402

SOURCES: Newspaper records of AAA applications, checked against lists of inhabitants in the Statistical Rolls to determine in-county residence of farmers. In-county applicants for wheat allotments based on samples, except for Greeley County, where they are complete. Statistical Rolls, Agriculture, contain the assessors' lists of farmers.

TABLE 19

RESIDENCE OF REPORTED NONRESIDENT FARMERS, KANSAS, 1936

Township	In-Co. Addresses	Post Offices in Adjacent Co. Actually In-Co. Residence	Apparent Total In-Co.	Actually Adjacent	Suitcase	Total
Garfield (Finney Co.)	137	30	167	6	2*	175
Pleasant Valley (Finney)	107	0	107	0	22	129
Foote (Gray)	72	0	72	4	12	88
E. Hess (Gray)	86	12 + 1F†	98 + 1F	2	2	103
Ingalls (Gray)	101	11 + 1F	112 + 1F	2	2	117
West Hibbard (Kearny)	45	0	45	1	12	58
Alamota (Lane)	61	3	64	3	2	69
Cleveland (Lane)	69	0	69	0	16	85
Spring Creek (Lane)	55	11 + 1F	66 + 1F	2	7	76
White Rock (Lane)	38	10 + 2F	48 + 2F	8	5	63
Isabel (Scott)	78	4	82	2	20	107
Whitewoman (Wichita)	77	8	85	3	24	112
Totals	926	88 + 1F	1,015 + 5F	33	126	1,179

SOURCE: Statistical Rolls (assessors' reports), 1936, by counties.

NOTE: A few farmers without addresses not counted.

* The assessor reported that suitcase farmers numbered fourteen but named only two.

† F signifies that although the family name of the farmer was found, his name was not; therefore, identification was not certain.

TABLE 20

PERCENTAGES OF WHEAT ABANDONED IN KANSAS

	1910–14	1915–19	1920–24	1925–29	1930–34
Farming Area Type 12*	66.3	45.9	27.1	39.3	22.4
Farming Area Type 10b†	26.4	42.9	24.9	13.5	27.9

SOURCE: J. R. Jacard, "Agricultural Production Trends 1910 to 1934, Kansas Type of Farming Areas for Area Agricultural Congress at Parsons, Jan. 29 and 30 (1935?)," mimeographed.

* Greeley, Hamilton, Kearny, Logan, Scott, Wallace and Wichita counties .

† Ford, Grant, Gray, Haskell, Meade, Morton, Seward, Stanton, and Stevens counties.

TABLE 21

AAA PAYMENTS IN 1935

County	Estimated Value of Wheat at 80¢ Bushel	AAA Payments	No. of Farms	Av. Value of Wheat per Farm	AAA Allot. per Farm
Cheyenne	$235,200	$174,814	1,091	$215.58	$160.23
Gove	0	316,492	890	0	355.61
Logan	0	112,225	541	0	207.44
Sherman	800	206,324	804	1.00	256.52
Wallace	0	42,619	410	0	103.95

SOURCE: *Colby Free Press-Tribune,* January 1, 1937. These statistics were included in a story entitled "What the AAA Program Meant in 1935."

TABLE 22

SUMMER FALLOW AND STRIP CROPPING, GREELEY COUNTY, KANSAS, 1936–40

Year	Summer Fallow (Acres)	Strip Cropping (Acres)
1936	15,000	30,000
1937	50,000	100,000
1938	70,000	120,000
1939	75,000	150,000
1940	90,000	180,000

SOURCES: Annual reports, Greeley County agent, 1938, 1939; *Greeley County Republican,* October 17, 1940.

TABLE 23

LAND USE, WHITEWOMAN TOWNSHIP, WICHITA COUNTY, KANSAS, 1939–40

1940 Averages

| | | Acres Planted | | |
| | | | Grain | Other |
Farm Acreage	Wheat	Barley	Sorghum	Crops
Suitcase Farms (18) 861.7	158.5	53.6	89.7	9.7
Local Farms (18) 1,091.1	210.4	72.5	50.0	40.1

1939 Averages

| | | Acres Harvested | | | |
| | | All Other | Fallow | Idle | Acres of |
Farm Acreage	Wheat	Crops	Acres	Acres	Crop Failure
Suitcase Farms (18) 861.7	114.4	9.7	274.3	49.8	144.6
Local Farms (18) 1,091.1	175.3	40.1	305.5	29.3	147.2

SOURCE: Compiled from Statistical Rolls, Agriculture, Wichita County, Kansas, 1940.

NOTE: One summer-fallow entry for each group was omitted because the acreage stated was too great to be possible. All suitcase farmers for whom the assessor's report appeared to be complete were included. The local farmers following them immediately in the record provided a reasonably representative sample.

TABLE 24

LAND USE, GREELEY COUNTY, KANSAS, 1939–40

1940 Averages

| | | Acres Planted | | |
| | | | Grain | |
Farm Acreage	Wheat	Barley	Sorghum	Other Crops
Suitcase Farms 865.4	261.7	50.9	44.6	70.5
Local Farms 1,356.5	161.5	98.4	221.6	159.1

1939 Averages

| | | Acres Harvested | | | |
| | | | Fallow | Idle | Acres of |
Farm Acreage	Wheat	Others	Acres	Acres	Crop Failure
Suitcase Farms 840.1	180.2	32.3	180.6	45.6	250.7
Local Farms 1,375.7	139.0	134.2	395.2	40.1	269.7

SOURCE: Compiled from Statistical Rolls, Agriculture, Greeley County, 1940.

NOTE: Suitcase farmers with a record of actual farming numbered thirty in 1940 and thirty-three in 1939. Local farmers, consisting of all local farmers in Colony Township and matching farmers in the other parts of the county, numbered ninety-five in 1940 and ninety-four in 1939.

247

TABLE 25
LAND OWNERSHIP IN COLORADO COUNTIES, 1936

County	% U.S.	% State	% Co. Tax Sale	% Corp.	% Resident	% Nonresident
Baca	.5	4.8	1.4	1.5	46.0	45.8
Bent	9.4	9.6	2.6	3.1	33.1	42.0
Cheyenne		4.9	4.9	11.2	24.4	54.6
Kiowa	.3	6.7	6.8	6.9	24.0	55.3
Kit Carson	.1	4.1	5.1	4.9	38.6	47.2
Lincoln	.3	8.6	4.6	9.4	34.7	42.4
Prowers	.7	5.3	2.2	11.1	37.0	43.7

SOURCE: "Land Use Survey of the Southern Great Plains Region, 1936, Progress Report," Resettlement Administration, Land Use Planning Division, Land Use Section, February 20, 1937.

NOTE: A few years later the acquisition of land for a land utilization project of the federal government raised substantially the percentage of land belonging to the United States government in Baca County.

TABLE 26
LAND USE, EASTERN COLORADO, EARLY 1950s

	Average Farm Land Acres	Average Cropland Acres	Cropland as % of All Land	Average Wheat Sown Acres		% of All Farm Land in Wheat	
				1951	Av. 1951–53	1951	1951–53
Suitcase Farms (231)	1196	966	80.8%	659	601	58.2%	54.4%
Local Farms (661)	1246	828	66.4%	473	428	38.1%	34.3%

SOURCE: 1954 ASCS wheat listing sheets for the following communities: community 2 in Bent County; Arapahoe, First View, Kit Carson, and Wild Horse in Cheyenne County; Towner and Haswell-Arlington in Kiowa County; Kim in Las Animas County; Karval in Lincoln County; and Anton in Washington County.

TABLE 27

COMPARISON OF FALLOW AND WHEAT ACREAGES, COLORADO, 1951–53
(IN NUMBERS OF FARMS)

	Fallow Equal to or Greater Than Wheat	Fallow Less Than Wheat but at Least One-half as Great	Some Fallow but Less Than One-half as Great as Wheat	No Fallow
Suitcase	54	29	20	20
Local	146	91	57	32

SOURCE: Colorado 1954 ASCS Wheat Listing Sheets for Bent County community; First View and Kit Carson in Cheyenne County; Haswell-Arlington in Kiowa County; Karval in Lincoln County; and Crowley County. In Crowley, which is partly irrigated, no farms with less than one hundred acres of cropland were counted.

NOTE: Those farms for which fallow records were not included were omitted. In all, 121 suitcase and 326 locally operated farms were classified.

TABLE 28

WHEAT ABANDONMENT IN COLORADO, 1951–53

Farmers	All Wheat Abandoned	At Least Part of Wheat Abandoned	Total
Suitcase	12	41	53
Local	17	66	83
	29	107	136

SOURCE: Based on comparison of cropland, acres of wheat planted, acres of fallow in a given year, from ASCS wheat listing sheets of 1954. Communities covered were Bent County number 2, First View and Kit Carson of Cheyenne, and Haswell-Arlington of Kiowa.

NOTE: The counts above are to be understood in terms of 312 crop years (104 x 3) for suitcase farmers and 762 (254 x 3) for local.

TABLE 29
LAND USE, WESTERN KANSAS, 1951–53

	Cropland			Wheat				Fallow	
	Acreage per Farm	Acreage	As % of All Land	Av. Acres Sown	As % of All Land	As % of Cropland		Acreage	As % of Wheat
Suitcase Farms (106)	634.8	481.3	75.0	297.6	46.9	61.8		241.3	81.1
Local Farms (108)	673.4	465.9	69.2	264.8	39.3	56.8		212.6	80.3

SOURCE: 1954 ASCS wheat lists, for Wichita, Sherman, Scott, and Grant counties.

TABLE 30

COMPARATIVE STATISTICS, PERSISTING AND NONPERSISTING FARMERS, 1954–61/62

	Farm Land, Av. Acres, 1954	Cropland, Av. Acres per Farm, 1954	Wheat, Av. Acres, 1951–53	Farms Containing 320 Acres Cropland or Less, 1954
Suitcase Farmers				
Persisting (86)	1,683.7	1,431.6	911.6	23
Nonpersisting (135)	885.3	669.9	410.7	60
Local Farmers				
Persisting (402)	1,387.7	936.2	493.7	94
Nonpersisting (259)	1,025.1	658.8	325.7	126

SOURCES: ASCS records for the following communities: community 2, Bent County; Arapahoe, First View, Kit Carson, and Wild Horse in Cheyenne County; Towner and Haswell-Arlington, Kiowa County; "B" or Kim, Las Animas County; Karval, Lincoln County; and Anton, Washington County.

TABLE 31

LAND USE AND PRODUCTIVITY, COLORADO COUNTIES, 1961–62

	Farmers	Farm Land Acres	Cropland Acres	Conservation Reserve Acres	Final Wheat Acres 1960 or 1961	Productivity*
Suitcase, Persisting from 1954	95	1,671.0	975.7	301.9	257.9	89.95
Suitcase, New since 1954	135	963.1	749.0	298.6	182.4	89.05
Locals, Persisting from 1954	341	1,714.4	962.7	199.5	299.9	97.45
Locals, New since 1954	186	1,054.13	649.8	201.2	172.0	91.51

SOURCE: ASCS records for either 1961 or 1962: number 2 in Bent County; Arapahoe, First View, Kit Carson, Wild Horse in Cheyenne County; Towner and Haswell-Arlington in Kiowa County; Flagler in Kit Carson County; Karval in Lincoln County. Final wheat is for preceding year. Productivity is for all cropland.

* Productivity not included for Flagler community.

TABLE 32

LAND USE, FARMERS NOT PARTICIPANTS IN CONSERVATION RESERVE, 1961 OR 1962

	Farm		Cropland			Wheat	
	Av. Acreage	% in Cropland	Av. Acreage	% in Wheat	Final Acreage		% Farm in Wheat
Suitcase (72)	1,255.1	76.2	956.6	39.6	379.2		30.2
Local (251)	1,191.2	70.7	841.6	37.2	313.0		26.3

SOURCE: ASCS wheat lists for community 2, Bent County; Arapahoe, First View, and Kit Carson in Cheyenne County; Towner and Haswell-Arlington, Kiowa County; and Flagler, Kit Carson County.

NOTE: Wheat acreages are for the year preceding, either 1960 or 1961.

252

TABLE 33
LAND USE, FARMERS PARTLY IN CONSERVATION RESERVE

	Farm Land Total Acres	Cropland		Conservation Reserve			Wheat		
		Cropland Acres in	% Farm in Cropland	Acres	% Cropland in Con. Res.	Acres	% Cropland in Wheat	% Farm in Wheat	
Suitcase Farmers (35)	2,730.3	1,526.5	55.9	366.7	24.0	437.4	28.7	14.6	
Local Farmers (102)	1,994.5	1,284.4	64.4	435.7	33.9	291.1	22.6	14.6	

SOURCE: ASCS wheat lists for Community 2, Bent County; Arapahoe, First View, and Kit Carson in Cheyenne County; Towner and Haswell-Arlington, Kiowa County; and Flagler, Kit Carson County.

NOTE: Wheat acreages are for the year immediately preceding, either 1960 or 1961.

TABLE 34

ACREAGES PLANTED AND LEFT FOR HARVEST, COLORADO COMMUNITIES, 1964–67

	No. of Farms	Wheat			Barley			Grain Sorghum		
		Av. Acres Planted	Acres Left for Harvest	% Left for Harvest	Av. Acres Planted	Acres Left for Harvest	% Left for Harvest	Av. Acres Planted	Acres Left for Harvest	% Left for Harvest
Part A: 1964										
Suitcase	119	331.4	121.1	36.6	12.9	3.7	28.5	39.0	31.6	79.4
Local	120	265.3	92.2	34.8	17.8	8.3	46.4	44.9	41.8	93.0
Part B: 1965										
Suitcase	168	505.2	115.9	22.9	.6	0	0	39.0	37.1	95.2
Local	166	312.3	84.2	27.0	.4	0	0	55.9	50.7	90.7
Part C: 1966										
Suitcase	46	383.0	365.8	95.5	.8	.8	100	3.2	3.2	100
Local	48	282.7	270.5	95.7	0	0	....	6.7	6.7	100
Part D: 1967										
Suitcase	41	458.9	264.2	57.6	0	0	....	60.5	60.5	100
Local	46	350.3	237.9	67.9	0	0	....	52.1	52.1	100
Part E: 1964–67*										
Suitcase	184	417.6	232.8	55.8	1.0	.2	21.0	26.6	23.3	87.7
Local	190	295.6	170.6	57.6	5.5	3.4	61.7	36.7	35.7	97.1

TABLE 34 (continued)
Part F: 1964–67†

Suitcase	374	429.8	164.5	38.3	4.5	1.3	28.4	37.0	33.8	90.7
Local	380	298.3	129.9	43.2	5.8	2.6	45.1	45.8	42.5	92.9

SOURCE: Performance records, County ASCS offices.

NOTE: Coverage is for all suitcase farms and matching local farms not in conservation reserve, 1964: Communities "B" and "C" in Baca County, Towner in Kiowa County; Arapahoe, First View, and Kit Carson in Cheyenne County; Karval in Lincoln County; Peconic, Burlington, Vona, Flagler in Kit Carson County; 1965: Communities in Baca and Kit Carson counties were omitted, the others were retained and Sheridan Lake, Brandon-Chivington, Eads, and Haswell-Arlington in Kiowa County were added; 1966 and 1967: Arapahoe, First View, and Kit Carson in Cheyenne County; and only Karval in Lincoln County. Percentages were figured on more exact acreages than the averages given to tenths of the acre.

• Three communities of Cheyenne and Karval, Lincoln County. The numbers of farms for the four-year totals are cumulative.

† Overall for communities covered. Totals are cumulative.

Bibliography

Unpublished Sources

Barber, E. Lloyd. "Variability of Wheat Yields by Counties in the United States." Mimeographed. USDA Bur. of Agr. Econ., September 1951.

Colorado. Agricultural Extension Service. "Annual Reports," by County Agents, 1916-67. Colorado State University, Fort Collins. Titles vary.

———. Akron Dryland Field Station "General Report," 1924-60. Also "Annual Report" and "Dryland Report." Earlier reports at Colorado State University; later at Akron.

"Decennial Census and Statistical Rolls" (assessors' reports), 1925, for Greeley, Hamilton, and Stanton counties, Kansas. Kansas State Historical Society, Topeka.

Falck, Depue; Greenslet, E. R.; and Morgan, R. E. "Land Classification of the Central Great Plains, Parts 4 and 5, Eastern Colorado." Mimeograph no. 56284. Geological Survey, U.S. Dept. of Interior. Washington, D.C., 1931.

Finnell, H. H. "How Much of the New Plow-up Is Good?" *Minutes,* Great Plains Agricultural Council, Southern Division. Mimeographed. Amarillo, January 5, 6, 7, 1948, pp. 54-56.

Greeley County, Kansas. "Commissioners' Journal," vol. 5 (1943-55). County Clerk's office, Tribune, Kansas.

———. File of Soil Blowing Complaints, 1961-68. County Clerk's office, Tribune, Kansas.

———. Land Deeds. Office of Register of Deeds, Tribune, Kansas.

———. United Agricultural Program Progress Report. (Prepared by J. E. Taylor, Chairman, Greeley County Planning Committee, after meeting, March 1941.) Manuscript. Greeley County Agent's office, Tribune, Kansas.

Hamilton County, Kansas. Land Deeds. Office of Register of Deeds, Syracuse, Kansas.

Jacard, J. R. "Agricultural Production Trends, 1910 to 1934, Kansas Type of Farming Areas for Area Agricultural Congress at Parsons, January 29 and 30" [1935?]. Mimeographed. Kansas State University, Manhattan.

257

Kansas. Agricultural Extension Service. "Annual Reports," by County Agents, 1918-63. Microfilm. Kansas State University, Manhattan. Titles vary.

———. "Assessors Reports," by counties, 1918-63. Microfilmed in part. Kansas State Historical Society, Topeka. Included are "Agricultural Statistical Roll" (through 1953), "Agricultural Statistical Schedule" (1954 to the present), and "Decennial Census and Statistical Roll" (1925 report, combined with census).

Kiowa County, Colorado. "Commissioners' Records," vol. 7 (1953-55); vol. 8 (1956-57). Courthouse, Eads, Colorado.

———. File of Soil Blowing Complaints, 1957-68. County Clerk's office, Eads, Colorado.

"Land Use in Baca County, Colorado, Based on a Field Survey." Mimeographed. Land Utilization Program. USDA Bur. of Land Econ., April 1, 1938. Denver Public Library, cataloged as A36.2: L/22/22.

"Land Use Survey of the Southern Great Plains Region, 1936, Progress Report." Mimeographed. Resettlement Administration, Land Use Planning Division, Land Use Section, February 20, 1937. In 1964, on file with the Extension Division, Kansas State University, Manhattan.

"Narrative Report of Wichita-Greeley County Farm Bureau, December 1, 1920, to November 15, 1921." Microfilmed. Kansas State University, Manhattan.

Peterson, J. Q.; Morgan, R. E.; and Greenslet, E. R. "Land Classification of the Central Great Plains, Part 2, Western Kansas and Southwestern Nebraska." Mimeograph no. 27749. Geol. Surv., U. S. Dept. of Interior. Washington, D.C., 1928.

Pevehouse, P. M. "Conditions in the Southwestern Wheat Area Which Affect the Rehabilitation Program (as Typified by Perkins Co., Nebraska)." Resettlement Admin. Research Bul. K-3. Mimeographed. May 1936.

Reed, Floyd K. "Winter Wheat, Total Acres Planted, 1939-1956." Mimeographed. Denver, n.d.

"Report on the Eleventh Conference of the Regional Advisory Committee on Land Use Practices in the Southern Great Plains Area," April 19 and 20, 1937. Mimeographed. Colorado Springs.

Stanton County, Kansas. "Commissioners' Journal," vol. 3 (1927-53). Courthouse, Johnson, Kansas.

———. File of Soil Drifting Complaints, 1955-68. County Clerk's office, Johnson, Kansas.

———. Land Deeds. Office of Register of Deeds, Johnson, Kansas.

Tribune (Kansas) Substation (also Branch Experiment Station). "Annual Reports," 1913-57. Kansas State University, Manhattan.

United States. Department of Agriculture. Agricultural Stabilization and Conservation Service (ASCS). "578" cards (performance records for individual farms), 1964-67. Baca County ASCS office, Springfield, Colorado; Cheyenne County ASCS office, Cheyenne Wells, Colorado; Kiowa County ASCS office, Eads, Colorado; Kit Carson County ASCS office, Burlington, Colorado; Lincoln County ASCS office, Hugo, Colorado.

———. "156" cards (records of individual farms in agricultural programs), 1961, 1962. Microfilmed. Colorado State ASCS office, Denver.

———. "156" cards (records of individual farms in agricultural programs), 1967. Microfilmed. Kansas state ASCS office, Manhattan.

———. "156" cards (records of individual farms in agricultural programs), 1968. Greeley County ASCS office, Tribune, Kansas; Hamilton County ASCS office, Syracuse, Kansas; Stanton County ASCS office, Johnson, Kansas.

———. Referendum lists, Greeley County, Kansas, farm owners and operators eligible to vote in 1963 wheat program referendum. State ASCS office, Manhattan.

———. Referendum lists, Haskell County, Kansas, farm owners and operators eligible to vote in 1963 wheat program referendum. State ASCS office, Manhattan.

———. Soil Bank acreage reserve statistics for Colorado, 1957, 1958. Denver.

———. Soil Bank acreage reserve statistics for Kansas, 1957, 1958. Manhattan.

———. Soil Bank conservation reserve statistics for Colorado, Denver.

———. Soil Bank conservation reserve statistics for Kansas, Manhattan.

———. Summary sheet WK-402, Greeley County, Kansas, wheat acreage figures for 1939. Federal Records Center, Kansas City, Missouri.

———. Summary sheet WR-504, Greeley County, Kansas, wheat acreage figures for 1940. Federal Records Center, Kansas City, Missouri.

———. Wheat Listing Sheets, Colorado, 1954, 1957. Federal Records Center, Denver.

———. Wheat Listing Sheets, Kansas, 1954, 1957. Federal Records Center, Kansas City, Missouri.

———. Wheat Listing Sheets, Kansas, 1959, 1960. Kansas State ASCS office, Manhattan.

United States. Department of Agriculture. Field Crops Statistics Branch,

Agricultural Estimates, Agricultural Marketing Service. Planted acreages of wheat for Colorado, 1931-38. Washington, D.C.

Personal Correspondence

Bader, Avis, long-time resident, Burlington, Colorado. June 21, 1969.

Boese, A. L., long-time resident and former AAA employee, Vona, Colorado. June 23, 1969.

Branson, Lester R., head specialist, ACP-SB, Kansas ASCS office, Manhattan. August 27, 1962.

Brown, W. O., real estate, Springfield, Colorado. January 10 and July 23, 1969.

Dansdill, Robert K., assistant state soil scientist, SCS, Denver. February 26, 1971.

Day, R. L., wheat farmer, Dodge City, Kansas. January 31, 1969.

Dutton, Darrell L., office manager, Hamilton County ASCS, Syracuse, Kansas. October 7, 1969.

Ediger, A. L., wheat farmer, Inman, Kansas. November 18 and December 11, 1968.

Freeman, Peter, a manager of Pawnee National Grasslands, employed since 1955, and long-time stockman, Chicago Ranch, Briggsdale, Colorado. November 1, 1969.

Forster, Kathlyn, office manager, later county executive director, Kiowa County ASCS, Eads, Colorado. January 31, 1964; May 5 and 24, 1966; April 14, June 20 and October 23, 1969; February 23, 1971.

Gaines, Arthur E., long-term resident, Flagler, Colorado. June 21, 1969.

Gifford, Frank, Secretary Kiowa County Soil Conservation District, Eads, Colorado. May 24, 1969.

Grant, Maxine, office manager, Baca County ASCS, Springfield, Colorado. December 19, 1963; October 24, 1968; July 31, 1969.

Greb, B. W., soil scientist, Central Great Plains Field Station, Akron, Colorado. June 13, 1963; December 7, 1964; November 12, 1968; October 16, 1969.

Gwin, Roy E., former county agent, Wichita County, Leoti, Kansas. August 24, 1965; November 10, 1966.

Harkness, C. W., wheat farmer, Garden City, Kansas. January 23, 1969.

Kane, Ray A., office manager, Weld County ASCS, Greeley, Colorado. October 7, 1969.

Kollmorgen, Walter M., Department of Geography, University of Kansas, Lawrence, Kansas. January 24, 1964.

Loeffler, M. John, Department of Geography, University of Colorado, Boulder, Colorado. June 6, 1963.

Mai, Arthur R., office manager, Wallace County ASCS, Sharon Springs, Kansas. October 24 and December 16, 1969; July 15, 1970.

Malin, James C., Kansas historian, Lawrence, Kansas. July 16, 1963; April 3, 1964.

McDonnell, Earl, ASCS office manager, Lincoln County, Hugo, Colorado. March 21, 1963; May 15, 1966; July 23 and November 7, 1969.

McFarland, C. L., county commissioner, Kiowa County, Towner, Colorado. May 6 and June 1, 1969.

Moody, Clifford, office manager, Arapaho County ASCS, Byers, Colorado. June 24 and July 1, 1963; September 30, 1968.

Nelson, Arthur R., state soil scientist, SCS, Salina, Kansas. December 11, 1964.

Novinger, Van L. M., long-time resident, Springfield, Colorado. February 26, 1964.

Pile, Margaret, clerk of district court, Tribune, Kansas. February 22 and July 23, 1969.

Simpson, H. H., Jr., office manager, Kit Carson County ASCS, Burlington, Colorado. July 12, 1963; April 10, 1964; June 5 and July 25, 1969.

Sitler, Harry G., agricultural economist, Economic Research Division, USDA, Colorado State University. May 22, 1963; August 19, 1969.

Smith, Don E., district soil conservationist, Soil Conservation Service, Simla, Colorado. July 1, 1969; July 10, 1970.

Snell, O. A., former wheat farmer and foreman, Garvey Farms, Carson City, Nevada. April 16, 1970.

Stinson, T. Bruce, long-term superintendent of Branch Experiment Station, Tribune, Kansas. January 20, April 3, July 10, 1963; December 13, 1965; June 13, 1966; March 3, July 25, 1969.

Voelker, Stanley W., agricultural economist, North Dakota State University, Fargo. May 15, 1963.

Wagner, Lloyd E., District Ranger, Comanche National Grassland, Forest Service, USDA, Springfield, Colorado. February 17 and May 16, 1969.

Waldren, Lloyd E., county executive director, Greeley County ASCS, Tribune, Kansas. January 13 and 30, 1969; February 3, May 18, and October 12, 1970.

Interviews

Benner, Velda, secretary, office of Kiowa County Agricultural Extension Agent. Eads, Colorado, June 10, 1966.

Boland, Wayne, Cheyenne County ASCS executive director. Cheyenne Wells, Colorado, November 21, 1968.

Bradbury, Arthur, county clerk, Kiowa County, Colorado. Eads, Colorado, October 16, 1968.

Branson, Lester R., head specialist, ACP-SB, Kansas state ASCS office. Manhattan, August 27, 1962; January 14, 1969.

Brown, Larry, production adjustment specialist, Colorado, state ASCS office. Denver, September 16, 1968.

Champe, John L., Lincoln, Nebraska. January 3, 1970.

Corns, Myrna, former resident of Burlington, Colorado. Lincoln, Nebraska. May 19, 1964.

Dansdill, Robert K., assistant Colorado state soil scientist, SCS. Denver, August 27, 1965.

Dutton, Darrell, office manager, Hamilton County, Kansas, ASCS committee. Syracuse, Kansas, November 14, 1968.

Eikelberry, Robert, soil correlator, Mid-West Region, Soil Conservation Service. Lincoln, Nebraska, February 2, 1962; September 8, 1970.

Fiss, Wilma, office manager, ASCS, Stanton County, Kansas. Johnson, Kansas, November 19, 1968.

Ford, R. D., county agent, Stanton County, Kansas. Johnson, Kansas, November 18, 1968.

Forster, Kathlyn, office manager; employed by Kiowa County ASCS committee since 1951. Eads, Colorado, July 11, 1966, October 16, November 20, 1968.

Fritzler, Myron, production adjustment program specialist, Colorado, State ASCS. Denver, September 16, 1968.

Grantham, E. H., real estate, Crowley County. Ordway, Colorado, June 10, 1966.

Greb, B. W., soil scientist, Central Great Plains Field Station. Akron, Colorado, June 8, 1960.

Harmon, Walter F., long-time stockman. Ordway, Colorado, June 10, 1966.

Holland, Marie, former AAA county office manager, then Greeley County ASCS office manager. Tribune, Kansas, August 21, 1961.

Holmes, Bryant, newspaper editor. Leoti, Kansas, November 16, 1968.

Kippes, Joe, former Stanton County AAA committee member. Johnson, Kansas, November 19, 1968.

Leonard, Warren, county commissioner, Lincoln County. Karval, Colorado, June 11, 1966.

McDonnell, Earl, office manager, Lincoln County ASCS committee. Hugo, Colorado, November 21, 1968; July 8, 1969.

Pearson, Franklin, assessor, Lincoln County, Colorado. Hugo, Colorado, June 11, 1966.

Pile, Margaret. Tribune, Kansas, November 16, 1968.

Reed, Floyd, Colorado state agricultural statistician. Denver, July 11, 1960.

Reed, P. L., long-time county commissioner, Kiowa County. Eads, Colorado, June 10, 1966.

Sandhouse, Herman, Adams County, Colorado, agricultural extension agent, 1929-44. Fort Collins, August 25, 1965.

Shull, Kenneth, production adjustment specialist, Nebraska state ASCS office. Lincoln, November 12, 1968; May 14, 1971.

Simpson, H. H., Jr., county office manager, ASCS Committee, Kit Carson County. Burlington, Colorado, August 24, 1961; November 21, 1968; July 8, 1969.

Sitler, Harry G., agricultural economist, Colorado State University. Fort Collins, Colorado, August 9, 1965.

Stavely, John O., long-time wheat farmer, Kiowa County. Haswell, Colorado, June 10, 1966.

Stevens, Morgan, Kiowa County agricultural extension agent. Eads, Colorado, October 16, 1968.

Stinson, T. Bruce, long-time superintendent of Tribune Branch Experiment Station. Tribune, Kansas, August 19, 1961, August 11, 1965; July 11, 1966; November 16, 1968.

Waldren, Lloyd E., office manager, Greeley County ASCS. Tribune, Kansas, November 15, 1968.

Wineager, Imogene, county clerk, Greeley County. Tribune, Kansas, November 15, 1968.

Government Publications

Arnold, G. H. "Farm Practices in Growing Wheat." In *USDA Yearbook, 1919*, pp. 123-50. Washington, D.C.: GPO, 1920.

Barber, E. Lloyd. *Meeting Weather Risks in Kansas Wheat Farming.* Agricultural Economics Report, no. 44. Kans. Agr. Exper. Sta., September 1950.

Bell, Earl H. *Culture of a Contemporary Rural Community: Sublette, Kansas.* Rural Life Studies, no. 2. USDA Bur. of Agr. Econ., Washington, D.C., September 1942.

Biennial Report of Kansas Board of Agriculture. Vols. 22-38 (1920-52). Topeka: Kansas Printing Plant.

Coffman, George W. "Corporations with Farming Operations." Agri. Econ. Report, no. 209. USDA Econ. Research Service, June 1971.

Colorado Agricultural Statistics. Colorado Department of Agriculture, with the USDA. Denver, 1920-68. (Titles vary.)

Conservation Reserve Program of the Soil Bank. USDA Inform. Bul. 185. Washington, D.C.: GPO, March 1958.

Cronin, Francis D., and Beers, Harold W. *Droughts: Areas of Intense Drought Distress, 1930-1936,* WPA, Division of Social Research, Research Bulletin, ser. 5, no. 1. USDA Agr. Econ. Bur. and Resettlement Admin. Washington, D.C.: January 1937.

Crop Report for Colorado. Bulletin no. 17. Colorado Dept. of Agr., with the USDA. Denver, September 1920. (See also *Colorado Agricultural Statistics.*)

———. Bulletin no. 53. Colorado Dept. of Agr., with the USDA. Denver, December 1923.

Drought and Wind Erosion Problems of the Southern Great Plains and a Conservation Plan for the Region. Report of the Soil Conservation Service to the Secretary of Agriculture on Problems of the Southern Great Plains, April 1954.

Edwards, A. D. *Influence of Drought and Depression on a Rural Community: A Case Study in Haskell County, Kansas.* Social Report, no. 7. Farm Security Admin. and USDA Bur. of Agr. Econ. Washington, D.C., January 1939.

Eikelberry, R. W., and Fly, C. L., eds. *Physical Land Conditions Affecting Use, Conservation and Management of Land Resources, Greeley County, Kansas.* USDA Soil Conservation Service and Kansas Agri. Exper. Sta. Manhattan, December 1956.

Farm Facts. Kansas Crop and Livestock Information, or Kansas Crop and Livestock Statistics. Report of the Kansas State Board of Agriculture, Topeka, 1949-1968.

———. *Problem Area Groups of Land in the Southern Great Plains.* USDA. Washington, D.C.: GPO, February 1939.

The Future of the Great Plains. Report of the Great Plains Committee. Washington, D.C.: GPO, 1936.

Hodges, J. A.; Elliott, F. F.; and Grimes, W. E. *Types of Farming in Kansas.* Kansas Agri. Exper. Sta. Bul., no. 251. Manhattan, August 1930.

Hunter Bryon; Moorehouse, L. A.; Burdick, R. T.; and Pingery, H. B. *Type of Farming Areas in Colorado.* Colo. Agr. Exper. Sta. Bul., no. 418. Fort Collins, September 1935.

Joel, Arthur H. *Soil Conservation Reconnaissance Survey of the Southern Great Plains Wind-Erosion Area.* USDA Tech. Bul., no. 418. Washington, D.C.: GPO, January 1937.

Johnson, W. D. *The High Plains and Their Utilization.* United States Geological Survey, 21st Annual Report, 1899-1900. Part 4, *Hydrology.* Washington, D.C.: GPO, 1901.

Kifer, R. S., and Stewart, H. L. *Farming Hazards in the Drought Area.* WPA, Division of Social Research, monograph 16. Washington, D.C.: GPO, 1938.

Nanheim, Charles W.; Bailey, Warren R.; and Merrick, Della E. *Wheat Production: Trends, Problems, Programs, Opportunities for Adjustment.* USDA Agr. Res. Service, Agr. Infor. Bul., no. 179. Washington, D.C.: GPO, March 1958.

Powell, John Wesley. *Report on the Lands of the Arid Region of the United States, with a More Detailed Account of the Lands of Utah.* United States Geographical and Geological Survey of the Rocky Mountain Region. 2d. ed. Washington, D.C., 1879.

Physical Land Conditions in Kit Carson County, Colorado. Physical Land Survey, no. 43. USDA Soil Conserv. Service. Washington, D.C.: GPO, 1949.

Prescott, Glenn C.; Branch, John R.; and Wilson, Woodrow W. *Geology and Ground Water Resources of Wichita and Greeley Counties, Kansas.* State Geol. Sur. of Kansas Bul., no. 108, April 1954.

Report of Soil Conservation Service: Problems of the Southern Great Plains. April 1954.

"The Report of the Eleventh Conference of the Regional Advisory Committee on Land Use Practices in the Southern Great Plains Area." April 19-20, 1937. Mimeographed.

Report of the Kansas State Board of Agriculture. Vols. 39-51 (1953-68). Topeka: Kansas Printing Plant.

Reynolds, John E., and Timmons, John F. "Factors Affecting Farmland Values in the United States." Research Bulletin, no. 566. Agr. and Home Econ. Exper. Sta. Iowa State University, February 1969.

Sauer, Carl O. "Land Resources and Land Use in Relation to Public Policy." Appendix 9, *Report of the Science Advisory Board,* July 31, 1933, to September 1, 1934. Washington, D.C., September 20, 1934, pp. 163-200.

Sitler, Harry G. *Economic Possibilities of Seeding Wheatland to Grass in Eastern Colorado.* ARS 43-64, USDA Agr. Res. Serv. Washington, D.C.: GPO, February 1958.

Stinson, T. B., and Laude, H. H. *A Report of the Tribune Branch Agricultural Experiment Station.* Agr. Exper. Sta. Bul., no. 250. Kansas State Agricultural College, Manhattan, March 1930.

Salmon, S. C., and Throckmorton, R. I. *Wheat Production in Kansas.* Kansas State Agr. Exper. Sta. Bul., no. 248. Manhattan, 1930.

Thornthwaite, C. W. *Atlas of Climatic Types in the United States, 1900-1939.* USDA Soil Conserv. Service Misc. Publ., no. 421. Washington, D.C.: GPO, 1941.

Underwood, John J. *Physical Land Conditions in the Western and Southeastern Baca County Soil Conservation Districts, Colorado.* Physical Land Survey, no. 30. USDA Soil Conserv. Service. Washington, D.C.: GPO, 1944.

United States. Bureau of the Census. *Fourteenth Census of the United States: 1920.* Washington, D.C.: GPO, 1922.

———. *Fifteenth Census of the United States: 1930.* Washington, D.C.: GPO, 1932.

———. *Sixteenth Census of the United States: 1940.* Washington, D.C.: GPO, 1942.

———. *U.S. Census of Agriculture: 1925.* Washington, D.C.: GPO, 1927.

———. *U.S. Census of Agriculture: 1935.* Washington, D.C.: GPO, 1936.

———. *U.S. Census of Agriculture: 1950.* Washington, D.C.: GPO, 1952.

———. *U.S. Census of Agriculture: 1954.* Washington, D.C.: GPO, 1956.

———. *U.S. Census of Agriculture: 1959.* Washington, D.C.: GPO, 1961.

Voelker, Stanley W. *Land-Use Ordinances of Soil Conservation Districts in Colorado.* Great Plains Council Publication, no. 5. Colorado Agr. Exper. Sta. Fort Collins, March 1952.

Wolfanger, Louis A.; Goke, A. W.; and Weakley, H. E. "Soil Survey of Deuel County, Nebraska." In *Advance Sheets, Field Operations of the Bureau of Soils, 1921.* Washington, D.C.: GPO, 1924.

Books

Barrows, Harlan H. *Lectures on the Historical Geography of the United States as Given in 1933,* edited by William A. Koelsch. University of Chicago, Department of Geography Research Paper, no. 77. Chicago, 1962.

Bowman, Isaiah. *The Pioneer Fringe.* American Geographical Society Special Publication, no. 13. Worcester, Mass.: Commonwealth Press, 1931.

Clements, Frederick E. *Climatic Cycles and Human Population in the Great Plains.* Carnegie Institution of Washington Supplementary Publication, no. 43. Washington, D.C., 1938.

———, and Chaney, Ralph W. *Environment and Life in the Great Plains.* Carnegie Institution of Washington Supplementary Publication, no. 24. Washington, D.C., 1936.

Hargreaves, Mary Wilma M. *Dry Farming in the Northern Great Plains, 1900-1925.* Cambridge: Harvard University Press, 1957.

Hewes, Leslie. "The Conservation Reserve of the American Soil Bank as an Indicator of Regions of Maladjustment in Agriculture, with Particular Reference to the Great Plains." In *Festschrift, Leopold G. Scheidl zum 60. Geburtsdag.* Vol. 2. Vienna, Ferdinand Berg & Son, 1967, pp. 331-46.

Johnson, Vance. *Heaven's Tableland: The Dust Bowl Story.* New York: Farrar, Straus & Co., 1947.

Kraenzel, C. F. *The Great Plains in Transition.* Norman: University of Oklahoma Press, 1955.

Malin, James C. *Winter Wheat in the Golden Belt of Kansas: A Study in Adaption to Subhumid Geographical Environment.* Lawrence: University of Kansas Press, 1944.

Pfister, Richard. "Water Resources and Irrigation." In *Economic Development of Southwestern Kansas,* part 4. Bureau of Business Research, University of Kansas, Lawrence, 1955.

Reitz, L. P., and Heyne, E. G. "Wheat Planting and Wheat Improvement in Kansas." In *Twenty-third Biennial Report of the Kansas Board of Agriculture, 1941 and 1942.* Topeka, 1942.

Saarinen, Thomas Frederick. *Perception of the Drought Hazard on the Great Plains.* University of Chicago, Department of Geography Research Paper, no. 106. Chicago, 1966.

Sears, Paul B. *Deserts on the March.* Norman: University of Oklahoma Press, 1935.

Svobida, Lawrence. *An Empire of Dust.* Caldwell, Idaho: Caxton Printers, 1940.

Taylor, Carl C. "The Wheat Area." In *Rural Life in the United States,* edited by Carl C. Taylor, pp. 383-90. New York: A. A. Knopf, 1949.

Thornthwaite, C. W. "The Great Plains." In *Migration and Economic Opportunity: The Report of the Study of Population Redistribution,* edited by Carter Goodrich. Philadelphia: University of Pennsylvania Press, 1965.

Webb, Walter Prescott. *The Great Plains.* New York: Ginn & Co., 1931.

Periodicals

Anderson, Clinton P. "Soil Murder on the Plains." *Country Gentleman,* September 1947, pp. 15, 83-85, 87, 88.

Asby, Richard. "Town Farming in the Great Plains." *Rural Sociology* 6 (1941): 341-43.

Belcher, J. C. "The Nonresident Farmer in the New Rural Society." *Rural Sociology* 19 (1954): 121-136.

Bird, John. "Great Plains Hit the Jackpot." *Saturday Evening Post,* August 30, 1947, pp. 15-17, 88, 90.

Borchert, John R. "The Dust Bowl in the 1970's." *Annals, Association of American Geographers* 61, no. 1 (March 1971): 1-22.

Carey, Henry L. "The Rise of Simon Fishman." *B'Nai B'rith Magazine* 48, no. 8 (May 1934), 274, 275, 300, 301.

Carlson, Avis D. "Dust Blowing," *Harper's Magazine* 171 (July 1935): 149-58.

Evans, Monroe. "Nonresident Ownership—Evil or Scapegoat?" *Land Policy Review* 1, no. 2 (July-August 1938): 15-20.

Fischel, V. C. "Ground Water Resources of Kansas." *Transactions, Kansas Academy of Science* 50, no. 2 (September 1947): 105-119.

Fuller, M. G. "The Land Purchase and Development Program in Baca Co., Colorado." *Soil Conservation* 5 (1940): 213-15.

Gray, L. C. "Federal Purchase and Administration of Submarginal Land in the Great Plains." *Journal of Farm Economics* 21 (February 1939): 123-31.

Hewes, Leslie. "Causes of Wheat Failure in the Dry Farming Region, Central Great Plains, 1939-1957." *Economic Geography* 41 (1965): 313-30.

———. "Traverse Across Kit Carson County, Colorado, with Notes on Land Use on the Margin of the Old Dust Bowl, 1939-1940 and 1962." *Economic Geography* 39 (1963): 332-40.

———. "Wheat Failure in Western Nebraska, 1931-1954." *Annals of the Association of American Geographers* 48 (1958): 375-97.

———, and Schmieding, Arthur C. "Risk in the Central Great Plains: Geographical Patterns of Wheat Failure in Nebraska, 1931-1952." *Geographical Review* 42 (1956): 375-87.

Kollmorgen, Walter M. "The Woodsman's Assaults on the Domain of the Cattleman." *Annals, Association of American Geographers* 59, no. 2 (June 1969): 215-39.

———, and Jenks, George F. "A Geographic Study of Population and Settlement Changes in Sherman County, Kansas, Part I: Rural." *Trans-*

actions, *Kansas Academy of Science* 54, no. 4 (December 1951): 449-94.

———. "Suitcase Farming in Sully County, South Dakota." *Annals, Association of American Geographers* 48, no. 1 (March 1958): 27-40.

"The Land of the Big, Rich, Freewheeling Enterprise in that Capitalistic Oasis, the Southwest, U.S.A." *Fortune,* April 1948, pp. 98-103.

Loomis, Charles P. "The Human Ecology of the Great Plains Area." *Proceedings of the Oklahoma Academy of Science* 17 (1937): 14-28.

Malin, James C. "Mobility and History: Reflections on the Agricultural Policies of the United States in Relation to a Mechanized World." *Agricultural History* 17, no. 4 (October 1943): 177-91.

———. "The Turnover of Farm Population in Kansas." *Kansas Historical Quarterly* 4 (1935): 339-72.

Roberts, E. D. G. "Land Utilization Program in the Southern Great Plains." *Science,* n.s. 88, no. 2283 (September 30, 1938): 289-92.

Szabo, M. L. "Characteristics of Non-resident Farm Operators on the Canadian Prairies." *Geographical Bulletin* 8 (1966): 279-303.

"Southwest Has a New Crop of Super Rich." *Life Magazine,* April 5, 1948, p. 23.

White, Owen P. "Wheat's Here to Stay." *Colliers,* January 2, 1932: 10-11.

Theses

Deal, Donald B. "Sidewalk Farming in the Specialized Wheat Region of Nebraska." Master's thesis, University of Nebraska, 1967.

Miller, Emy K. "Corporation Farming in Kansas." Master's thesis, University of Wichita, 1933.

Newspapers
Colorado

Bent County Democrat, 1945-50, 1953-56.
Burlington Call (Kit Carson County), 1943.
Cheyenne County News, 1933-34, 1943-48.
Democrat Herald (Baca County), 1927-38, 1954.
Denver Post, various dates, 1940s.
Flagler News (Kit Carson County), 1935.
Kiowa County Press, 1930-33, 1945-50, 1954-55.
Kit Carson County Record, 1919-21.

Lamar Daily News (Prowers County), 1939.
Ordway New Era (Crowley County), 1946-51, 1954.

Kansas

Colby Free Press-Tribune (Colby County), 1930s.
Dighton Herald (Lane County), 1933.
Dodge City Journal (Ford County), 1933.
Elkhart Tri-State News (Morton County), 1933.
Garden City News (Finney County), 1933.
Goodland News-Republic (Sherman County), 1933.
Gove County Advocate, 1933.
Grainfield Cap Sheaf (Gove County), 1933.
Grant County Republican, 1933-34.
Greeley County Republican, 1919-47, 1953-57.
Grinnell Record-Leader (Gove County), 1933.
Hoxie Sentinel (Sheridan County), 1933.
Hugoton Hermes (Stevens County), 1933.
Jacksonian and Gray County Record (Gray County), 1933.
Johnson City Pioneer (Stanton County), 1925-39, 1944.
Lakin Independent (Kearney County), 1930s.
Leoti Standard (Wichita County), 1933, 1935.
News Chronicle (Scott County), 1933.
Oakley Graphic (Logan County), 1933, 1936.
Republican Gazette (Gove County), 1933.
St. Francis Herald (Cheyenne County), 1933.
Satanta Chief (Haskell County), 1922-26.
Selden Independent (Sheridan County), 1933.
Sherman County Herald, 1933-36.
Southwest Daily Times (Seward County), 1933.
Southwest Tribune (Seward County), 1933, 1970.
Sublette Monitor (Haskell County), 1922-26, 1928, 1933-35.
Syracuse Journal (Hamilton County), 1924-35, 1943-46, 1957-59.
Tiller and Toiler (Pawnee County), 1933.
Topeka Capital, 1923.
Western Times (Wallace County), 1933, 1935.

Missouri

Kansas City Star, 1939.

Nebraska

Chapell Register (Deuel County), 1914-15.

Maps and Plats

Colorful Colorado (map). State Department of Highways, Colorado, 1966. (Includes National Grasslands.)

Greb, B. W. "Wheat Producing Areas of Colorado" (manuscript map). N.d.

Hammond, Edwin H. "Classes of Land-Surface Forms in the Forty-eight States, U.S.A." Map Supplement Number 4, *Annals, Association of American Geographers,* 54, no. 1 (March 1954).

Official Grant Farm Plats, 1963. Owners and operators of farms, Grant County, Kansas.

Pleistocene Eolian Deposits of the United States, Alaska, and Parts of Canada (map), comp. by the National Research Council Committee for the Study of Eolian Deposits, Division of Geology and Geography. Geological Society of America, 1952.

United States. Department of Agriculture. Agricultural Stabilization and Conservation Service (ASCS). Communities of Colorado, ASCS subdivisions of counties (map). State ASCS Office, Denver.

———. Forest Service. *Comanche National Grassland, San Isobel National Forest,* Colorado. GPO, n.d.

———. Soil Conservation Service (SCS). "Horse-Rush Creek Soil Conservation District" (manuscript map). N.d.

———. *Progress in Soil Conservation Work Completed in Soil Conservation Districts* (map). December 21, 1951.

Acknowledgments

The completion of this study would have been impossible without the assistance of several agencies and many individuals, named and unnamed in this report. Acknowledgment is due several agencies. Financial support by the University of Nebraska Research Council over the years is gratefully acknowledged. The cooperation and thoughtful assistance by state and county officers of the Agricultural Stabilization and Conservation Service (ASCS) of the United States Department of Agriculture were indispensable. Valuable contemporary records that, in the main, could not be duplicated elsewhere were made available at the following repositories: the Kansas State Historical Library, Topeka; the State Historical Society of Colorado, Denver; the C. Y. Thompson Library of the University of Nebraska; the federal records centers of Denver and of Kansas City, Missouri; the Agricultural Extension Service of Kansas State University, Manhattan; and the Agricultural Extension Service of Colorado State University, Fort Collins. The county clerks and registers of deeds of Greeley and Stanton counties, Kansas, and of Kiowa County, Colorado, provided important source material for a portion of the study.

The list of individuals who contributed valuable information or guidance in the research is long. Henry Christensen, Colorado state executive director, and Wendell Becraft, Kansas state executive director of the ASCS, made available records in the state and county offices and authorized the use of those stored in the federal records centers. Lester R. Branson, head specialist, ACP-SB, Kansas state ASCS office, Manhattan;

Larry Brown and Myron Fritzler, ASCS production adjustment specialists for Colorado; and Kenneth Shull, ASCS production adjustment specialist for Nebraska, provided necessary information for the effective use of records and assisted in other ways. The ASCS county office managers, later called county executive directors, almost without exception went beyond the call of duty in supplying data and aiding in their interpretation. Special mention should be made of Mrs. Maxine Grant, Baca County, Colorado; Mrs. Kathlyn Forster, Kiowa County, Colorado; Earl McDonnell, Lincoln County, Colorado; and H. H. Simpson, Jr., Kit Carson County, Colorado. Sincere thanks are also due E. H. Pubols, center manager, Denver Federal Records Center, and later E. S. Howard, acting center manager; Frank Lilley, chief, reference branch, and William J. Caby, supervisor, reference service branch, Kansas City Federal Records Center; Eugene D. Decker, archivist, Kansas State Historical Society; Wayne R. Collings, librarian, C. Y. Thompson Library, University of Nebraska; Robert Eikelberry, soil correlator, Mid-West Region, Soil Conservation Service, Lincoln; J. R. Jacard, retired faculty member, Kansas State University; B. W. Greb, soil scientist, Central Great Plains Field Station, Akron, Colorado; and T. Bruce Stinson, long-time superintendent of the Branch Experiment Station, Tribune, Kansas. The frequent citations of Stinson and Kathlyn Forster in the study give only incomplete evidence of my heavy dependence on these knowledgeable participants in and observers of regional events. To all those named in the text, footnotes, and bibliography, as well as many others not named, I am grateful for assistance rendered, often without a record being made of their contribution.

Special recognition is due those fellow workers whose handiwork and judgment speak for themselves in the maps and graphs so essential in the presentation of the results of the investigation. Yeoman service was rendered by Joseph A. Bunik, Donald B. Deal, Emmett A. Gillaspie, Jr., Jerry L. Livingston, Wayne A. Seim, Larry Schweitzer, Larry L. Teply, and Paul Wilson as cartographic assistants.

Finally, I wish to recognize the many contributions of my wife, Elma, who made this a joint effort. Her assistance was indispensable. It included the drudgery of copying thousands of names and statistics, expertly recognizing pertinent items in old newspapers and reports, and serving as a critic of the manuscript.

Leslie Hewes

Index

AAA: allotments of wheat acreage, 6, 21–22, 37, 52; applications for allotments, 22, 51, 77, 84; controls by, 4, 102, 119; controls in Greeley County, 86–88, 97–100; payments by, 3, 51–52, 91, 96, 98, 119, 131, table 21

Abandonment: of farms and cropland, 80, 81, 83, 117, 164–69; of crops, see Wheat, abandonment of

Absentee: defined, 4; ownership, see Nonresident owners and ownership

Acreage reserve of the Soil Bank, 139

Adams County, Colorado, 74, 81, 139

Advance and retreat of farming, 2–3, 178–79

Agricultural Adjustment Administration: see AAA

Agricultural Development Company: see Kansas Agricultural Development Company

Agricultural machinery: see Farm machinery

Agricultural policies, 3–4

Agricultural Stabilization and Conservation Service: see ASCS

Aicher, L. C., 47

Alva, Oklahoma, 114, 126, 127

Amarillo, Texas, 147

Anderson, Clinton P., 117

Anton community, Washington County, Colorado, 125, 176–77, fig. 38

Arapahoe community, Cheyenne County, Colorado, 125

Arkansas City, Kansas, 110

Arlington, Kiowa County, Colorado, 106. See also Haswell-Arlington community, Kiowa County, Colorado

ASCS, 7, 134–35, 144, 147, 150, 155–56

Assessors, Kansas, 11, 12, 20, 93

Baca County, Colorado: early wheat farming, 34, 73, 77–81; early suitcase farming, 78–81; old settlers were stock raisers, 78; wheat abandonment, 83, 180, 182; abandoned farmhouses, 81; relief payments, 84; suitcase farmers in 1954, 126; land not available to suitcase farmers, 128; operation by Baughman, 118, 129; Comanche National Grassland, 133, 184; acreage reserve, 139; dust blowing, 161; blowland and the absentee, 167–69; land utilization project purchase price, 183; little recent suitcase farming, 184

Barrows, Harlan H., 2

Baughman, J. W., 78, 110, 117, 129, 130, fig. 24

Baughman Land Company, 110,

275

172, fig. 24
Bell, Earl H., 4, 63
Belpre, Kansas, 99
Bennett, Colorado, 127
Bent County, Colorado, 109, 115–16, 121–23, 125, 140, 177
"Big farming," 8, 42
Bird City, Kansas, 8
Blakemore ranch (or farms), 107–8
Blowing dust: *see* Soil blowing
Blowland violations, 166, 170–74
Boulder, Colorado, 32, 55
Bowman, Isaiah, 3, 184
Brandon, Kiowa County, Colorado, 106, 107, 111, 117
Brandon-Chivington community, Kiowa County, Colorado, 125
Breaking of prairie or sod, 75, 117, 178–79; Greeley County, Kansas, by Fishman, 13, 15, 17, 75; for Fishman, 17, plate 2; in Hamilton County, 31–33, 60; in Stanton County, 38–39, 41, 90; in Haskell County, 42–44, 117; Wheat Farming Company broke prairie land, 46; in Colorado early, 15, 74–78; later breaking in western Kansas, 98, 100, 102–3; in Kiowa County, Colorado, 104–5, 108, 109, 112, 113, 118; elsewhere in eastern Colorado, 104, 110, 114–18, 132; sod crop given for breaking, 117
Bucklin, Kansas, 78
Burlington, Colorado, 13, 15, 16, 18, 70

California, 55, 123, 127
Cañon City, Colorado, 147
Carmen, Oklahoma, 110
Carpenter, Jim, 108
Census farms, 125
Ceresco, Nebraska, 16, 69
Cherokee, Oklahoma, 39, 126–27
Cheyenne County, Colorado, 75, 76, 104, 113–15, 125, 126, 129, 131, 140, 144, 157–58, 180, 183
Cheyenne County, Kansas, 51, 86
Cheyenne County, Nebraska, 170

Cheyenne Wells, Cheyenne County, Colorado, 114
China, 55
Cimarron, Kansas, 39, 60
Cimarron River High Plains, 79
Climate, variation of, 1, 3, 179, 183–84
Clinton, Missouri, 60, 69
Coats, Pratt County, Kansas, 62
Colby, Kansas, 8, 100, 107, 117
Collingwood Grain Company, 39
Collingwoods, 39, 83, 91
Colony Township, Greeley County, Kansas, 17, 20, 22–25, 27, fig. 5, tables 11 and 12
Coloradoans, 55, 126–27, 146–47, 149
Colorado Rockies, 55, 127, 146
Colorado Springs, Colorado, 55, 127, 146–47
Comanche National Grassland, 133–34, 184
Conservation reserve of the Soil Bank, 4, 139–40, 144–46, 148, 150–52, 177, 185, fig. 30, tables 31 and 33
Copeland, Kansas, 43, 78
Corporations, 15, 33, 46–47, 59, 60–61, 66, 70, 185
County agents, agricultural extension service, 20, 106, 112
Crop failure: *see* Wheat, abandonment of
Cropland, increase in, 104, 105, fig. 16
Crowley County, Colorado, 105–6, 109, 123, 125, 128, 140
Cullison, Kansas, 99
Custom farming: *see* Suitcase farmers, custom farming for

Denver, Colorado, 14, 77, 114, 127, 146–47
Depression, agricultural, 3
Deuel County, Nebraska, 8
Dodge City, Kansas, 43, 55, 101, 107, 127, 147
Drought, 3, 10, 27, 69, 70, 116, 120–21, 138, 157, 178

Dry-farming movement, 2
Dumas, Texas, 114
Dunham, H. C., 42, 58
Dust blowing: *see* Soil blowing
Dust Bowl, 1, 3, 68, 70, 117–18, 120, 138, 161, fig. 1

Eades, Kiowa County, Colorado, 106, 108, 111
Edwards, A. D., 43, 56, 67
Eikleberry, Robert, 165
Elbert County, Colorado, 104, 131, 132
Elevator, grain, 13, 14, 61, 100
Ellis County, Kansas, 46
Enid, Oklahoma, 127, 147
Evans, Morris, 162–63, 169
Excess acres, 157–58

Fallow and fallowing: early examples of, 14, 33, 47, 78, 81; important by 1939, 87, 94–95, tables 22, 27; often neglected in second suitcase farming frontier, 101, 112, 136; later use of, 105, 107, 109, 123, 135, 137
"Farming the government," 3, 86
Farm machinery, 6, 8, 9, 13, 14, 15, 16, 18–19, 33, 35–36, 42, 46, 58–59, 63, 64, 70, 74, 78–79, 99, 102, 111, 112, 114–15, 154, fig. 12; transport of, 6, 8, 35–36, 46, 154
Fencing, 13, 15–16, 20, 31, 38, 75
Fine, Lou, 13
Finnell, H. H., 117
Finney County, Kansas, 51, 56, 68, 134, 143
Fisher, Fred E., 22, 33
Fisher ranch, 22, 58
Fishman, Simon: early farming in Kansas, 9, 12–15, 19, 45; land development in Kansas, 14–15, 17, 30; in Nebraska, 15; in Colorado, 15–16, 59, 75; as innovator, 14, 15, 30; miscellaneous, 58, 59, 60, 75
Fishman land company, 13

Ford County, Kansas, 50
Forster, Kathlyn, 112, 119, 122, 153, 154, 185
Fowler, Kansas, 78, 79
Fransman, Pete, 109

Gamble, suitcase farming as, 38, 115, 118, 136
Gano, George E., 96, 99–100, 110, 117
Garden City, Kansas, 55, 99, 127, 147
Garvey, Ray H., 100, 106–8, 110–11, 117, 124, 126
Garvey-Kriss farms, 106–7, 117
Geographical distribution of suitcase farming: *see* Suitcase farmers, distribution of
German-Russians, 93
Government payments, 3, 91, 96, 185–86. *See also* AAA: Acreage reserve of the Soil Bank; Conservation reserve of the Soil Bank; Relief payments
Grain elevator: *see* Elevator, grain
Grain sorghum, 95–96, 105, 152, 157–58
Grant County, Kansas, 35, 51, 53, 56, 83–84, 91, 134, 143, 164–66
Gray County, Kansas, 50, 51, 52, 66, 84
Great Bend, Kansas, 55, 78, 114, 127, 147
Great Plains, 1–2, 69, 138, 181–82
Great Plains Committee, 2
Greeley County, Kansas, 83, 84–89, 95–96, 124, 140, 146, 147, 153, 164, 171–72, 176, 179, fig. 37; as part of suitcase farming frontier, 11–30, 50, 51, 53, 55, 58, 59, 62–69, 97–101, tables 1–12
Greeley County Republican, quoted, 12–16, 19, 21

Hamilton County, Kansas, 83, 86, 124, 146, 153, 165–66, 179, fig. 15b; as part of suitcase farming frontier, 31–37, 50, 51, 52, 53, 55,

56, 58, 59, 60, 62, 64, 66, 67–68, 101–3, fig. 15a, tables, 13, 14
Hammond, Edwin H., 128
Harrison Township, Greeley County, Kansas, 12, 17, 18, 20, 23, 27
Haskell County, Kansas, 83, 84, 92, 143, 147, 176, fig. 37; early suitcase farming, 41–44, 50, 51, 56, 65, table 16
Haswell, Kiowa County, Colorado, 106–8, 111, 113, 118, 121–22, fig. 22a. *See also* Haswell-Arlington community, Kiowa County, Colorado
Haswell-Arlington community, Kiowa County, Colorado, 122, 126, 137, 146, 148, 150, 151, figs. 22b, 32a, 32b
Hays, Kansas, 46, 47, 58
Herd law, 20, 31
Hopkins, Tom F., 41, 42, 43, 78
Horace, Greeley County, Kansas, 12, 24
Housing shortage, 99, 101, 103, 118
Hutchinson, Kansas, 43, 55, 96, 100, 101, 127, 147

Idle land, 164–69
Improved land, 49, 56, 63, 64, fig. 10
In-county farmers growing wheat, 53, table 18
Innovation and innovator, 1, 14, 15, 30, 48, 50, 58, 59, 64, 81, 102, 105, 110, 111, 116, 117, 118, 177
Irrigation, unfavorable to suitcase farming, 134, 143, 148

Jenks, George F., 4
Joel Report, 164–69
Johnson, Stanton County, Kansas, 38, 91

Kansas Agriculture Development Company, 12, 14
Kansas and Kansans, 74, 79, 81, 126, 146, 147, 149, 150
Kansas City, Missouri, 17, 55

Karval community, Lincoln County, Colorado, 110, 157–58
Kearny County, Kansas, 6, 52, 53, 56, 66, 83, 143
Kiowa County, Colorado, 104, 140, 153, 157, 172–74, 176–77, 180; as part of suitcase farming frontier, 76, 104–13, 125, 126, 128, 129, 130
Kippes, Joe, 40
Kit Carson County, Colorado, 16, 73, 75, 126, 127, 128, 130, 131, 153, 157, 184
Kollmorgen, Walter M., 4, 149
Kriss, John, 100, 106, 107, 117
Kucera, Frank, 19, 58

Lamont Township, Hamilton County, Kansas, 34–36
Land boom, 57, 102, 112, 126–27
Land development, 13–15, 114, 118, 129
Land use: *see* Out-of-county farmers; suitcase farmers
Land utilization projects, 119, 129, 132–34, 183, 184, fig. 25
Land values, 43, 182–83, fig. 40
Larned, Kansas, 32, 55, 147
Leoti, Kansas, 109
Leonard, Warren, 110
Liberal, Kansas, 42, 78, 80, 108, 129
Lincoln County, Colorado, 104, 109, 110, 157–58
Loess, 128, 185
Logan County, Kansas, 8, 53, 56, 83, 86, 156
Loomis, Charles R., 179
Loveland, Colorado, 81, 146
Lyons, Kansas, 33, 47, 58

McAdams, James, 42, 58
McDonald, Kansas, 39
McDonnell, Earl, 119
McPherson, Kansas, 55
Malin, James C., 19, 60
Manila, Iowa, 17, 61, 69
Martin, I. E., 32
Martin, Ike, 34
Minneola, Kansas, 42

Molz, Christian, 23, 32, 34
Montezuma, Kansas, 80
Moore County, Texas, 66
Morton County, Kansas, 56, 65, 66, 83, 149, 179, 183, 184
Moscow, Stevens County, Kansas, 51, 58
Moundridge, Kansas, 55

National grasslands, 133–34, 184
Nebraska and Nebraskans, 15, 17, 55, 126, 127
Nelson, Anton, 16, 19
New farmers, grew most wheat, 20, 34–35, 40, 45, table 17
Newhouse, Mirt, 32
Newton, Kansas, 39
Nonresident, defined, 4
Nonresident farmers, residence of, 53–54, table 19
Nonresident owners and ownership, 3, 37, 44, 57, 65–67, 88, 93, 102, 128–31, 143, 183, 185, figs. 14, 24, 29; early delaying effect of, 57; had land largely in crops and wheat, 43–44, 103, 112, 121, 131; abandonment by, 117, 118, 164–69; and dust, 4, 75, 161–74
Nonresidents distinguished, 6–7

Oklahoma and Oklahomans, 41, 80, 108, 114, 121, 126–27, 146
Omaha, Nebraska, 31, 36, 114
Ordway, Crowley County, Colorado, 110
Oskaloosa, Iowa, 61
Otero County, Colorado, 131, 132, 133, 140
Out-of-county farmers: in western Kansas from adjacent counties, 23, 53–54; geographical distribution of, 49–52; land use by, 23–25, 37, 41, 59, tables 5, 16; number and percentage of wheat farmers, 23, 36–37, 41, 49–50, 51, fig. 7, table 4; tenure of, 26, 29, tables 11, 12; yields of, 27–28, 37, 41, tables 9, 10, 14

Pawnee County, Kansas, 51
Pawnee National Grassland, 133
Paying for land with one crop, 43, 69, 91
Performance records, 156–58, table 34
Perkins County, Nebraska, 148–49
Persistence of farmers, 29, 141–42. *See also* Suitcase farmers, persistence of
Pile, Margaret, 17
Plains, Kansas, 33, 39, 91
Place relations: *see* Suitcase farming, spatial aspects of
Plow-up: *see* Breaking of prairie or sod
Powell, John Wesley, 2
Prater, Fred, 78
Pratt, Kansas, 32, 39, 55, 78, 147
Pretty Prairie, Kansas, 147
Productivity index, 150, table 31
Profitability: *see* Suitcase farming, profitability of; wheat, profitability of
Prowers County, Colorado, 79, 80, 125, 126

Railroad, 8, 12, 38, 44, 57, 77, 106
Real estate promotion, 13, 14, 15, 17, 18, 30, 55, 59, 75, 76, 99, 114, 115, 117, 126, 129
Relief payments, 84
Residence of Greeley County wheat farmers, table 4
Risk, 3, 68, 69. *See also* Wheat, abandonment of

Saint John, Kansas, 55, 80
Satanta, Kansas, 39, 42
Satchel farmer, 5
Sauer, Carl O., 2
Scott County, Kansas, 56, 65, 83, 134, 143
Searcy, F. A., 61
Sell, Aaron, 99, 100, 101
Seward County, Kansas, 58, 83
Sheridan Lake, Kiowa County, Colorado, 106, 125

Sherman County, Kansas, 51, 56

Shore, E., 38, 62

Sidewalk farmers and farming, 5, 7, 19, 24, 25, 40, 42, 57, 58, 109, 116; as pioneers in wheat farming, 25, 57, table 7

Simpson, H. H., Jr., 153

Sledd Farm Corporation, 33, 47, 58

Smid boys, 14

Smoky Township, Sherman County, Kansas, 44–45, 48

Snell, O. A., 8, 100

Sod-breaking ordinance, 4, 113–15, 131–32, 134, fig. 25

Soil Bank: acreage reserve, 139; conservation reserve, 4, 140, 144–46, 151, 177, 185, fig. 30, table 33

Soil blowing, 27, 75, 80, 87, 118, 121, 161–74

Soil drifting: *see* Soil blowing

Spangler, James, 60, 69

Speculation and speculators, 2, 7, 25, 44, 57, 58, 61, 69, 70, 103, 113, 114, 117–18, 130, 185

Stafford, Kansas, 77, 99, 100

Stanton County, Kansas, as part of suitcase farming frontier, 37–41, 50, 51, 53, 56, 83, 84, 86, 90, 143, 166–67, 179, fig. 37, table 15

Stavely, B. A., 126

Stinson, T. Bruce, 11, 23, 154

Strip cropping, 87, 88, 89, table 22

Suitcase farmers: addresses of, *see* sources of (below) ; became residents, 14, 17, 18, 19, 30, 38, 62, 79, 91, 109, 115, 141, 148; early big farming by in Nebraska, 8, 9; early big farming by in Kansas, 13, 16, 20, 22, 33, 34, 39, 42, 46, 47, 58; later big farming by in Kansas, 100; early big farming by in Colorado, 78–79; later big farming by in Colorado, 107, 108, 114–15, 116; Coloradoans, 55–56, 126–27, 146–47, 149; crowded out back home, 61, 79, 101; custom farming for, 7, 96, 100, 110, 153; defined, 4, 5; de-scribed, 5, 6, 7, 20, 80, 85, 177; distribution of, 24–25, 49–53, 124–26, 140–41, 148–49, figs. 5, 7, 17, 18, 19, 26, 27, 33, 34, 36, tables 4, 5; dust hazard, 4, 7, 27–28, 76, 80, 87, 92, 98, 102, 116, 121, 122, 161–74; early wheat farmers, 8–9, 12, 19, 20, 31–32, 40, 44–45, 57, 77, 78, 106, 108, 109, 110, 111–12, 116; farmed at home also, 6, 34, 35, 60, 61, 64, 69, 153; farmed both in and out of county, 153; former residents, 17, 30, 45, 55–56, 69, 127, 145–47, 148; home bases, *see* sources of (below); innovators, 14, 15, 30, 42, 48, 58, 59, 71, 74, 81, 105, 111, 117–18, 177; involvement in actual farming, 7, 60–61, 153–54; Kansans, 74, 79, 80, 81, 126, 127, 146–47, 149–50; land use, 94–96, 112, 115, 134–38, 141–43, 150–52, 177, tables 23, 24, 29, 30, 31, 32, 33, 34; persisting vs. nonpersist-ing, 141–43, table 30; persisting vs. new, 150–52, table 31; Ne-braskans, 15, 17, 55, 126, 127; occupations of, 61, 69; Oklaho-mans, 41, 80, 108, 114, 121, 126–27; percentage of wheat farmers, 75, 80–81, 88–89, 90, 92, 140, 148, 149, figs. 17, 18, 26, 27, 33, 34; change in percentage, 88, 122–24, 134, 148, figs. 28, 35, 37, 38; per-sistence of, 29–30, 36, 62, 81, 141–42, 148; sources of in early Kan-sas, 17, 31, 36, 39, 41, 43, 47, 54–56, figs. 4, 6a, 6b, 8, 9; sources of in early Colorado, 74, 78–80, 81; later sources of, 89, 91, 93, 99, 102, 126–27, 146–47, figs. 21, 22a, 22b, 23, 31, 32a, 32b; tenure of, 60, 129, 142, 152–53; Texans, 84, 115, 126, 127, 146, 149; town dwellers, 4, 33, 35, 61, 127, 146–47; under-reported, 6, 9, 11–12, 14, 18, 21, 32, 35, 45, 52, 124; wheat emphasis, 17, 26, 33, 35,

44, 57–59, 77, 78, 106, 108, 111, 112, 115, 124, 135, 142, 151, 152; yields, 13, 14, 19, 27, 37–38, 41, 59, 74, 107, 109, 155–56, 158, tables 1, 3; young, 60–62, 78, 91. *See also* Out-of-county farmers; Suitcase farming

Suitcase farming: beginning of, 8–9; decline of, 76, 81, 83–89, 95–96, 121–24, 134, 143, 175–77; resumption of, 97–103, 104; interpretation of, 3, 63–71, 129; hypothesis of, 3, 63, 178–79; ecology of, 178–84; spatial aspects of, 63–64, 128, 175, fig. 36; dependence on absentee ownership, 65–67, 129; risk, wheat failure, and speculation, 2, 3, 22, 57, 61, 68–69, 70, 103, 113–15, 117–18, 130, 136, 184, 185; profitability of, 22, 34, 43, 46, 69, 70, 71, 114, 177–78, 181–82; "paid for land with one crop," 43, 91; often a sideline, 61, 69, 144. *See also* Out-of-county farmers; Suitcase farmers

Summer fallow: *see* Fallow and fallowing

Syracuse, Kansas, 23, 24

Tax sales, 65, 130

Tenure: *see* Out-of-county farmers; Suitcase farmers

Terrell, Monroe, 115

Texans, 84, 115, 126, 127, 146, 149

Thomas County, Kansas, 46, 50, 56

Timpas sod-breaking district, 131

Towner, Kiowa County, Colorado, 76, 106, 112, 148, 151, 154, 155

Town farmers: *see* Sidewalk farmers and farming

Tribune, Greeley County, Kansas, 24, 99, 101

Tribune Township, Greeley County, Kansas, 12, 20

Trueds, 16, 18, 19, 58

Ulysses, Grant County, Kansas, 35

United Farms Corporation, 33

Wallace County, Kansas, 46, 50, 51, 53, 56, 83, 86

Wallins, 16, 18, 19

Warner, Fred, 42, 58

Water supply, 24–25, 67–68, 93, 99, 103, 164

Weld County, Colorado, 81, 127

Wetzels, 17, 19, 61, 69

Wheat: abandonment of, 28, 38, 68, 83, 85, 92, 121, 136–37, 139, 157–58, 179–80; acreage, changes in, 21, 73, 77, 84–85, 105, 113, table 1; acreage of suitcase and out-of-county farmers early in Kansas, 12–14, 16–17, 19, 23, 31–35, 38–42, 44, 46–47, 59–60, tables 2, 5, 6, 7, 13, 15; later in Kansas, 138, 152, tables 23, 24, 29; in Colorado, 109–16, 136–37, tables 26, 27, 30–34; areas, figs. 2, 20; failure, *see* Abandonment of (above); farmers as percentage of all farmers, 52–53; 125; planted by new farmers, 20, 34–35, 40, 45, 78, 108, table 17; profitability of, 91, 114, 178, 181, 183; yields, 3, 4, 13, 14, 19, 27, 37, 38, 41, 59, 74, 107, 109, 155–56, 158, tables 1, 3

Wheat Farming Company, 46–47, 58

Whitewoman Township, Wichita County, Kansas, 93, table 23

Wichita, 22, 32, 55, 56, 100, 108, 110, 114, 127, 147

Wichita County, Kansas, 53, 55, 56, 64, 65, 83, 92, 94, 124, 143, 176

Wilson, Clement, 17, 18

Wind erosion: *see* Soil blowing

Wind erosion index, 165–69

Woodman, A. E., 31, 32, 36, 61

Yields: *see* Wheat, yields

Zook, Z. B., 32.

DATE DUE